KU-597-890

AMBIVALENT ANTI-COLONIALISM

The United States and the Genesis of West Indian Independence, 1940–1964

Cary Fraser

Contributions in Latin American Studies, Number 3
Joseph Arbena, *Series Adviser*

GREENWOOD PRESS
Westport, Connecticut • London

Library of Congress Cataloging-in-Publication Data

Fraser, Cary.
Ambivalent anti-colonialism : the United States and the genesis of West Indian independence, 1940-1964 / Cary Fraser.
p. cm.—(Contributions in Latin American studies, ISSN 1054-6790 ; no. 3)
Includes bibliographical references and index.
ISBN 0-313-28795-3 (alk. paper)
1. West Indies, British—Relations—United States. 2. United States—Relations—West Indies, British. 3. Great Britain—Colonies—America—History. 4. Nationalism—West Indies, British—History—20th century. I. Title. II. Series.
F2131.F73 1994
327.730729—dc20 93-10372

British Library Cataloguing in Publication Data is available.

Copyright © 1994 by Cary Fraser

All rights reserved. No portion of this book may be reproduced, by any process or technique, without the express written consent of the publisher.

Library of Congress Catalog Card Number: 93-10372
ISBN: 0-313-28795-3
ISSN: 1054-6790

First published in 1994

Greenwood Press, 88 Post Road West, Westport, CT 06881
An imprint of Greenwood Publishing Group, Inc.

Printed in the United States of America

The paper used in this book complies with the Permanent Paper Standard issued by the National Information Standards Organization (Z39.48-1984).

10 9 8 7 6 5 4 3 2 1

Copyright Acknowledgment

An earlier version of chapter 1 appeared as "Understanding American Foreign Policy Towards the Decolonization of American Empires, 1945-1964," *Diplomacy and Statecraft* 3 (March 1992). Reprinted by permission of Frank Cass & Co Ltd, London.

Contents

Acknowledgments

Thanks are due to the Swiss Federal Commission for Overseas Scholarships, the Social Science Research Council, the MacArthur Foundation, the Harry S. Truman Foundation, Cornell University, and the Graduate Institute of International Studies for the support provided at various stages for the completion of this study.

To the staff of the Public Record Office and the Institute of Commonwealth Studies in London, the National Archives in Washington, the Roosevelt, Truman, Eisenhower, Kennedy, and Johnson Presidential Libraries, Cornell University, the University of Maryland, and the University of the West Indies, I extend heartfelt gratitude for the services provided during my visits to their collections.

I would like to thank Locksley Edmondson and Arch Dotson at Cornell University for the support and consideration I received during my all too brief stay in Ithaca. Arch went beyond the call of duty in helping me to settle into life at Cornell. Locksley provided me with a sense of the possibilities of the nebulous project which I had undertaken as a dissertation.

To Catherine Kelleher and Karen Dawisha, I must express my immeasurable gratitude for the assistance I obtained during my stay at the University of Maryland. At Maryland, I enjoyed being part of the community built around the Center for International Security Studies, and for that experience Catherine bears a major responsibility.

To Richard Rockwell and Richard Moss of the SSRC, I must express gratitude for their quiet and unstinting help during my fellowship from the SSRC-MacArthur program. They were instrumental in providing me the opportunity to become part of the SSRC-MacArthur network, and together with Ruth Adams, encouraged me to repay my debt to the program by working at the SSRC. I can only try to assure them that this study seeks to establish an historiography which bridges scholarship from various national perspectives. I hope it lives up to the iconoclastic goals of the SSRC-MacArthur program.

The study was produced with invaluable support from three scholars--Yves Collart, Anthony Hopkins, and Shahram Chubin--whose collective wisdom encouraged me to go well beyond my original conception of the project. My frequent and prolonged absences from Geneva while doing the research for this project did not allow me to see them very often, but it made our few meetings all the more meaningful. My thanks goes to them for having suffered with considerable patience the vagaries attendant upon my life as a *gastarbeiter* in Switzerland and the United States of America.

To my wife, Teri, my daughter, Ayesha, my extended family, and friends, who have had to endure my absences, lack of contact, and occasional bouts of disquiet, I say thanks for the patience. To Ana Romero, Rudolph Graham, Michael Lashley and others of the West Indian intellectual community in Geneva I owe a considerable debt.

I wish to thank everyone who helped me during the evolution of my thinking and research over the past several years as I prepared this manuscript.

AMBIVALENT ANTI-COLONIALISM

Introduction

This study seeks to fill a gap in the historiography of the Caribbean and that of American foreign policy in the Caribbean. It is only in recent years that the history of American relations with the Commonwealth Caribbean territories has been the focus of scholarly inquiry. Although the reasons for this are complex, the lack of importance assigned to these territories in American foreign policy is one explanation. Another factor lies in the history of these territories that for so long was defined by their relationship with Britain tended to attribute slight importance to the American connection. There has been the inclination to assume that the United States only emerged as a major consideration in the life of these societies since their accession to independence in the 1960s and 1970s.

This study attempts to revise those perceptions. It demonstrates that a sustained process of interaction between the United States and the British colonies in the Caribbean began in 1940 and had a critical impact upon the evolution of events in these societies over subsequent decades. The emergence and consolidation of nationalist movements in the British colonies over the period 1940-64 led to the British withdrawal from the region and the assertion of American hegemony over these territories. During this period, the level of American interest fluctuated in response to developments within these territories, as a function of its relationship with Britain, and as a consequence of shifts in perceptions of American policymakers about security requirements in the Caribbean and the wider international system.

In plotting the course of Anglo-American-West Indian relations over the period, it became clear that these relations could not be divorced from the decolonization process that swept the international system after World War II. As the issue of the Atlantic Charter in 1941 and the India Crisis of 1942 demonstrated, the demands of non-European nationalists had begun to assume critical momentum during that war. Relations among the American government, its British counterpart, and West Indian nationalist movements were conducted against the backdrop of the challenge to colonial rule in other regions; and the introduction of constitutional reform in Jamaica during the war was linked to the impact of events in Asia. The ascendancy of the nationalist movements in the British West Indian colonies cannot be considered without reference to those wider global processes and the challenge to the system of racial segregation in the United States by minority groups, particularly black Americans.

The focus of this study is the interaction among West Indian nationalists, American policymakers, and their British counterparts. The story is woven around several themes; first, the evolution of the West Indian quest for political independence; second, the British effort to reconcile its desire to remain a major power through an alliance with the United States while confronting a sustained challenge to British imperial authority during and after the war; and third, the American dual effort to impose order upon the newest entrants into the historic American sphere of influence in the Caribbean by establishing limits to their participation in the wider international system. This policy toward the British colonies was being conducted in tandem with an effort at the level of the Anglo-American relationship to manage the process of British disengagement from empire. These themes provide the elements of continuity for the study over the period 1940-64.

Rather than a history of American foreign policy toward the Caribbean, the study is designed to be an exercise in international history--exploring how the challenge to European empire shaped events and policies in the United States, Great Britain, and the Caribbean. It represents an effort to weave together American diplomatic history, British imperial history, and West Indian history to demonstrate that the study of decolonization requires historians to transcend a variety of fields that may be compartmentalized by cultural, disciplinary and national boundaries.

Beginning in 1940 with the Bases-for-Destroyers Deal and the Havana Conference, the United States sought to ensure its security through the assertion of its "right" to intervene in the political evolution of the territories. The fear of a German victory in Europe in mid-1940 raised the fundamental issues of dealing with the existing European colonies in the Western Hemisphere and preventing their transfer to Germany in the event of the latter's triumph.

The study ends with the electoral defeat of the Jagan government in British Guiana in December 1964. By mounting a campaign to unseat Jagan American policymakers demonstrated their willingness to impose limits upon the ideological, domestic and foreign policies of the nationalist movements and newly independent states of the Commonwealth Caribbean. The effort to unseat Jagan because of his openness to Marxist-Leninist ideology and ties with the Communist world reflected, as in 1940, the American desire to maintain the Caribbean as its *chasse-gardée*. Jagan's removal also represented some compensation for the loss of Cuba and provided an opportunity to demonstrate America's vigor in preventing further encroachment upon its sphere of influence.

For the British, the Bases-for-Destroyers Agreement represented the abdication of their exclusive authority over the British Caribbean and the beginning of a special relationship with the United States. It represented a conscious effort to secure American support for the maintenance of British power in the international system. In 1940 this support was sought to provide Britain with the resources necessary to halt the German military advance in Europe. The 1940 agreement, in hindsight, signaled the beginning of the British transition from an equal to the United States in international affairs to the status of junior partner in the Anglo-American alliance.

During the period 1960-1964, the pattern that had been set in 1940 revealed its enduring qualities as Britain reversed its support for Jagan and joined in the campaign to force him from office. The British reversal demonstrated Britain's sensitivities to the security concerns of its senior partner and its acknowledgment of American primacy in the Caribbean. This deference to America in the Caribbean was reciprocated by American support for British policy in Southern Africa, American assistance in the creation of a British nuclear force, and collaboration to maintain sterling as an international currency.

For West Indian nationalists, the Bases-for-Destroyers Deal represented both a threat and an opportunity. The threat of incorporation into the American colonial system within the Caribbean, and the opportunity to exploit American anticolonial rhetoric to reinforce the emerging challenge to British colonial rule. In 1940, the nationalists were forced by the exigencies of the wartime situation and imperial policy to accept the Bases-for-Destroyers Deal and the American military presence. On the threshold of independence in 1960, West Indian nationalists forced the British and American governments to revise the 1940 agreements and to respect West Indian nationalist sensibilities.

By 1964, West Indian nationalists were largely accepting of the reality that political independence marked a transition into the American sphere of influence. In their efforts to deal with the legacy of colonial rule and constraints upon the structural transformation of their economies, the West Indian nationalists began to solicit American investment and technology. They also explicitly defined themselves as part of the West. Cheddi Jagan, who fought to stretch the ideological limits of that sphere of influence, paid the price of being forced from office. His removal from office in 1964 was a signal to the rest of the Commonwealth Caribbean of the limits of American tolerance.

Thus, the period 1940-1964 represented a process of transition for all the parties--America, Britain, and the West Indies. This study seeks to sketch that process of transition and the interactions among the various parties. Given the relatively unmapped nature of the terrain and the lack of scholarly attention to this tripartite relationship, the study cannot be considered definitive. Rather, it has been conceived as a means of opening the subject to wider study.

While a plethora of studies have analyzed American policies toward the Caribbean, the focus of most of these studies has been the Spanish-speaking Caribbean, Haiti, and Central America. Those studies dealing with the entire Caribbean Basin have generally carried a section devoted to an examination of the Dutch- , French- , and English-speaking territories.[1] However, there has been little attempt to examine the American relationship with the Commonwealth Caribbean as a distinct subregion within the wider Caribbean. For most American scholars, there is little recognition of the distinctiveness of the Commonwealth Caribbean and, as a consequence, little attention has focused upon the rise of West Indian nationalism and the American response to that phenomenon.

In the early post-1945 period some attention was paid to the region by metropolitan visitors whose focus was on the conditions for, and process of, colonial reform in these territories. The usefulness of these early monographs lies in their provision of a point of departure for present-day researchers and for their depiction of contemporary concerns.[2]

Paul Blanshard's monograph represents the compilation of his observations developed during his service as a member of the staff appointed to the Anglo-American Caribbean Commission (AACC) during the war. Blanshard revealed himself to be a critic of the colonial policies pursued by both Britain and the United States, and highlighted the gap between the platitudinous rhetoric emanating from the respective imperial capitals and the reality in the colonies. He was particularly severe upon the colonial bureaucracies, the autocratic nature of colonial authority, and the lack of economic viability of the territories due to their dependence upon sugar production.

Blanshard also examined the challenge to white colonial authority in these territories, and the strong reaction from local inhabitants to American efforts to introduce Jim Crow practices in the British Caribbean territories. The rejection of this aspect of American culture reflected the broader challenge to white rule and the demands for the introduction of democracy in these colonies. Blanshard's work explicitly advanced the view that the failure to provide economic and political reform would only intensify the crisis and redound to the benefit of the Soviet Union.

Annette Fox's treatise sought to provide a framework for American policymakers to deal with the crisis of colonial authority in the Caribbean. While not sharing Blanshard's exposure to these societies, Fox advanced similar arguments for colonial reform. For Fox, only the Soviet Union stood to benefit from the outbreak of conflict in the colonies, and American policy should have been directed at preventing the expansion of Soviet influence. As a consequence, Fox gave enthusiastic support to the work of the Caribbean Commission as a means of providing local representation to colonial subjects, and as a channel for increased levels of metropolitan support for economic reform in the colonies.

Bernard Poole's book was a study of the origins and structure of the Caribbean Commission. Like Blanshard and Fox, Poole's point of departure was the crisis of colonial rule in the Caribbean. His central argument was that the Caribbean Commission was the embodiment of the concept of *Partnership* coined by Lord Hailey as the basis for continued colonial rule in the Caribbean. The new rationale for colonial rule was inevitable in the wake of the discredit of the concept of *Trusteeship* by the unrest of the 1930s. With the imperial mission refurbished, the Caribbean Commission was viewed as the mechanism through which a brighter material future could be developed for the subjects of colonial rule.

Mary Proudfoot's study was a comparative view of American and British colonial policies. It added little to the work done by its predecessors and, despite an exhaustive description of these policies, the book offered little insight into American attitudes to colonial rule in the post-1945 period.

More recently, Herbert Corkran, Jr. offered a monograph that chronicled the evolution of the Anglo-American Caribbean Commission and its successor institutions over the period 1942-69. Despite its detailed account of the vicissitudes confronted by these agencies in their efforts to promote cooperation among Caribbean territories, Corkran's work also lacked original insight into the roots and evolution of American policy toward the Commonwealth Caribbean.[3]

Two scholars have recently begun to explore American policy towards the Commonwealth Caribbean during World War II. Both have used the declassified records located at the National Archives of the United States of America. Annette Palmer's dissertation explored the American entry into the Caribbean, the course of the war and the role of American forces in the area, and some of the social and political consequences of the American presence.[4] It represented the first systematic treatment of American policy in the Commonwealth Caribbean during the war.[5]

Palmer's work showed the American desire to assure its security in the region in the wake of the German military successes of 1940. This bid for security spurred the expansion of the American military presence in the British territories. Palmer recounts the details of the military activities of the American forces and their success in containing the damage inflicted by German submarine warfare. The study also explored the manner in which the initial welcome offered to the Americans was soured by the attempts to introduce Jim Crow practices in these territories and stimulated political activity by the emerging nationalist movements.

Howard Johnson published two articles in 1984 analyzing the evolution of American policy toward the British colonies over the period 1940-45.[6] In these two articles, Johnson explored the roots of American involvement in the British Caribbean and argued that security concerns were the dominant influence upon American policy. The fear of unrest in both the American and British colonies in the region was perceived as a critical factor in encouraging American involvement in the region. In addition, American anxieties about secure access to the region's petroleum and bauxite resources were of critical importance. American and British recognition of the inadequacies of British policy in wartime led to suggestions for Anglo-American collaboration that resulted in the creation of the AACC.

This process of collaboration, in Johnson's view, institutionalized an American role in the British colonies and allowed the United States to influence British colonial policy in the region. This influence was exercised in 1942 to push the British into accelerating the pace of colonial reform that later led to the introduction of a new constitution in Jamaica in 1944. Fears of unrest in the region in 1942, together with the collapse of European empires in South East Asia, fueled American concerns and contributed to this American activism on behalf of British colonial subjects. Johnson also argued that the AACC served as a mechanism for the expansion of American commercial interests in the British colonies, in keeping with the general thrust of American foreign economic policy.

While these latter studies have focused exclusively upon the evolution of American relations with the British colonies over the wartime period, this study attempts to explore those relations in a wider context. The study is largely based upon records of the State Department found at the National Archives in Washington. Other records were located at various presidential libraries around the United States. Some of the records of the State Department dealing with the British Commonwealth have not yet been opened, despite the expiration of the thirty-year limit under which files are generally kept classified. In addition, individual documents were withdrawn on grounds of national security from various files to which I had access, at both the Archives in Washington and at some of the presidential libraries.

For Chapter 6 of the study, I have used a mix of official documents, newspapers, and secondary literature to explore American policy toward British Guiana from 1957 to 1964. The files of the Department of State for the period 1960-64 have not yet been released and, as an alternative, I have relied extensively upon the *New York Times* for information on the Kennedy administration's policies toward that colony. The declassification of the State Department's files may later suggest modification of the details of those policies, but I am of the view that the accounts in the *New York Times* are an accurate reflection of the outlines of that policy. The few records of the Kennedy administration that are open to public scrutiny have been used, where possible, to corroborate or provide nuanced understandings of accounts drawn from the *New York Times*.

A visit to the Public Record Office in London in 1985 provided me with some of the British Foreign Office records used in Chapter 3. For the rest of the study, I have relied upon secondary sources for the elucidation of British policy toward the West Indies and the United States. Given the volume of material released by the National Archives, it would have been a life's work to use British Colonial Office and Foreign Office files in the preparation of this study.

On a visit to Jamaica in 1988, I utilized the library of the University of the West Indies at Mona for access to unpublished secondary materials not widely available. The published materials on the West Indies, including the work of West Indian historians and political scientists, used in this study were obtained in Geneva, London, and Kingston.

Notwithstanding the problems of access to primary sources in the United States, and a reliance on secondary sources for information on the United Kingdom and the British West Indies, it has been a fascinating experience trying to reconstruct the past from records and literature having multiple perspectives. It has led to a measure of simplification, if not superficiality, in the study but it is a risk that any enterprise of this nature will experience. I can only hope that the information provided, and the opening of a field of intellectual inquiry will be seen as a measure of compensation for any faults in the study.

NOTES

1. A typical example of this approach is Robert D. Crassweller, *The Caribbean Community: Changing Societies and United States Policy* (New York: Praeger Publishers, 1972).

2. Paul Blanshard, *Democracy and Empire in the Caribbean* (New York: Macmillan, 1949); Annette Baker Fox, *Freedom and Welfare in the Caribbean* (New York: Harcourt Brace, 1949); Bernard L. Poole, *The Caribbean Commission: Background of Co-operation in the West Indies* (Columbia: University of South Carolina Press, 1951); and Mary Proudfoot, *Britain and the United States in the Caribbean* (London: Faber & Faber, 1954).

3. Herbert Corkran, Jr., *Patterns of International Co-operation in the Caribbean, 1942-69* (Dallas: Southern Methodist University Press, 1970).

4. Annette Palmer, *The United States and the Commonwealth Caribbean, 1940-45* (Ph.D. diss., Fordham University, 1979).

5. Two articles dealing with earlier periods are Fitz Baptiste, "The United States and West Indian Unrest, 1918-39," *Working Paper No.18* (Jamaica: ISER/UWI, 1978); and Ann Spackman, "The Role of Private Companies in the Politics of Empire: A Case Study of Bauxite and Diamond Companies in Guyana in the early 1920s," *Social and Economic Studies,* 24, no. 3 (1975), 341-78.

6. Howard Johnson, "The United States and the Establishment of the Anglo-American Caribbean Commission," *Journal of Caribbean History*, 19, no.1 (1984), 26-47; and Howard Johnson, "The Anglo-American Caribbean Commission and the

Extension of American Influence in the British Caribbean, 1942-1945" *Journal of Commonwealth and Comparative Politics* 22, no.2 (1984), 180-203.

1

Colonialism and U.S. Foreign Policy

Over the decade of the 1930s the colonial issue was a major challenge to the legitimacy of colonialism as a framework governing the relations between the major powers and the wider world. As it unfolded, the crisis of the colonial order had destabilizing effects upon the international system and set the stage for the process of decolonization that shattered the European-centered order that had evolved over the previous century. Its impact upon the international system was a reflection of both its global spread and its complexity. The American colonial possessions were not immune to this rising challenge to the colonial order but, for the purposes of this study, discussion will be restricted to demonstrating how American colonial policy influenced its responses to European colonialism after 1945.

The crisis revolved around three major issues. First, it was a conflict over the rules governing the international flows of capital and goods that arose out of the collapse of the international trading and financial systems and the resulting Great Depression. The breakdown of these systems caused a return to mercantilism and managed trade among the major economic powers. The British system of imperial preferences was only the most extensive of the mercantilist trade regimes enacted in the 1930s. All of the major industrial and colonial powers pursued similar strategies in the 1930s as a means of achieving a high degree of self-sufficiency. One major benefit of this scheme was the system of guaranteed markets that imperial trading systems provided for both manufactured goods and raw materials. This return to mercantilism triggered a critical, at times hostile, response from the United States whose fiscal and trade policies had contributed significantly to the breakdown of the trading system in the first place. The foreign trade of the United States had been adversely affected by the establishment of these mercantilist regimes among its competitors and the economic dislocation created crisis conditions inside the United States itself. The American campaign for the end of colonialism during the 1930s was one response to the reemergence of mercantilism as the framework governing international commerce.[1]

Second, the claim for colonies by Germany, Japan, and Italy, and their military and diplomatic activities prior to 1939 in pursuit of those claims, were catalysts for the growth of international tensions and the outbreak of the European war in 1939. The lack, or inadequacy, of their own colonies was a major irritant to these countries. In the early twentieth century, colonies served as an index of power and influence among the major powers, and German, Italian, and Japanese pretensions to major power status were diminished by their have-not status. The revival of Germany's claim to colonies during the 1930s, arising out of the perceived injustice of the Versailles settlement following World War I, opened the way for German efforts to refashion the map of Europe. While the seriousness of Germany's colonial claims under the Third Reich was questionable, these pretensions served to cast doubt on the legitimacy of the status quo and the balance of power in Europe.[2] The colonial issue had become a major irritant in the interwar period and threatened the stability of the post-1919 European state system.

The resurgence of imperialism in the 1930s also manifested itself in Japanese and Italian efforts to expand their colonial holdings in Asia and Africa respectively. The expansionist policies of these two powers and the failure of the other powers to impose constraints upon their activities undermined the concept of collective security upon which the interwar system had sought to base itself. This failure of collective security to prevent military conflict within the context of colonial expansion served to symbolize the link between colonialism and international instability. Japanese colonial expansion in Asia also threatened the balance of power in the area, raised tensions with Britain and the United States, and provoked military confrontation with the Soviet Union and China. Thus, the threat of colonialism to the international system extended from Europe into Africa and Asia, affected American interests in the latter area, and paved the way for the global extension of any conflict.

Third, there was the crisis of colonial rule in the colonies. As a consequence of the dislocation caused by the international economic crisis, social and political unrest wracked the colonies. These disturbances in the colonies became linked to the emergence of elites within the non-European world who sought to challenge imperial rule in the colonies, calling into question the benefits of colonialism, and demanding changes in the relationship between the colonizers and the colonized.[3]

Implicit within the challenge to colonial rule was a rejection of European pretensions to racial supremacy and a civilizing mission in the non-European world. Nazi views on race represented only a more strident and extreme version of the racial attitudes that underlay many European perceptions of the non-European world. European rejection of Nazi racial theories and views only served to strengthen and embolden these elites in their challenge to European rule. Furthermore, the carnage of World War I; the emergence of the Soviet Union as an alternative model of political, social, and economic development; and the open debate on the future of Western society that dominated the 1930s all provoked a reassessment in the non-European world of Europe and its culture.[4]

The outbreak of unrest in the tropical colonies served as an indicator of dissatisfaction with colonial rule, and provoked a reassessment of the colonial situation within the metropoles. This reassessment included the search for a new ideological and institutional framework for colonial rule. This search became embroiled in the heated debate over the morality of imperialism. American criticisms of European colonialism; the Pandora's box opened by the rationale for stripping Germany of its colonies, that is, the fitness or lack thereof of certain states to be colonial powers; and the perceived link between imperialism and the onset of war all fueled the ideological debate on colonialism. This debate not only raised the issue of which variant of imperialism was the most beneficent and thus deserving of continued existence but also brought into question the very existence of colonialism itself.

Through its various facets, the crisis of the colonial order in the 1930s revealed a complex interplay of motives and events that assumed a central role in international affairs. The colonial issue ranged across the economic, political, and ideological dimensions of the relationships between the European and non-European worlds. It was also a detonator of the conflict between the major powers that led inexorably, it seems in hindsight, to the outbreak of war in 1939.

This crisis of colonialism became even more acute with the onset of World War II. The war saw the establishment of Japan's short-lived dominance in Asia and the Pacific. Its rapid military rout of the European powers and the United States in the area, and its promotion of anti-European nationalism among the Asians made it a major contributor to the evolution of the colonial issue in the post-1945 period. The promulgation of the Atlantic Charter by the United States and Britain in 1941, and its subsequent adoption by non-European nationalists, boded ill for European attempts to reassert colonial rule after 1945. Finally, the prestige and influence of the two rhetorically anticolonial major powers, the United States and the Soviet Union, had been considerably enhanced by the end of the war. This raised expectations that the two powers would live up to their wartime rhetoric. These expectations may have demonstrated a certain measure of naiveté, but the diminution of the power and influence of the European imperial states offered the nationalist groups in the colonies more room to maneuver against their European overlords through appeals to these two states for assistance.

After 1945, the colonial issue became much less complex at the level of the international system. In essence, it centered around the efforts of the major European colonial powers to reassert and/or extend their empires, and the challenge to this process by nationalist elites in the various territories. An important element in this dialectic of imperial reassertion versus nationalist challenge was that the major colonial powers sought to offer reformed colonialism as their response to the crisis of colonial rule that had become manifest over the preceding decade and a half. For the colonial powers, the central concern was to devise the institutional mechanisms that would ensure the implementation and supervision of the new colonial dispensation--a process that envisaged a token increase in representation at the level of colonial government and a policy of greater participation by colonial elites in colonial administration.

This attempt to implement a new colonial dispensation was confronted by the declining legitimacy of colonial rule among colonial subjects. This loss of legitimacy, suffered by both the concept and practice of colonial rule, was accompanied by new internal alignments within the colonial territories where the elites challenging colonial rule had acquired, or were in the process of acquiring, increasing legitimacy vis-à-vis the colonial governments. Further, these elites had developed links with nationalist elites in other colonies. These links helped to transform the challenge to the European reassertion of empire from one concerning individual territories to one that increasingly became important to other colonies, within and across empires.[5] These linkages among groups across territories were extended by the growth of contact between nationalist groups in the colonies and influential groups or institutions in the metropoles. In effect, in the metropoles groups of collaborators arose who provided support to nationalists in the colonies in their quest for changes in colonial rule.[6]

Consequently, after 1945, there was a significant shift in the balance of forces between the colonizers and the colonized. The latter increasingly gained the initiative in the struggle to determine the political status of the colonial territories and accelerated the pace of change beyond the expectations of, and preparedness for, change in the metropoles. Inevitably, the conflicting perspectives on the extent and pace of change between the colonizers and the colonized triggered a series of crises--India, Indonesia, Ghana, Indochina, Kenya, and Algeria. Every crisis had an impact far wider than its immediate boundaries upon the pace, direction, and extent of challenge to colonial rule in other territories.

There was a fundamental continuity in the colonial issue over the 1930s and the wartime and postwar periods. The crisis of colonial rule in the 1930s raised grave doubts about its legitimacy, and the course of World War II undermined colonialism even further. It finally succumbed to the nationalist challenge after 1945. Despite this basic continuity, an evolution had also occurred. In the post-1945 era, the colonial issue had evolved from a complex multidimensional problem in international relations to a much simpler dialectic of conflict between the colonizer and the colonized. The terrain of conflict had shifted to the colonies, but important groups within the metropole had also begun to take sides in the evolving struggle, as would other parties from outside the various imperial systems.

For any understanding of American policy toward decolonization after 1945, the initial American response to the nationalist challenge that began in the 1930s is a useful point of departure. Throughout the 1930s, the American response to the colonial issue was shaped by the desire for the restoration of an international trading order that would help to ease the painful consequences of the Great Depression on the American domestic political economy. Of primary concern were efforts to dismantle trade barriers to contain the spread of European mercantilism and to prevent the establishment of a Japanese-led economic community in Asia.[7] In brief, American concerns with access to markets and opportunities for investment were critical factors influencing the American demands for an end to imperialism.

During the war, American endorsement of the Atlantic Charter, its attempts to obtain a British commitment to implementing colonial reform in India, and the proposal to prevent the restoration of French rule in Indochina have all been represented as evidence of American, and particularly Franklin Roosevelt's commitment to the cause of anticolonialism.[8] While these declarations and policies did enjoy significant support from various American constituencies, it is not clear that Roosevelt's policies represented anything more than perspicacity in recognizing the growing force of nationalism that would sweep the non-European world.[9] This foresight on the part of Roosevelt could also be interpreted as a tactic for signaling support for Asian nationalism as a means of countering Japanese wartime propaganda of Asia for Asians.[10]

The ambiguities surrounding Roosevelt's policy toward Indochina, and eventually France, is certain cause to question the strength of Roosevelt's endorsement of non-European nationalism.[11] Roosevelt's acceptance of the restoration of French rule in Indochina, and his support for the American extension of its empire through the acquisition of control over the Japanese mandate-territories in the Pacific, certainly contradicted his earlier attitudes. Whatever his personal views, Roosevelt's wartime policies reflected a pragmatic use of support for non-European nationalism as a means of enlisting support from domestic and foreign constituencies for the war effort and wartime foreign policy.[12]

Roosevelt's death in April 1945, prior to the war's end, brought Harry S. Truman to office. Truman's lack of expertise in foreign affairs opened the way for the State Department, and its Europhile leadership, to exert greater influence over American policies.[13] Moreover, the perspicacity that Roosevelt and a few other American officials displayed in recognizing the force of non-European nationalism, was lacking in the new president and in the more influential sections of the State Department.

Another factor influencing American policy was the defeat of Germany and Japan, which accelerated the search for a postwar settlement in Europe. This settlement moderated American demands for an end to colonialism. The support of the European colonial powers for American policies in Europe was too valuable an asset to be jeopardized by challenging their status as colonial powers. By the time of the San Francisco Conference establishing the United Nations, American policy had shifted decisively toward support for the European efforts to reassert control over their empires."[14]

It would be easy to assume that from the San Francisco Conference onward, the American support for non-European nationalism was lukewarm. However, it would seem that the American response to non-European nationalism as part of its foreign policy after 1945 is a much more complex and tortuous story. It is a fact that the two major wars in which United States military forces have been involved since 1945, that is, Korea and Vietnam, have both been wars resulting from the superimposition of major power conflicts upon civil wars arising out of the decolonization process. Obviously for the United States, decolonization after 1945 has posed problems as great, if not greater, than those posed by the issue of maintaining stability and peace in Europe.

This complexity has eluded much of the conventional views of the history of American policy toward the disintegration of European imperial systems. American policy toward decolonization in the non-European world has traditionally been studied at two levels. First, it has been studied to establish the extent of American influence on the evolution of the ideology of colonialism.[15] Second, it has been examined in specific contexts of decolonization; that is, American policy toward decolonization in particular regions such as Africa or Asia, or toward individual countries such as India or Indonesia.[16]

Two main approaches have dominated these studies: the first sees the United States pursuing a policy of anticolonialism, rooted in its own historical experience of throwing off the shackles of colonial rule and hostility to colonialism as a constraint on the right of a people to self-determination.[17] The second view is that of American anticolonialism serving as a cover for the pursuit of its own political, strategic, and economic advantage in the non-European world at the expense of the other colonial powers.[18]

However, recent studies of American policy toward decolonization in various areas provide a less simplistic evaluation of that policy as it evolved after 1945. Rather than viewing American policy as predetermined, either by idealism, or by a search for its own advantage vis-à-vis its European partners, the recent literature has illustrated the uncertainties that surrounded and helped to shape American policy. As a result, that policy is shown to be the product of its considerations of which side to support, at what point of time, and for what purpose, given the imperatives of wider American concerns, particularly the fear of the spread of communism.[19]

While these various approaches have been useful for the elucidation of the details of American policy, they are inadequate as explanations for the seemingly contradictory policies followed by the United States in confronting decolonization in the non-European world. These approaches fail to explain why the United States at times viewed self-determination and decolonization as incompatible, as in the case of Vietnam, after the signing of the 1954 Geneva Accord. They do not adequately explain the suspicion of American motives and policies demonstrated by both the nationalists and the European powers when the United States sought to project itself as an intermediary between the protagonists. Explanations are also necessary for America's desire, as the dominant power in the international system seeking stability and the maintenance of the status quo, to use both the retention of empire and decolonization as instruments for achieving stability.

Given the postwar dialectic of European reassertion of empire and the nationalist drive for decolonization, one would have assumed that the policy choices open to American policymakers, either driven by ideology or by the desire to expand at the expense of the European powers, would have been simple: support decolonization. Similarly, if there was hesitancy in American policy toward decolonization, does this not imply a lack of vision among policymakers about the necessity to deal with the issue until the pace of events had overtaken them? If American policy was opportunistic, is it possible to identify a pattern that underlies this pragmatism? As stated earlier, these approaches to the study of American policy on decolonization are inadequate in providing an explanation for the complexity of that policy in the post-1945 era.

In view of the inadequacies of these approaches, the rest of this chapter is devoted to elucidating a framework for the analysis of United States' policy toward decolonization after 1945. This framework situates the policy toward decolonization at the center of American global policy and shows how the colonial issue was intimately linked to the evolution of this global policy.

The perception of American policymakers since 1945 that the United States is the guarantor of stability in the international system, and ultimate guardian of the perimeters of the non-Communist world--best articulated as Containment--has been the central pillar around, and upon, which American post-1945 foreign policy has been elaborated.[20] The preeminence of containment in American policy after 1945 created a situation in which practically every other element of policy became a function of containment. Inevitably the American response to decolonization became an integral part of the wider strategy of American foreign policy.

This is the first and most important factor to be established when analyzing the American response to decolonization since 1945. Anticolonialism, for United States policymakers, did not exist as an independent policy. The extent of support for non-European nationalism among American policymakers was critically dependent upon its ability to serve the perceived requirements of containment. In essence, the American response to non-European nationalism became intrinsic to the debate on the mechanics or tactics of implementing containment. There was no blanket endorsement of non-European nationalism or self-determination for non-

Europeans. Endorsement was done on a case-by-case basis and as a response to the perceived ideological coloring of nationalist factions.

This attitude toward non-European nationalism emerged as early as the late 1940s, as was evidenced by the difference in the American response to the nationalist movements in Southeast Asia. In the case of Indonesia, the United States swung its support behind Sukarno's faction of the nationalist movement against Dutch efforts to reestablish control over Indonesia after that faction put down a Communist uprising in 1948. However, uncertain about the ideological credentials of the Vietnamese nationalist leadership, because of its ideological inclusiveness and its incorporation of Communist factions, the Americans responded by pursuing a policy aimed at the destruction of the movement.[21]

The second aspect of American policy that needs to be taken into account is the fact that the right to self-determination and its corollary, political independence, became part of the arsenal of propaganda directed against the Soviet Union and its assertion of control over a sphere of influence in Eastern Europe. In using the right to self-determination as a club with which to attack the Soviet Union and communism, the United States portrayed itself as a champion of that right. American policymakers considered self-determination and independence to be incompatible with the creation of a state patterned on any variant of Marxism-Leninism. American policymakers, pursuing containment of the Soviet Union and its allies, considered the right to self-determination and the process of decolonization to be incompatible with and opposed to the spread of communist influence in the international system.[22]

The adoption of anticolonialism as an instrument of containment was not the only factor influencing American policy towards non-European nationalism. American policy had shifted because American aid for European reconstruction and the restoration of the North Atlantic-dominated trading system had specifically provided for the opening of the European colonial possessions to American capital flows. The opening of imperial barriers satisfied the search for commercial advantage that had underpinned much of the American anticolonialist rhetoric of the prewar and wartime periods.[23] With American commercial concerns appeased, and anticommunism of much greater import to policymakers, American anticolonialism languished.

A further element to be considered in analyzing American policy toward non-European nationalism is the existence of the perception, widely shared among American policymakers prior to 1960, that non-European peoples under colonial rule were unfit for self-government. They were generally of the view that self-government could be achieved only after the necessary tutelage in the principles of western political ideologies and systems had been imparted to colonial subjects. This perception of nonwhites as lacking the qualities necessary to exercise power was replicated in American society through discrimination against racial minorities. It was also a product of the American ideology of colonial rule that underpinned the administration of American colonies. From the perspective of non-Americans, it was inconsistent, if not hypocritical, for American policymakers to be ardent advocates of non-European nationalism while continuing to practice segregation in domestic politics. The twin challenges of decolonization and the civil rights movement forced American policymakers and the wider society to reconsider the notions of European racial superiority that underlay American attitudes to nonwhites.[24]

In addition, by supporting a period of tutelage and gradual progress toward decolonization, American policymakers could argue that stability would be assured and radicalism (read communism) avoided. Conveniently, it also served to provide them with a rationalization of their inability, and/or unwillingness, to pursue a policy of vigorous support for an end to European empire in the non-European world.

This identity of views with the colonial powers on the need for gradualism to determine the pace of decolonization was further strengthened by the adoption of a policy of allowing the colonial powers to set the agenda and timetable for decolonization. In the interim, the United States made the requisite placatory noises about its commitment to decolonization. The decision to defer to the colonial powers set American policy upon a course that was responsive to events rather than pursuit of its own initiatives. Of equal importance, American policymakers tended to view events affecting the colonies through the prism of perceptions advanced by the colonial powers. The importance accorded to Western Europe in American global strategy, created a context in which commonality of views was perceived as central to the maintenance of alliance cohesion. Any willingness on the part of the United States to initiate an independent policy was subject to the perceived necessity to compromise with its allies on an issue of profound importance to them. As a result, American policy became hostage to these considerations.[25]

An influential factor affecting American policy was the desire to shape its policy toward nationalism in the non-European world with a view to maintaining the stability of its allies in Europe. In the case of France, the critical European actor in the North Atlantic Treaty Organization (NATO), American policy toward the decolonization of the French empire was particularly concerned with ensuring that the process of decolonization did not destroy the right wing and moderate parties in France. American policymakers feared the creation of conditions for the reemergence of the Parti Communiste Français (PCF) as the major political force in France itself.[26] Given the instability of the Fourth Republic and its continuing state of crisis as it responded to the wars of national liberation in Indochina and Algeria, it was clear that the process of decolonization could have serious impact on the stability of political system in the metropole itself. Consequently, American policy toward decolonization transcended the non-European world, and was sensitive to the impact of the process upon the domestic political systems of the member states of NATO. In this context, given the importance assigned to Western Europe in American global strategy, the United States increasingly became identified as a guarantor of European empire and power in the non-European world. John Foster Dulles, early in his tenure as secretary of state, pointed to this perception of American policy among people in the Near East and South Asia.[27]

A further consideration for American policymakers was the economic contribution of the colonies to the process of economic recovery in Western Europe and Japan in the aftermath of the war. It is again not surprising that the United States became actively involved in Southeast Asia after the military victory of the Chinese Communists in the civil war. By attempting to deny the People's Republic of China the opportunity to trade with Japan and the West, the United States consciously sought to divert Japanese economic and trade ties to Southeast Asia as a means of compensating for the rupturing of Sino-Japanese ties.[28] The elevation of Southeast Asia to a status rivaling that of Europe in American global policy had much to do with its perceived importance as a source of economic support for Japan and Western Europe in the aftermath of the war. With Eastern Europe increasingly integrated into the Soviet sphere of influence, and Latin American exports denominated in dollars, Southeast Asian exports were considered as an absolute necessity for European and Japanese recovery. The importance of Southeast Asia transcended its role as a major supplier of raw material resources for Western Europe and Japan. To both France and the United Kingdom, their colonies were important dollar earners, and sources of invisible and service incomes for the metropole.[29]

Although European recovery depended upon American assistance, the colonies were also of critical importance to postwar reconstruction and the maintenance of a semblance of independence. The American decision to support the French in Vietnam, the British in Malaya, and initially, the Dutch in Indonesia, was a consequence of its acceptance of European efforts to reassert control over their respective imperial domains. However, with the onset of guerrilla insurgencies during 1948-49 in Malaya, Burma, Indochina, the Philippines, and Indonesia led by nationalist and Communist forces, American policy began to shift.

Confronted by a series of insurgencies construed as a coordinated effort by the international Communist movement to challenge Western control over Southeast Asia, and its access to the resources needed for Western European and Japanese recovery, American policy toward the region focused upon preventing the emergence of any new Communist state in the area. This shift in policy was pursued with the recognition that the colonies were integral to the process of economic reconstruction in Europe and Japan, and to the political stability of France in particular.

The outbreak of the Korean War led to the institutionalization of the globalist vision of containment, that is, the necessity to respond to every perceived threat to American authority outside of Europe. It also led to the expansion of the American commitment to its European allies in their efforts to restore their imperial systems. The United States, by late 1950, had come to recognize that European and Japanese recovery required control and/or access to the resources of the European colonies. With few exceptions, such control/access depended upon the reassertion of empire. Prior to 1950, the United States was hesitant to endorse such a policy openly. After the outbreak of the Korean War, the Truman administration was increasingly willing to move toward such a position under the guise that the threat to the European empires was Communist inspired.[30]

It can be argued that from 1945 to 1953, that is, from the last days of the Roosevelt administration to the signing of the Korean Armistice, these were the main considerations influencing American policy on dealing with non-European nationalism. However, from 1953 onward, several events both inside and outside of the United States began to influence policy. As a consequence, American support for the continuation of European colonialism as a mechanism for maintaining stability in the international system began to be attenuated.

The frustration felt by American voters about the conduct and progress of the Korean War was a critical determinant of the 1952 presidential elections. The Republican victory marked a return of American conservatism to the White House, and that conservatism was particularly manifest in the fiscal policies adopted by the new administration. Demonstrating a vigorous commitment to balanced budgets, President Dwight D. Eisenhower pursued a policy of pruning military expenditure as part of the economic and fiscal policies of his administration. This fiscal conservatism was instrumental in the endorsement of the strategy of Massive Retaliation--reliance on the threatened use of its nuclear advantage in the face of perceived challenges to American interests.

While this strategy did not forfeit reliance on military instruments to pursue American foreign policy, it implied a willingness to use nuclear diplomacy and a selective approach to the use of force. It represented a retreat from the Truman Administration's stance that every sign of instability in the international system necessitated a call to arms. This retreat also implied a willingness to utilize other instruments such as covert action, negotiations, and, increasing reliance on alliances, to pursue the goal of containment of the Communist countries.[31] The willingness to utilize a wider range of instruments to pursue its strategy of containment had noticeable consequences for the Eisenhower administration's policies toward non-European nationalism and the process of decolonization.

By reducing its own conventional forces, and signaling to its European partners that they were expected to assume a greater role in providing for the defence of Europe, the Eisenhower administration forced the European colonial powers to come to terms with their own military weakness. They were unable to maintain adequate military forces to meet the demands of NATO and the challenges from insurgent colonial populations. The European colonial powers were forced toward an accommodation with non-European nationalism through a recognition of their own weakness and the determination of the Eisenhower administration to limit military expenditures.

In addition, the Eisenhower administration demonstrated its willingness to exercise its influence on the European colonial powers to pursue policies in keeping with the American vision of the world--a vision which did not foresee American blanket endorsement for the continuation of European empire. This did not signify that the Eisenhower administration was prepared to champion anticolonialism. Rather, it became clear that the Americans were not prepared to blindly follow the European lead on colonial issues and preferred to distance themselves from the Europeans in embarrassing situations. In addition, the Eisenhower Administration sought to persuade the Europeans to move in a timely fashion on the issue of decolonization but were not prepared to pursue such a policy publicly. It preferred to exert pressure behind the scenes to push the European colonial powers toward an accommodation with non-European nationalism.[32]

The best example of this policy was the effort by the Eisenhower administration to prevent the Anglo-French-Israeli operation against Egypt in 1956, and the subsequent humiliation of the three states by the administration for having flouted American advice on the issue.[33] Similarly, prior to Dienbienphu, the United States had sought to encourage France to adopt a more progressive policy in Indochina as a way out from the humiliation inflicted by the VietMinh on the French military. This willingness to distance itself from European efforts to maintain their empire was, as in the case of the Truman Administration, conditional upon the successor regime being perceived as non-Communist. This element of continuity between the Truman (Democratic) and Eisenhower (Republican) administrations reflected the consensus among American political elites that communism was the antithesis of self-determination, and thus not to be considered a legitimate variant of nationalism. It was this conception of communism as illegitimate that led the Eisenhower administration to subvert the Geneva Accord on Vietnam.

A further consequence of American reliance on nuclear weaponry and of its increasingly global reach was the requirement for a system of forward bases to facilitate its deployment of military force. The need for these bases from which to project military power had emerged as a constant in American strategic thinking after 1945. Under the various administrations, it became clear that American access to bases in the colonial territories of the European powers was a significant factor influencing American policy toward the decolonization of European empires. The failure of the United States to prevent the Suez episode may have been the result of a British and French miscalculation about the extent to which the United States was dependent on their goodwill. However, it demonstrated that both the Europeans and Americans were cognizant of the implications for the projection of American and Western influence in the non-European world when non-European nationalists sought to change the terms of access to strategic areas. The need for overseas bases was integral to American strategic and military thinking and became a bargaining card within the NATO alliance.

But it was not only the accession of the Eisenhower administration to office that forced a shift in American policy toward non-European nationalism. The 1954 United States Supreme Court ruling in *Brown v. Board of Education* that segregation was unconstitutional transformed the debate and context of American politics. That decision was a powerful catalyst for the rise of the civil rights movement that challenged both the political structures in the United States and the self-image of the United States as a champion of freedom. The unwillingness of Americans to be identified with the suppression of non-European nationalism was undoubtedly influenced by the emergence of the civil rights movement. For the first time in the twentieth century, American segregation and its corollary--the denial of rights to racial minorities--were facing a major challenge to their survival. As the guarantor of security for the European colonial powers, the United States under Eisenhower found itself confronting a dual challenge from the nonwhite world inside and outside of the United States. In this context, the Eisenhower administration had to tread carefully around this dual challenge, as its response to the decolonization process and the civil rights movement had implications simultaneously for both domestic and foreign policy.

These shifts in the domestic political climate of the United States were buttressed by the changing international climate that followed the Korean Armistice and the decision to partition Korea. The death of Joseph Stalin opened the way for a moderation of tensions between the United States and the Soviet Union. The Austrian Treaty of 1955 and the Geneva Accord on the future of Indochina provided opportunities for a rapprochement among the major powers. The relaxation of tensions occasioned by changes of leadership in both the United States and the Soviet Union, and the commencement of fruitful negotiations on issues that had exacerbated tensions among the major powers, were also contributory factors to the shift in American foreign policy toward a wider range of instruments of containment.

The evidence of European economic recovery by 1953-54 with the successful isolation of the Italian and French communist parties provided the basis for the European states to seek a greater role in international affairs. Efforts by the British Prime Minister Winston Churchill to encourage a summit meeting between the leaders of the two major European alliances after the death of Stalin was one sign of this revival of European diplomacy. The Geneva Accord on Indochina, which was negotiated without a formal American role in the settlement, was further proof of European reassertion of autonomy in international affairs. In addition, the growing political, military, and economic linkages among the European member states of NATO made it clear that America's immediate postwar challenges had been successfully overcome. Increasingly, the sense of panic and crisis that had dominated

American policy from 1947 onward could be tempered by the relative stability enjoyed by the European states.

Similarly in Asia, the military stalemate in Korea, the suppression of communist-led insurgencies in Southeast Asia with the exception of Indochina, and, the emerging evidence of Sino-Soviet tensions within the Communist world, all pointed to the possibility that the United States could afford to relax its confrontational stance to challenges in the international system. The establishment of treaties with various regional groupings, including Australia, New Zealand, and the Southeast Asia Treaty Organization (SEATO) in the Pacific, and in South and Southwest Asia through the Central Treaty Organization (CENTO), served to formally broaden the security responsibilities facing the United States and to reassure United States policymakers that their objective of containing the Communist powers was being achieved. In addition to these alliances some of which had been instituted by the Truman administration, the United States under Eisenhower also sought to devolve some of the responsibilities for containment upon its alliance partners. These alliances represented a retreat from the willingness of the Truman administration to shoulder the burden of pursuing containment.

Finally, the emergence of the nonaligned movement at the Bandung Conference in 1955, demonstrated that the non-European world was seeking to widen its options away from the bipolar vision that sought to extend itself outside of the division in Europe. This attempt by Yugoslavia and many leading non-European states to distance themselves from the conflict between the major alliances was aimed at establishing greater room for maneuvering for the weaker states in the international system. Nonalignment emerged as an umbrella for change that would not be automatically perceived as threatening to the two major blocs in the international system.

While these signs of a changing domestic and international context were instrumental in shifting U.S. policy toward non-European nationalism, the decision by the Soviet Union to provide substantial economic assistance to various states in the non-European world changed the terms of Soviet-American competition for the support of these states. Thereafter, while the competition in Europe remained essentially military in terms of deployment and technological sophistication of weapons and forces, Soviet-American competition increasingly centered upon ideological and economic competition in the non-European world.

The Soviet Union also demonstrated its support for non-European nationalism by providing arms to states and political movements that were targets of pressure by the Western powers. This willingness to challenge the traditional dominance of the West in the non-European world added a military dimension to the competition between the two major alliance systems amid their efforts to win the hearts and minds of the non-European world.

Inevitably, the issue of decolonization became one of the areas of competition between the Communist countries and the members of NATO. As a consequence of this active courtship of nationalists by the Communist states, the United States under the Eisenhower administration began to demand a renunciation of ties with, or support from, the Communist countries as evidence of legitimate nationalism. Ideological purity was no longer the sole prerequisite of non-European nationalism if it wished to be recognized by the United States. Anticommunism in all of its forms was now a fundamental principle of legitimate nationalism in American eyes.

The challenge to Western dominance in the non-European world was not restricted solely to the Soviet Union, however. Increasingly, the People's Republic of China, radicalized by the Great Leap Forward campaign and the Sino-Soviet competition over their respective claims to leadership of the non-European world, began to assert a policy independent of and on occasion at cross purposes with that of the Soviet Union. In addition, as in the case of Egypt, other states began to provide support for the movements challenging colonial rule. This broadening of the sources of support for the challenge to colonial rule signaled the emergence of a much more complex international environment within which the United States continued to pursue its strategy of containment of the Communist world.

Notwithstanding this evolving international system, there was little American effort to reassess the multifarious sources of change operating therein. Rather, the view remained that communism constituted the greatest threat to the international system. Containment of the Communist powers was seen as the key to stability in the international system. While there was an effort to increase the use of other instruments of containment, such as covert action, negotiations, and economic aid, there was little effort to reassess the validity of containment as a strategy for dealing with an international system that had become more complex. The myopia conferred upon American policymakers by the bipolar lenses through which they viewed the world, effectively hindered their ability to develop a more nuanced appreciation of the dynamics that were forcing changes in the international system.

This intellectual rigidity was due in part to the McCarthy era which had effectively pilloried communism and also ostracized nonconformism from the body politic. McCarthyism had created an atmosphere in which departing from the consensus on foreign policy, where containment was the official orthodoxy, could open the path to political, professional, and personal marginalisation. The shadow of McCarthyism and the hysteria it generated had effectively closed the avenues for political debate in the United States. The impact of this social movement on the entire body politic and particularly on foreign policy elites in the United States cannot be underestimated. Its effects, and the style of politics it represented, have persisted beyond the demise of the senator whose name and modus operandi had defined the phenomenon.[34]

In effect, the Eisenhower administration was operating in the context of a dynamic and changing international environment and an ideologically rigid domestic arena. The rigidity of the domestic environment placed effective constraints upon any ability, or inclination, to introduce significant modification of American foreign policy. It was this gap opened by the rigidity of United States domestic politics and the fluidity in the international system that may have contributed to Eisenhower's image as passé and ineffectual in the 1960 presidential campaign. The criticism of the administration was particularly severe on the issue of the perceived lack of preparedness of American military capabilities in light of Soviet technological advances, particularly in rocket development.

The challenge to the inadequacy of the massive retaliation strategy had begun well before the 1960 presidential campaign. As early as the Gaither Committee report of 1957 that had recommended major increases in defense spending, there had emerged a tendency to criticize the basic premises, as well as the actual implementation, of massive retaliation as too limited and without sufficient credibility to deter change in the international system.[35] The Cuban Revolution and its subsequent challenge to American hegemony in its traditional sphere of influence; the outbreak of civil war in Laos and the resumption of the Vietnamese civil war; the growing influence of Nasser's Egypt in North African and Middle East politics; the radicalization of the Algerian challenge to French colonial rule; Sputnik and its revelation of the advance of Soviet technology, and the consequent recognition that even Fortress U.S.A. would no longer be immune from nuclear war; all occurred during the closing years of Eisenhower's period in office. This multiplication and diversification of the challenge to America's pretensions to the status of guardian of and arbiter of change in the international system must have been jarring to the Eisenhower Administration that had been so critical of Truman's handling of foreign affairs.

For an administration that had come into office on a campaign platform promising a rollback of the Communist world, the overthrow of Mohammed Mossadegh in Iran and Jacobo Arbenz in Guatemala were distant victories and of little relevance to the campaign of 1960. In effect, the presidential campaign in 1960 was a forum for the debate over the instruments and strategies of containment--debate which had begun in the aftermath of the 1956 election.[36]

The victory of John F. Kennedy in the 1960 campaign led to the emergence of the strategy of flexible response, which, as Gaddis has shown, was a revised version of the globalist strategy of containment applied by the Truman administration after 1950.[37] The premises of flexible response remained those of the Truman and Eisenhower administrations. The United States was the guarantor of stability in the international system and it was incumbent upon the United States to act as the final arbiter of change therein. Further, the central objective of the United States remained containment of the Communist countries and their allies and the prevention of the emergence of new Marxist-Leninist regimes.

These elements of continuity with its predecessors were incorporated into the strategy of flexible response. It was a strategy that required an increase in the range of instruments with which to pursue containment, incorporating a greater reliance on conventional and special military forces and the conception of a ladder of escalation through which threats to American security could be met and confronted. Further, there was a pronounced emphasis on meeting the challenge of the Soviet Union and China in the non-European world. While the Berlin crisis of 1961 revealed the continued primacy of Europe in American foreign policy, the Kennedy administration sought to focus on competing in the non-European world against the Communist states. In addition, the administration had brought with it an element of American culture that would put a distinctive stamp on its period in office--the concept of the detailed management of social change referred to as nation-building. The illusion of its ability to control the process of change in the international system was a central feature of the Kennedy administration and a motive force behind its policies.[38] This was the major distinction that demonstrated a difference from the preceding administrations. Where the Truman and Eisenhower administrations had perceived themselves as guarantors of the postwar world and the final arbiters of change in the international system, the Kennedy administration sought to establish America as the manager of change in the international system and in individual societies. It was, perhaps, this illusion that was the single most important factor in paving the way for the American disaster in Vietnam.

Another element of continuity between the Eisenhower and Kennedy administrations was the sensitivity displayed toward the impact of the civil rights movement on both domestic and foreign policies. According to Mahoney, John F. Kennedy, whose record on the civil rights movement could not be construed as an endorsement of its objectives, deliberately courted the liberal wing of the Democratic party by articulating a relatively progressive stance on the issue of decolonization. This stance on decolonization was a critical factor in gaining the support of the black vote in the 1960 election that Kennedy won by a narrow margin over Richard Nixon.[39] Once in office, it was difficult for Kennedy to depart from the policies he had articulated on decolonization, given the need to maintain support from the domestic constituencies that he had courted during the election campaign.

While the stance on decolonization was a mechanism for securing support from domestic constituencies, the Kennedy administration was also concerned about the support from the Communist states given to nationalists who challenged America's European allies. It was feared that this policy would provide substantial benefits to these states and undermine American influence in the international system.[40] Thus, the rhetorical support accorded by the Kennedy administration to the need for change in the non-European world was directed at pre-empting the Soviet and increasingly the Chinese challenge to the American role of arbiter of change in the international system.

As had been the practice of its predecessors, the Kennedy administration sought moderate and safe nationalists whose anticommunism would be the best guarantee against the radicalization of non-European nationalism. For the new administration, Fidel Castro's Cuba was a challenge to the American sphere of influence in the Caribbean and testimony to both the inadequacy of the American response to non-European nationalism and the success of the Communist challenge. Similarly, the Guinean decision to break its ties with France and move into a closer relationship with the Soviet Union was seen as proof of the radicalization of non-European nationalism.

But if the Kennedy administration was willing to preempt the challenge by the Communist states in the non-European world, however, this willingness was compromised by the reluctance to provoke a confrontation with a European ally. This was the case of the administration's policy toward Portugal and its African colonies. There were early efforts to pressure Portugal to start preparations for decolonization, but divisions within the administration hampered this policy.[41] The dispute revolved around the need for continued access to the Azores base leased by the United States from Portugal. This base was considered critical to the American ability to act quickly and reinforce its deployments in Europe. The reluctance of Antonio Salazar's Portugal to respond to the growing demand for independence in Africa was accompanied, as in the earlier cases of Holland in Indonesia and France in Vietnam, by a willingness to use American-supplied arms to repress the nationalist movements in its colonies. Portugal was able to resist American pressures because of its recognition that the Azores base was an ace with which to trump the Americans' game.

Eventually, as occurred under both Truman and Eisenhower, the Kennedy administration capitulated to Portugal's refusal to bend to American pressure. In the wake of the Berlin crisis of 1961, when the importance of the Azores base as a transit point for American forces being sent to reinforce NATO forces in Europe was emphasized, American policy was dominated by the need to maintain access to the base. Despite its rhetoric, the Kennedy administration was unprepared to break with Portugal over the latter's unwillingness to shed its colonies. The continued preeminence of Europe in American diplomacy remained a constraint upon its policy toward non-European nationalism, even under an administration committed to inducing a shift in policy toward the non-European world.

Thus, from Truman to Kennedy, American policy was shaped by the demands of European security, pursuit of vigorous anticommunism, and the need to reconcile domestic and foreign policy concerns about dealing with the nonwhite world inside and outside of the United States. These were the fundamental parameters, within which the various administrations formulated their policies toward the decolonization process sweeping the European empires. These parameters, in a certain sense, dictated the continuities evident in American policies from Truman to Kennedy. While all the administrations may have maintained a consistent rhetorical commitment to end colonialism in the non-European world, the demands of policy created an ambivalence about actually translating that rhetoric into policy.

These continuities in policy across administrations, despite rhetorical and contextual differences, reflected the hold of the bipartisan consensus that accorded primacy to Europe in American strategy and policy. Despite ideological differences and different policy emphases in domestic policy, the sanctity of the consensus on foreign policy led to the adoption of similar policies by Republicans and Democrats in dealing with a changing international environment. The bipartisan consensus on policy of the 1945-69 period effectively constrained any radical departure in American strategy. That consensus conditioned the response of policymakers and revealed the inadequacy of the American response to a rapidly changing environment. The decision to escalate the war in Vietnam, and the consequences of that decision for American domestic and foreign policy demonstrated the failure of American policymakers to understand the appeal and power of non-European nationalism.

For purposes of greater clarity, one can argue that there were four phases through which United States policy passed over the period from 1945 to 1964: (1) 1945-47; (2) 1947-53; (3) 1954-60; (4) 1961-1964. While the continuities in American policy toward non-European nationalism from Truman to Kennedy must constrain any attempt to establish clear distinctions among the various administrations, these four phases have significantly different characteristics that suggest the need for some temporal demarcation.

The first period, 1945-47, was dominated by the search for a postwar settlement in Europe among the major Allied powers, with the rapid development of an Anglo-American entente versus the Soviet Union. The division of the spoils of war was the basis for renewed conflict in Europe. Equally important was the fact that Britain's claim to a pivotal role in the balance of power in Europe had been seriously undermined by the war. The waning of British power, the emergence of the Soviet Union as the dominant military power in Europe, and the patent weakness of Europe in the wake of the war, made it evident that early expectations of an autonomous postwar Europe were not immediately attainable. It can be argued that the decision to terminate Lend-Lease Act arrangements, and the rapid American demobilization reflected the American expectation that there would be an expeditious return to normalcy.

With regard to American policy toward non-European nationalism, it can be argued that Roosevelt's death accelerated the retreat from support for non-European nationalism. The reemergence of the department of state as the dominant institution overseeing American foreign policy, as opposed to its lack of influence during Roosevelt's tenure, saw the rapid return to prominence of the Europhiles whose major concern was the restoration of Europe to preeminence and the downgrading of other regions in American policy. The withdrawal of support to the VietMinh, the unwillingness to challenge British and Dutch efforts to restore Dutch rule in Indonesia, and the general acquiescence in European efforts to reassert their imperial pretensions, all pointed to the abandonment of support for non-European nationalism. As in the case of Europe itself, American policymakers seemed to believe that the Europeans would be able to induce their rebellious subjects to return to the fold of European imperial rule.

The proclamation of the Truman Doctrine in 1947 (the second period), by contrast, revealed that the stability of Europe and any continuation of Britain's role in Europe required the commitment and support of the United States. The Truman Doctrine, the Marshall Plan, the establishment of NATO, and the decision to establish American bases in Britain were all concrete demonstrations of the American commitment. Between the two sets of events was a period of flux as the United States awaited Europe's recovery, and Europe sought an American commitment to support a postwar European order. The European desire for the American commitment was rooted in the fear that the United States would again refuse a major role in Europe, as it had done after World War I.

The growing recognition that European recovery and reassertion of empire were inextricably linked led to the shift in American policy from 1948 to 1953. This period was marked by the increasing support accorded by the United States to the European efforts to reassert their empires. The shift in American policy was achieved through the globalization of the Communist threat, by depicting both the establishment of the People's Republic of China and the outbreak of insurgencies in Southeast Asia as evidence of Communist challenges to the establishment of a Western dominated order in the region. The exception was Indonesia, where the United States supported Sukarno as a moderate nationalist against its Dutch ally and against the Indonesian Communist party. American policy during this period was largely supportive of European reassertion of empire. This was especially evident in the military support accorded to the French in Indochina. American purchases of Malayan rubber which helped the British to revitalize the Malayan economy while the imperial government was conducting a counterinsurgency campaign against the Communist-led guerrilla movement was further evidence of this policy.[42] American attitudes to non-European nationalism had shifted decisively toward supporting the European powers in their efforts to reassert their empires during this critical period.

By 1954, with the economic recovery of Europe, the death of Stalin, and the relaxation of tensions occasioned by the end of the Korean War, the signing of the Austrian Peace Treaty, and the accession to office of Eisenhower in the United States, American policy began to shift toward encouraging the European powers, particularly France and Britain, to come to terms with non-European nationalism. As earlier indicated, this encouragement was perceived as the means for undermining the growth of the influence of the

Communist powers in the international system. The Eisenhower administration feared that European obstinacy would lead to the radicalization of non-European nationalism and the establishment of ties between nationalist movements and the Communist powers. Nonetheless, the third period (1954-1960) did not see the Eisenhower administration break away from the ambivalence surrounding American policy toward non-European nationalism. In the case of Vietnam, while accepting the establishment of North Vietnam, it sought to make permanent the partition of Vietnam in violation of the Geneva Accord that had outlined provisions for the reunification of the country after national elections. Similarly, there was little preparation and little warmth for the onset of decolonization in sub-Saharan Africa--despite rhetoric to the contrary.[43]

In a sense, the Eisenhower administration marked a period of transition in American policy towards non-European nationalism. From 1948 to 1953, American policy largely encouraged the European reassertion of imperial authority. After 1960, the Kennedy administration was prepared to encourage the European colonial powers to accelerate the pace of decolonization. The Eisenhower administration was pulled in different directions by the European reluctance to abandon their imperial domains and its recognition of the power of non-European nationalism. A victim of circumstances over which it could exercise little control, the administration was in the final analysis unable to develop a coherent policy toward non-European nationalism.

The fourth period, 1961-1964, marked the most open advocacy by the United States of the cause of non-European nationalism, both rhetorically and in the exercise of political will. But the rigidities of the American political system, particularly the Manichaean views of policymakers and the bipartisan consensus on foreign policy, set constraints upon Kennedy's ability to initiate the radical departure that his administration's rhetoric conjured up. In the case of Portugal and its African colonies, the limits of the Kennedy administration's efforts were revealed. There was no great willingness to pursue a strategy of confrontation with a European ally. In the case of the Belgian Congo, the Kennedy administration's unwillingness to abandon its predecessor's opposition and hostility to the Lumumbist faction of the nationalist movement and its support for a leadership considered more pliable by its European allies revealed the basic continuity of the American policy--rhetoric notwithstanding. Satisfying European concerns and destroying radical nationalists was of greater import than supporting the principle of self-determination.

In addition to this periodization of American policy, the fact that the United States was itself a colonial power should also help to shape assessments of American policy toward decolonization. Prior to and after World War II, the United States was one of the major colonial powers. Its Territories, the term used to describe these colonial holdings, included Alaska, Hawaii, Puerto Rico, and the U.S. Virgin Islands. The Philippines, which gained independence in 1946, had also been a colony of the United States since the

Spanish-American war of 1898. These holdings were extended in 1945 by the American assumption of trusteeship responsibilities over the Japanese mandate territories in the Pacific. The acquisition of these territories as an extension of American colonial holdings was done at the urging of the military. American postwar strategy in the Pacific included plans for control over these islands. There was little ambivalence about American colonialism being extended to accommodate its post-1945 security interests.

On the other hand, the demands of Alaska and Hawaii for full incorporation as states in the American political system were met in 1959. In the case of Puerto Rico, it acquired the status of free associated state with the United States, a legal situation that left it neither a state within the United States, nor a full-fledged colony. The Virgin Islands remain a colony though with a considerable measure of self-government. More recently, in the 1980s, there have been efforts to terminate the trusteeship status over the former Japanese mandate territories in the Pacific, not without some difficulty.

Behind these changes has been a willingness on the part of the United States to accede to some of the changes demanded by the inhabitants of these territories. In effect, there has been a stated willingness to respect the right of self-determination of the inhabitants of these territories. The United States held its grant of independence to the Philippines as a model for the Europeans to follow and moved with relative dispatch after 1945, to implement changes in the political dispensation governing its various colonial territories. It is arguable that it was this relative flexibility and willingness to provide for self-determination for its own colonial territories that shaped the perception of the United States as an anticolonial power.

However, this relative flexibility in American policy embodied the ambiguities and contradictions shaping American policy toward non-European nationalism in the post-1945 world. Both colonialism and anticolonialism had some utility value in American foreign policy--the former as an instrument of security policy. The latter was a means of demonstrating its ideological commitment to "the right of self-determination" as part of its propaganda campaign against the communist group of states and as a way of inferring its moral superiority vis-à-vis its European allies. It was this paradox of support for both colonialism and anticolonialism that constrained American policymakers in their dealings with non-European nationalism and made them responsive to, rather than initiators of, change in the non-European world. It was also this paradox that made the United States the target of ire from both its European allies and non-European nationalists.

NOTES

1. For a discussion of American commercial policy in the 1930s see Jeff Frieden, "Sectoral Conflict and Foreign Economic Policy, 1914-1940," *International*

Organization 42, no. 1 (1982), 59-90; Lloyd Gardner, *Economic Aspects of New Deal Diplomacy* (Madison: University of Wisconsin Press, 1964), passim; and Richard N. Gardner, *Sterling-Dollar Diplomacy* (London: MacGraw-Hill, 1969), passim.

2. For Anglo-German negotiations and the colonial issue see A. Edho Ekoko, "The British Attitude Towards Colonial Irredentism in Africa in the Inter-War Years," *Journal of Contemporary History* 14, no. 2 (1979), 287-307; and R. John Pritchard, "The Far East as an Influence on the Chamberlain Government's Pre-War European Policies," *Millennium* 2, no. 3 (1973-74), 7-23.

3. Central to this presentation is the view that the decolonization process after 1945 cannot be properly understood without reference to events in the individual colonies in the 1930s, and the impact of the unrest of the 1930s on the emergence of new leadership and the realignment of forces within the colonies. Shifts in metropolitan policy prior to the war represented the efforts to come to terms with crisis in both the international system and in the colonies. For a discussion of the economic roots of the unrest, see A.G. Hopkins, *An Economic History of West Africa* (London: Longman, 1973), 237-91; and J. Ayodele Langley, *Pan-Africanism and Nationalism in West Africa, 1900-1945* (London: Oxford Press, 1973), 195-240.

4. This aspect of the historiography of colonialism is still very neglected; that is, How did the European crisis of the 1914-45 period affect the emerging crisis of European rule in the non-European world? The focus on the colonialism-nationalism axis often neglects the considerable variety of intellectual influences on nationalist thought prior to 1945--variety that was an integral part of the pre-1939 period.

5. See Yves Collart, "Limites à la decolonization," *Relations Internationales*, no. 18 (1979), 115-30.

6. The concept of collaboration as an instrument of colonial expansion has been used by Ronald Robinson to explain the establishment of the European empires in Africa and Asia. See Ronald Robinson, "Non-European Foundations of European Imperialism: Sketch for a Theory of Collaboration" in Roger Owen and Bob Sutcliffe (eds.) *Studies in the Theory of Imperialism* (London: Longman, 1972). I would argue that in the process of decolonization, nationalists in the colonies used collaborators in the metropole to expedite European political disengagement in the colonies. Thus, colonization and its antithesis, decolonization, represented a process of collaboration, or, more accurately, interpenetration of various societies set in train by European imperial expansion. This revised concept of collaboration can be extended into the postcolonial period where the framework of collaboration has emphasized the economic dimension of the relationship, such as trade and investment issues, and political and military cooperation in facilitating further decolonization as, for example, in Zimbabwe, or in the Eastern Caribbean; or, as in the case of Franco-Moroccan collaboration, for purposes of military intervention in Francophone Africa.

7. See Gerald K. Haines, "American Myopia and the Japanese Monroe Doctrine," *Prologue*, 13, no. 2 (1981), 101-14.

8. For favorable assessments of Franklin D. Roosevelt's anticolonialism, see F. R. Dulles and G. E. Ridinger, "The Anti-Colonial Policies of Franklin D. Roosevelt," *Political Science Quarterly* 70, no. 1 (1955), 1-18; and William Roger Louis,

Imperialism at Bay (New York: Oxford University Press, 1978), passim. For more measured assessments see Walter LaFeber, " Roosevelt, Churchill, and Indochina: 1942-45," *American Historical Review* 80, no. 5 (1975), 1277-95; John J. Sbrega, "The Anti-colonial Policies of Franklin D. Roosevelt: A Reappraisal," *Political Science Quarterly*, 101, no. 1 (1986), 65-84; Lowell T. Young, "Franklin D. Roosevelt and America's Islets: Acquisition of Territory in the Caribbean and in the Pacific," *The Historian* 35, (1972-73) 205-20; and Robert Dallek, *Franklin D. Roosevelt and American Foreign Policy, 1932-1945* (New York: Oxford University Press, 1979), passim.

9. Roosevelt's friend Rexford Tugwell, who went on to become Governor of Puerto Rico, provided an interesting assessment of Roosevelt's attitude to non-European nationalism. According to Tugwell, "Franklin felt that the independence movement, so powerful in India, was latently just as insistent elsewhere and that it must eventually prevail. He had no intention of committing the United States to the impossible task of checking these aspirations. On the contrary, he was dedicated to self-determination." See Rexford G. Tugwell, *The Democratic Roosevelt* (New York: Doubleday, 1957), 592.

10. For a discussion of the appeal of Japanese propaganda to Asians and concerns about the potential consequences of this for the war see Christopher Thorne, *The Issue of War* (New York: Oxford University Press, 1985), 144-210.

11. Roosevelt displayed little tolerance, if not outright contempt, for Burmese nationalists at the same time that he expressed his sympathy for Indian nationalists in 1942. The instrumentalist dimension of Roosevelt's support for non-European nationalism is explored in Dallek, *Roosevelt and American Foreign Policy*, 326-27.

12. See chapter 3 where I explore Roosevelt's sensitivity to domestic constituencies, particularly black Americans, on the colonial issue. Roosevelt's sensitivities in this regard predate World War II as Dallek shows in his analysis of Roosevelt's policy toward the Italian invasion of Ethiopia. See Dallek, *Roosevelt and American Foreign Policy*, 112-113. In the Phillipines, the terms for that colony's independence had been set by the Roosevelt administration. However, caution should be exercised in viewing this act as symbolic of Rooosevelt's anticolonial views. In the United States,considerable support for Phillipine independence existed in Congress among protectionist-minded representatives who wished to reduce American imports of goods from the Philippines. While reflecting some sentiment in favor of ending America's imperial role, the agreement on Philippine independence was also a product of the growth of American protectionist sentiment in the 1930s. For a discussion of the factors shaping American policy toward the Philippines, see Julius W. Pratt, "Anticolonialism in United States Policy" in Robert Strausz-Hupé and Harry W. Hazard, *The Idea of Colonialism* (London: Atlantic Books, 1958), 126-28.

13. See George Herring, "The Truman Administration and the Restoration of French Sovereignty in Indo-China," *Diplomatic History* 1, no. 2 (1977), 97-100; and, Barry Rubin, *Secrets of State* (New York: Oxford University Press, 1985), 65-68.

14. Ibid; and Lisle Rose, *Dubious Victory*. (Kent, Ohio: Kent State University Press, 1973), 175-81.

15. For example, Louis, *Imperialism at Bay*; Kenneth J. Twitchett, "The Intellectual Genesis of the League of Nations Mandates System," *International Relations* 3, no. 1 (1966), 16-39.

16. For example, Gary Hess, *America Encounters India, 1941-47* (Baltimore: Johns Hopkins University Press, 1971); Robert J. MacMahon, *Colonialism and Cold War* (Ithaca, N.Y.: Cornell University Press, 1981); and Thomas J. Noer, *Cold War and Black Liberation* (Columbia: University of Missouri Press, 1985).

17. See Louis, *Imperialism at Bay*; Julius W. Pratt, "Anti-colonialism in United States Foreign Policy," in Robert Strausz-Hupé and Harry W. Hazard (eds.), *The Idea of Colonialism* (London: Atlantic Books, 1958); and, Foster Rhea Dulles and Gerald E. Ridinger, "The Anti-Colonial Policies of Franklin D. Roosevelt". William Roger Louis' position would shift by 1985 to a more nuanced view of American policy. See note 18.

18. William Roger Louis, "American Anti-Colonialism and the dissolution of the British Empire," *International Affairs*, 61, no. 3 (1985), 395-420; Amikan Nachmani, "It's a Matter of Getting the Mixture Right: Britain's Post-War Relations with America in the Middle East," *Journal of Contemporary History* 18, no. 1 (1983), 117-40; and Kenneth J. Twitchett, "The American National Interest and the Anti-Colonial Crusade," *International Relations* 3, no. 4 (1967), 273-95.

19. Robert J. MacMahon, *Colonialism and Cold War*; Thomas J. Noer, *Cold War and Black Liberation*; Lisle Rose, *Roots of Tragedy*, Westport, Conn.: Greenwood Publishing Corporation, (1976); Steven Metz, "American Attitudes toward Decolonization in Africa," *Political Science Quarterly* 99, no. 3 (1984), 515-34; Ritchie Ovendale, "Britain, the United States, and the Cold War in Southeast Asia, 1949-1950," *International Affairs* 58, no. 3 (1982), 447-64; and Andrew J. Rotter, "The Triangular Route to Vietnam: The United States, Great Britain, and Southeast Asia, 1945-50," *International History Review* 6, no. 3 (1984), 404-23.

20. The best overview of containment is found in John Lewis Gaddis, *Strategies of Containment* (New York: Oxford University Press, 1982). While having reservations about some of Gaddis' arguments, I have relied on his descriptions and his analysis of the major shifts in U.S. policy over the period 1945-64. Some of the arguments I advance over the rest of the chapter would suggest a need for a revision of Gaddis' conceptual framework and some of his arguments. The minor consideration paid to the non-European world (outside of Vietnam and the PRC) and U.S. efforts to implement containment therein, represents the most visible weakness in Gaddis' work.

21. For various perspectives on the differences in U.S. policy toward Indochina and Indonesia, see MacMahon, *Colonialism and Cold War*, 304-16; Evelyn Colbert, "The Road Not Taken". *Foreign Affairs* 51, no. 2 (1973), 608-28; and George McT. Kahin, "The United States and the Anticolonial Revolutions in Southeast Asia, 1945-50," in Yonosuke Nagai and Akira Iriye (eds.), *The Origins of the Cold War in Asia* (Tokyo: University of Tokyo Press, 1977), 338-61.

22. Kahin argues that U.S. policymakers assumed that the challenge to European empires was a process in which it was possible to distinguish between communists and nationalists "that the two could never genuinely fuse." See Kahin, "The United States

and the Anti-Colonial Revolutions in Southeast Asia, 1945-50," 349. However, Kahin's argument is equally valid when applied to American attitudes toward alliances between non-Communist and Communist forces in Europe. American policymakers were consistently hostile to attempts by non-Communist parties to establish coalitions with Communists in France and Italy throughout the post-1945 era. The point here is that American policy toward non-European nationalists paralleled its attitudes in Europe, reinforcing my argument that the response to decolonization was part of the wider strategy of American foreign policy.

23. For a discussion of American use of E.R.P aid to gain access to European colonies see Robert A. Pollard, *Economic Security and the Origins of the Cold War, 1945-50* (New York: Columbia University Press, 1985), 197-203; and Alfred E. Eckes, Jr., *The United States and the Global Struggle for Minerals* (Austin: University of Texas Press, 1979), 157-62.

24. Richard Nixon's report on his visit to Africa in 1957 explicitly addressed this issue and the predicament it posed for American policymakers. According to Nixon, "We cannot talk equality to the peoples of Africa and Asia and practice inequality in the United States." "The Emergence of Africa: Report to President Eisenhower by Vice-President Nixon," *Department of State Bulletin*, 36, no. 930, April 22, 1957, 635-40.

25. The consistency of this element in U.S. policy can be observed from the decision at the San Francisco Conference in 1945 to support the European efforts to reassert their control over their empires, through the U.S. backing of French policy in Indochina and North Africa in the 1950s, to the deference exhibited toward Britain's and Portugal's policies in Southern Africa in the 1960s and early 1970s.

26. For a discussion of the post-1945 problems of France and the role of the colonial myth in rendering the Fourth Republic fragile, see D. Bruce Marshall, *The French Colonial Myth and Constitution-Making in the Fourth Republic* (New Haven, Conn.: Yale University Press, 1973), passim; and Tony Smith, *The French Stake in Algeria, 1945-62* (Ithaca, N.Y.: Cornell University Press, 1978), passim. For coverage of U.S. policy toward France after 1945, see Townsend Hoopes, *The Devil and John Foster Dulles* (Boston: Little, Brown, 1973); Irwin M. Wall, *L'influence americaine sur la politique francaise, 1945-1954* (Paris: Balland, 1989); William Burr, "Marshall Planners and the Politics of Empire: The United States and French Financial Policy, 1948," *Diplomatic History* 15, no. 4 (1991), 473-94; and Geoffrey Warner, "The United States and the Rearmament of West Germany, 1950-54," *International Affairs* 61, no. 2 (1985), 279-86.

27. FO 371/103515, "Text of Radio Address by the Honorable John Foster Dulles, Secretary of State, on his recent trip to the Near East and South Asia," June 1, 1953.

28. For U.S. perceptions of Southeast Asia after 1945, see Ovendale, "Britain, the United States, and the Cold War"; Rotter, "The United States, Great Britain, and Southeast Asia, 1945-50"; Michael Schaller, "Securing the Great Crescent: Occupied Japan and the Origins of Containment in Southeast Asia," *Journal of American History* 69, no. 2 (1982), 392-414; Yoko Yasahura, "Japan, Communist China, and Export

Controls in Asia, 1948-52," *Diplomatic History* 10, no. 1 (1986), 75-89; Robert Blum, *Drawing the Line* (New York: W.W. Norton, 1982); Pollard, *Economic Security and the Origins of the Cold War*, 186; and Nicholas Tarling, "The United Kingdom and the Origins of the Colombo Plan," *Journal of Commonwealth and Comparative Politics* 24, no. 1 (1986), 3-34.

29. Ibid; see also "PPS/51" in Anna Karsten Nelson (ed.) *The State Department Policy Planning Papers, 1947-1949* (New York: Garland Publishing, 1983).

30. For a discussion of the economic contribution of the colonies to Europe, see Karsten, "PPS/51"; and P. W. Bell, "Colonialism as a Problem in American Foreign Policy," *World Politics* 5, no.1 (1952), 86-109.

31. For a discussion of the instruments of containment under the Eisenhower administration, see Gaddis, *Strategies of Containment*, 127-97.

32. Telegram, Hildreth to Dulles, May 22, 1953. Hildreth reported meeting Nehru who raised the issue of decolonization in Africa. "I said United States was faithful to its traditions in these matters and would like nothing better than to work openly for political liberty, but that we did not (repeat not) feel we could afford open break with British and French in this matter." *Declassified Documents Reference Service* 8, no. 1 (1982) DOS 000932.

33. Letter, Eisenhower to Swede Hazlett, November 18, 1957. *Declassified Documents Reference Service* 8, no. 4, (1982) WH002931. In the letter Eisenhower indicated that "had we published an account of the long, patient and hard work we did with the British and French, as well as the Israeli, in order to prevent the attack on Egypt and in making plain what would be our attitude in the event of such an attack was undertaken, there would have been the greatest political trouble in Britain, and probably in France. So we just had to let people think that we acted on the spur of the moment and astonished our friends by taking the action we did. Actually, they knew exactly what we'd do."

34. For a discussion of the phenomenon and its links to both domestic politics and foreign policy of the United States, see Richard M. Freeland, *The Truman Doctrine and the Origins of McCarthyism* (New York: Alfred A. Knopf, 1972); and Richard M. Fried, *Nightmare in Red: The McCarthy Era in Perspective*. (New York: Oxford University Press, 1990).

35. See Gaddis, *Strategies of Containment* 184-86.

36. Ibid., 187-99.

37. Ibid., 204.

38. The Alliance for Progress was probably the most grandiose realization of this vision.

39. Richard D. Mahoney, *JFK: Ordeal in Africa* (New York: Oxford University Press, 1983), 30-31.

40. Gaddis, *Strategies of Containment*, 198-236.

41. Mahoney, *JFK: Ordeal in Africa*, 209-22; and Noer, *Cold War and Black Liberation*, 64-82.

42. For a discussion of US policy in Malaya during this period, see Pamela Sodhy, *The US-Malaysian Nexus* (Kuala Lumpur, Malaysia: Institute of Strategic and International Studies, 1991), 49-97.

43. See Martin Staniland, *American Intellectuals and African Nationalists, 1955-1970* (New Haven, Conn.: Yale University Press, 1991), 27-28.

2

The Crisis of Colonial Rule in the Caribbean

As in the rest of the colonial world of the 1930s, the British colonies in the Caribbean were rocked by unrest arising out of the economic downturn induced by the breakdown of the international monetary and trading systems in the 1920s and 1930s. The effects of the collapse of commodity prices on sugar and other agricultural products from the British Caribbean were compounded by the convergence of long- and short-term factors that had adverse effects upon the colonial order in these societies.

The outbreak of disturbances in St. Kitts in 1935, followed by strikes and riots in many other territories over the three succeeding years was evidence of the grave popular dissatisfaction which had taken root in the area.[1] For Britain, the unrest in these colonies mirrored in other colonies in Asia and Africa was an indication that its reputation as a colonial power was at stake. Moreover, the upheavals and subsequent reports on their roots in the Caribbean represented an indictment of British colonial rule. The cumulative effect of these events was the revelation of the bankruptcy of the contemporary order in the region. In summary, the jewels in the crown of the first empire had become the millstones of the second empire. Despite the transformation of Britain from the poor cousin of Europe into *primus inter pares* in a European-dominated world order, these most ancient of colonies in the British empire were evidence of stagnation, rather than the injection of progress implied in the apologia for imperialism and colonial rule in the nineteenth and twentieth centuries.

The crisis of colonial rule in the British Caribbean revealed the dual nature of the problems to be confronted. In the first instance, the evidence of the economic decline, political decay, and social dislocation underlying the outbreak of unrest across the entire region, pointed to the need to confront these realities at the level of individual territories. In the second, the renewed importance of the empire to Britain, and the need to provide for a new ispensation within the framework of empire became salient. The evidence of profound crisis in the colonial order of the British Caribbean confronted the imperial government with a major challenge.

The collapse of sugar prices, and the decline in profitability of the sugar industry, can be considered the catalyst triggering the unrest in these territories.[2] However, other factors set the stage for the crisis in the political economy of these colonies. The problems confronting the sugar industry were only one manifestation of the lack of economic dynamism of these territories. Despite increasing levels of production and efficiency in the utilization of inputs, British West Indian sugar production remained caught between the growth of cane-sugar production in other areas of the Caribbean (for example, Cuba and Puerto Rico), in Mauritius and in the Pacific, and the growth of a subsidized beet-sugar industry in Europe.

The emergence and expansion of these other sugar producing centers reduced the share of the British Caribbean in the international sugar market, and the increased competition from these other producers forced the British West Indies sugar industry toward greater reliance upon preferences within the British imperial system to survive. The emergence of Puerto Rico and Cuba as major sugar producers had an especially significant impact on the British West Indies after the Spanish-American War of 1898. The American market was effectively closed to sugar exports from the British West Indies through the American introduction of preference for exports from Puerto Rico and Cuba.[3] Consequently, by the closing years of the nineteenth century, the British West Indies were locked into the British imperial system by their dependence upon the preferences granted by Britain and Canada. This dependence upon imperial preferences was further reinforced by the lack of competitiveness of other agricultural crops. Despite some diversification, notably into bananas, nutmeg, cocoa, citrus, coffee, and arrowroot, these crops succumbed to competition from other producers within and outside of the British Empire.[4] Sugar remained king despite all the adversities it faced.

This mutually reinforcing framework of specialization and dependence in the external relations of the British West Indies was buttressed by the lack of change in the domestic economy. The access to the imperial exchequer and markets effectively provided a buffer for the sugar interests in the colonies and removed incentives for restructuring the economies of these territories. The margin of profitability offered by imperial preferences was sufficient to enable the sugar industry and the plantation system to survive.

Despite the acquisition of land by free laborers, the emergence of a viable peasantry was constrained by the continued domination of the plantation economy in these territories.[5] The cultivation of alternative crops was largely undertaken by the peasant sector, though official support for the peasantry did not emerge until the late nineteenth century.[6] However, competition from other producers and lack of adequate preferences within the empire effectively hindered the development of these crops as alternatives to sugar cultivation. Notwithstanding these attempts at diversification, plantations remained the dominant unit of production throughout most of the British West Indies. Trade, fiscal policy, and in effect government policy remained hostage to plantation interests as these territories struggled to maintain their viability in the face of an increasingly adverse external environment.

This long-term situation of specialization, dependence, and rigidity of the economy of the British West Indies, was exacerbated by developments in the 1920s and 1930s. While the price of sugar rose during and immediately after World War I, the price declined thereafter. By the late 1920s, the United Kingdom had to increase the level of preferences accorded to the British West Indies sugar industry to give the industry breathing space to become more efficient.

Throughout the 1930s sugar production consistently exceeded demand. The major trading countries established the International Sugar Agreement (ISA) to limit production and exports, thereby stabilizing the market. For the British West Indies, the agreement imposed limits upon the output of the sugar industry for its duration. As a consequence, the crisis of the 1930s made it imperative for alternatives to the sugar industry to be found. Over the decade, it had become evident that the political economy of these territories was in need of reform and reorganization. One serious concern was finding ways to reduce the burden that preferences for the British West Indies sugar industry placed upon the imperial exchequer.[7]

Beyond the convergence of these long- and short-term threats to the sugar industry, the other parts of the agricultural sector in the British West Indies were in as serious, or even more precarious, condition. For cocoa produced in Grenada and Trinidad, notwithstanding its higher quality, the emergence of lower-cost producers in Brazil and Africa posed a serious threat to the survival of this crop in the long-term. In 1939, the industry was reported to have been living on credit for several years past, with the hope that there would be an upswing in prices.[8]

For bananas, which had become a major export for Jamaica, the Windward Islands, Dominica, and British Honduras, the spread of leaf spot disease had proved a serious constraint upon production. Decreasing production and the outbreak of the war triggered an increase in prices, but the long-term future of the crop was bleak.[9]

In the citrus industry, production in Jamaica was hampered by low prices and poor cultivation practices. In Dominica, hurricane damage and disease presented serious constraints to growers. Both of these territories were confronted by competition from Palestine and a decline in purchases by the United States that compounded the difficulties facing the West Indian industry. It was testimony to the state of the agricultural economy in the British West Indies that outside of sugar, citrus was perceived to be the only agricultural export crop for which there was the possibility of expansion. However, even that possibility was considered uncertain.[10] Other agricultural crops suffering adversely in the 1930s included copra and rice. The coconut industry was suffering from a lack of capital investment. Rice as an export crop was important only to British Guiana, and the colony's markets were threatened by imports into the British West Indies from India and Burma.[11]

As a consequence, according to the West India Royal Commission: "misfortune had overtaken the producers of most of the alternative agricultural commodities in which the West Indies had found relief from the sugar depression of the nineties. . . . the position of the producers of such commodities as cocoa, coconuts, citrus, limes, bananas, coffee, rice and nutmegs has become so serious that in recent years there has been a decided movement back to sugar, though this has been lately checked by the operation of the International Sugar Agreement."[12] The future of the economies of the British West Indian territories looked decidedly grim.

A fundamental cause of this precarious situation in the West Indies in the 1930s was the continued prevalence of absentee landownership. This phenomenon had been a perennial problem for the West Indies since the establishment of the sugar industry as the major economic activity. The absence of the owners from these territories meant that these economies were dependent upon the whims of people for whom the problems were divorced from their everyday life. Moreover, the fundamental dynamic of the economy remained external to the economy of these territories. For the owners of the land, the sources of capital investment, the organizers of the transportation services to and from these territories, and for the metropolitan government, the central concern was the profitability and survival of the sugar industry. There was little concern with the other areas of the agricultural economy and their importance to these territories.[13]

Within the scheme of empire, the British West Indies remained a major source of raw sugar to meet the needs of the metropolitan economy. The returns on investment in the sugar industry guaranteed by the grant of imperial preferences was the central concern of both investors and the metropolitan government. Given this framework, profits derived from sugar were used for diversification of investment by shareholders in other parts of the empire and to support their standard of living in Britain. Taxes paid to local government went toward the maintenance, construction, and rehabilitation of the infrastructure necessary to maintain the profitability of the sugar industry. There was little concern with the investment of profits derived from sugar into economic diversification of the territories themselves, or of improving and creating the infrastructure necessary for the social welfare of the inhabitants of these territories.

In effect, for more than a century after the end of slavery, the conception of the British West Indies remained that of sugar islands among investors and governments, both local and metropolitan. Metropolitan policy remained responsive to sugar interests in London, and colonial governments were held hostage to the demands of the sugar industry in the various territories. Thus, absentee landlords, both by their control of land and capital in the British West Indies and their influence with the metropolitan government, were able to perpetuate the primacy of sugar in these colonies.

This situation of crisis throughout the economy of the British West Indies was further exacerbated by the closure in the 1920s and 1930s of traditional outlets for migration from these territories. From the late nineteenth century, migration had emerged as an alternative to the unemployment and underemployment that prevailed in the British West Indies. Barbadian and Eastern Caribbean migration to Trinidad and British Guiana had been one outlet for the surplus population of the former territories. Jamaicans moved to work in Cuba and established settlements on the Central American mainland, notably in Nicaragua, Costa Rica, and Honduras. The construction of the Panama Canal had also served as a magnet for migrant labor from Jamaica and Barbados, and many of these laborers had remained in Panama or in the Canal Zone. There was migration to the United States, particularly to New York City. In that city a generation of black political activists whose roots were in the West Indies, emerged in the 1920s and 1930s, and their work helped to spearhead the rise of various strains of black political activism that would subsequently influence nationalism in the West Indies and Africa.[14]

In the wake of the economic dislocation of the 1930s, the traditional outlets for migration from the British West Indies began to close. These closures removed a safety valve for these territories. Cuba and Panama began to introduce controls on migrant labor from the British West Indies, as did Trinidad. In addition, there was a net increase in returning migrants from the United States and other areas as the Depression set in.[15]

This migration had been important to the British West Indian colonies in several ways. First, it reduced population pressure on the land in the labor-surplus territories. This outflow was undoubtedly a major factor in the maintenance of social stability in these colonies. It is arguable that migration of labor constituted both a cause and a consequence of the survival of the plantation system in the British West Indies. It reduced pressure to reorient the economy and landholding systems to accommodate the growth in population. Without the pressure of rising population, there was little incentive for the landholding systems to be modified. Second, the migration reduced unemployment and underemployment in these territories. It was evident, from the late nineteenth century onward, that there was little scope for the expansion of either the economy, or the demand for labor employed in these territories. Third, migration offered employment and remuneration to workers from these colonies. Their remittances helped to maintain their families and communities in these territories.

By the 1930s an additional stimulus to migration from the region began to exert its influence upon these territories. Improvements in health care across the region had led to the lowering of mortality rates and a resultant rise in the rate of natural increase of the population.[16] The decrease in mortality rates implied that population growth was accelerating. Either an increase in migration or economic expansion and diversification had to occur to cope with this growth in population. Unfortunately, the economic crisis within the region and the closure of the traditional outlets for the migration from the colonies combined to offer little hope for immediate relief. Population pressure was intensifying upon these territories at a time when both their long-term viability and their short-term ability to adjust to the contemporary crisis had been compromised.

These economic and demographic pressures combined in a sociopolitical framework that could best be described as an anachronism in the fourth decade of the twentieth century. According to the Moyne Commission, the principle along which colonial government was organized in the British colonies was based on models drawn from the nineteenth century. It was based upon the view of government as the guardian of law and order.[17] Without exaggeration, it could be argued that the function of government was primarily repressive, with minimal consideration paid to others that fell within the purview of the state.

However accurate the view of the Moyne Commission, prior to 1940 the fundamental responsibility of colonial government was perceived to be the maintenance of a climate conducive to the well-being of investors in London and their agents in the colonies.[18] At both the territorial and metropolitan levels, colonial government was conceived as administration on behalf of the colonist.[19] Innovativeness in government, or activism on behalf of the nonwhite subjects who formed the majority in these territories were not considered virtues to be displayed by colonial service officials. Their future career opportunities were dependent upon the assessment of their performance by prominent colonists, or their associates, and other connections in the metropole.[20]

Nowhere was this conception of government more evident than in the systems of administration in existence in the British colonies prior to 1944. In all of these colonies, the function of the restrictive franchise, based upon property and income qualifications, was to prevent the emergence of legislatures dominated by the nonwhite majorities in the population. The Crown colony system of government for these territories, while rhetorically presented as a device to allow the colonial office to impartially discharge its responsibilities to the inhabitants of these colonies, actually functioned to perpetuate white minority rule in these territories.[21] Similarly, the existence of ancient constitutions in Barbados, the Bahamas, and Bermuda which conferred a measure of self-government and authority upon legislatures in these islands was not an anomaly. The relatively large white communities in these islands could be trusted, and actively endeavored, to perpetuate white minority rule.

Just as important, the consensus on government as the perpetuation of white minority rule--shared by the Colonial Office and colonists--was instrumental in perpetuating the rigidity of West Indian political economy up to the middle of the twentieth century. Control over the territorial governments by white minorities in collaboration with the colonial office meant that, apart from the (mis)fortunes of the sugar industry, relatively little attention was paid to the problems affecting West Indian society. The eruption of unrest in the 1930s and the findings of the Moyne Commission point to this ethos of neglect that informed colonial administrations in the British West Indies.[22]

The best indicator of this neglect was the situation facing the laboring classes in these colonies. The end of slavery in the British West Indies in the fourth decade of the nineteenth century had created an agricultural proletariat. This proletariat was largely dispossessed of land for exploitation on its own behalf, and planter organization, with government support, to prevent the emergence of a labor market in which laborers would be able to organize for purposes of industrial action.[23] In essence, after emancipation, labor organization represented slavery continued by other means--indentured labor; planter collusion to set wage levels; refusal to legislate labor ordinances or enforce those in existence; and ultimately, use of local militias and imperial forces to suppress discontent arising out of adverse conditions affecting local labor. This enduring hostility to the self-organization of labor in the British West Indies continued until the 1930s and was shared by governments in the metropole, and those in the territories, and among the landed and commercial interests in the colonies.[24]

It is significant that it was not until the accession to government by the Labour party in Britain that the issue of labor legislation in the colonies began to be addressed.[25] More importantly, the unrest throughout the 1930s in the West Indies and other areas of the empire forced the metropolitan government to recognize that hostility to labor unions in the colonies had to be abandoned. Instead, cooperation with the Trades Union Congress in the United Kingdom was instituted to promote and support union development in the colonies as a means of stabilizing the industrial climate.[26] The inclusion of a provision in the Colonial Development and Welfare Act 1940 making the enactment of a labor code in any colony a condition for receipt of funds under this act was one indication of this shift in policy by the metropolitan government. The fact that it was not until a century after the end of slavery that the issue of rights for the free labor produced by emancipation in the West Indies was addressed is one indication of the lethargy and neglect which shaped the context and practice of colonial rule, especially as it affected colonial subjects.

Compounding the ethos of neglect that informed colonial administration was the admitted lack of competence of officers entrusted with such administration. The Moyne Commission pointed to the need for the improvement in material incentives and rewards accruing to colonial service officers to attract more qualified personnel.[27] There was also a lack of stability and continuity in the colonial administration because of mobility within the colonial service. There was a relatively quick turnover of personnel in the West Indies that did not facilitate the development of a long-term view of the problems of individual colonies. One reason for this rapid turnover of staff was the fact that the West Indies was perceived to be a backwater of the empire. Appointments in Africa and Asia were considered to be more prestigious and financially lucrative than in the West Indies. Service in the West Indies also tended to be perceived as useful only insofar as it opened the door to an appointment elsewhere.[28] Given these career imperatives, it was perhaps inevitable that there would be little willingness on the part of individual colonial service officials to develop a long-term conception of their role or that of government in the West Indies.

These were not the sole handicaps afflicting the caliber of British personnel appointed to colonial administrations in the West Indies. As T. S. Simey has argued, psychological maladjustment, alienation within their own society, and subsequent problems of adjustment in the colonies were responsible for a relatively significant rate of "invaliding from the tropics" among colonial service officers.[29] This problem was further compounded in the British West Indies by the emergence of a highly educated middle class.[30] Trained largely in denominational schools because of the lack of government support for state schools, the avenues for social, political, and economic mobility were blocked by the operation of the colonial system. The existence of a restricted franchise effectively hindered the ability of members of this class to increase their influence within the institutional framework of colonial rule, and constrained their development of popular support. Further, the institution of Crown colony government effectively implied that the rise of individuals to prominence and political office was more often a function of their relationship with the Governor. It was rarely based upon the ability to articulate and represent the concerns of their fellow colonial subjects. Notwithstanding these constraints, this colored middle class agitated from the nineteenth century onward for greater measures of self-government to be introduced in the colonies, and up until the 1942, these demands remained largely unfulfilled. Despite their education and internalization of the values of British colonialism, including loyalty to the Crown, their political advancement remained blocked by the determination of the metropolitan and local governments to maintain colonial administration as an exclusive preserve for the colonists.[31]

Appointments to senior positions within the local administrations were also blocked by the practice of recruiting overseas personnel to staff these slots. By the 1930s, with the competence of some British appointees in question, the continuation of this practice in a context where local personnel with both the intellectual capacity and educational background to fill these positions were to be found, created the conditions for conflict and increased criticism of the colonial administrations by colonial subjects. The extension of this practice of white supremacy into the private sector was another dimension of the problem affecting the colored communities in these islands.[32] As in the colonial administrations, coloured mobility was constrained by the operation of the white supremacy ethic in the life of these colonial societies.

By the time the Moyne Commission arrived in the British West Indies, the bitterness underlying this conflict had increased and the Commission reported this growth in racial tension.[33] This increasing evidence of racial animosity was an indication of the white-coloured divide along which colonial society was beginning to crumble. It also represented the increasing challenge to the conception of colonial society as a bastion of white privilege. The emergence of a highly literate, aware, and articulate colored middle class rooted in the professions, the teaching community, and the lower levels of the colonial administration, had been a gradual process building over the century after the end of slavery. The creation of an educational system in the colonies had largely been achieved through missionary activity with minimal support from the colonial administrations, and it was largely through this system that the education of the middle class had been achieved. Nonetheless, by the 1920s the growing influence of this class in colonial society had been recognized and their demands for a greater role in control over the colonial order had begun to pose a dilemma for the existing colonial dispensation. As the Moyne Commission phrased it:

> the discontent that underlies the disturbances of recent years is a phenomenon of a different character, representing no longer a mere blind protest against a worsening of conditions, but a positive demand for the creation of new conditions that will render possible a better and less restricted life. It is the coexistence of the new demand for better conditions with the unfavourable economic trend that is the crux of the West Indian problem of the present day.[34]

Intrinsic to this demand for the creation of new conditions was the growing clamor for a greater degree of self-government from the middle class that the Moyne Commission acknowledged but was unwilling to endorse. However, it did indicate a willingness to support a measure of colonial reform through the lowering of property and income qualifications necessary to exercise the vote.[35] In effect, by the time the Moyne Commission had taken its evidence in the colonies, it was clear that the emergence of this colored middle class and the constraints it faced within colonial society had created a level of tension that further undermined the existing order.[36]

The growing demand for changes in the colonial system represented a search for new rules-of-the-game, or put another way, a new dispensation in these territories. The rise in racial tensions observed by the Moyne Commission could not be divorced from these changes taking place. One side was demanding an end to their exclusion from privilege on grounds of race, and the other was resisting as far as possible this assault on their bastion. It was also a demonstration of the fact that government by and on behalf of colonists was under question. The challenge to the restrictions on the franchise was the initial effort by colonial subjects to improve their position within the colonies.

As John Mordecai has argued, the riots in the 1930s transformed the climate in the colonies.[37] The upsurge of working-class militancy also brought into question the operation of the colonial order. This militancy helped to provoke metropolitan sensitivity to criticism about colonial policy. It was in this context of the challenge to colonial rule, both within and outside the empire, that there was the emergence of a new political alliance across the British West Indies. It was a coalition in which the middle classes in the various territories joined with the working class to advance an agenda of mutual interest for the workers, unions and other legislation protective of their rights; for the middle class, universal suffrage, constitutional reform, and self-government.[38] This process of realignment transformed the politics of these colonies. The alliance between these hitherto separate constituencies was evidence of the changing political climate in the colonies.

The establishment of this alliance was best demonstrated by the emergence of Norman Manley in Jamaica and Grantley Adams in Barbados. Both were lawyers who, by virtue of their work in providing legal services for laborers involved in the riots, became leaders of the new alliance in their respective territories.[39] In addition, their activities in meeting with leaders from other territories in the British West Indies in various contexts during the 1930s began to lay the basis for a challenge to colonial rule that transcended any single territory. The demand for federation, self-government, and trade unions, all assumed a regional salience before the outbreak of war and even before the arrival of the Moyne Commission in the British West Indies.[40]

This new alliance of the middle and working classes and its activism both within and across individual territories was accompanied by an intensified intellectual and political debate around the issue of the future of the West Indies. The context of crisis in the British West Indies was one factor prompting this debate. However, developments in the United States, particularly the growing influence of organized labor, the New Deal administrations of Franklin D. Roosevelt from 1933 onward, and the growth of black and Pan-African nationalist influences in which Jamaican Marcus Garvey and other American-based West Indians played a major role, all contributed to the discussion about the future of the British West Indies. Similarly, the emergence of the Soviet Union as a model of political development and the rise to prominence of the Labor Party in Britain itself, contributed to the new political consciousness and debate in the British West Indies. The writings of West Indian intellectuals demonstrated the sweep of the debates.[41]

The certainties of the colonial order were being eroded by this period of social economic and intellectual ferment in the British West Indies and the wider world. The unrest and the findings of the Moyne Commission confirmed the necessity for change and an urgent response.

Given the prior record of colonial administration in the British West Indies, it is not surprising that the Moyne Commission's recommendations opted for a strategy of gradual and incremental improvement in conditions in the British West Indies. Its major recommendation, subsequently adopted and enshrined in the Colonial Development and Welfare Act 1940, was for an increase in expenditure by the metropolitan treasury to finance improvements in welfare and social conditions in the British West Indies. This gesture was portrayed as a significant departure in metropolitan policy toward the Empire. This portrayal neglected to inform world opinion that the new policy was necessary to respond to the level of deprivation found in the British West Indies--deprivation that had its roots in decades of imperial neglect. The decision to prevent the publication and dissemination of the Moyne Commission report was based on the fear of its potential propaganda value to British enemies during the war.[42] The new policy was a reflection of the measure of embarrassment that the Moyne Commission report represented to the imperial government, as much as it bespoke the implementation of a new colonial dispensation. Beyond the recommendation to loosen the strings of the imperial purse to finance social development and welfare in the British West Indies, the Moyne Commission report advocated increased financial support for the sugar industry. It also advocated that a portion of such increased support should be earmarked for financing improvements in the living and social conditions of the workers. The commission categorically rejected industrial development in these territories and argued that the sugar industry and agriculture in general were, in their view, the sole viable bases for the British West Indian colonies.[43]

On the political and administrative side, the expansion of the franchise (though without the extension of universal suffrage) and improvements in conditions and emoluments for expatriate staff (to attract more competent officials) were recommended.[44] In the area of social and welfare issues, a considerable increase in expenditure and the creation of a special organization to supervise and implement schemes for such expenditure were advocated.[45] It is not clear whether the creation of this parallel bureaucracy was recommended because of a lack of confidence in the competence of the existing colonial administrations, or because it would avoid the control of the budgets of individual colonies by parsimonious Treasury officials.[46]

In any event, responsibility for this new experiment in colonial policy devolved upon this supracolonial bureaucracy. Of even greater importance, it represented a shift in the center of gravity in colonial administration. The new dispensation would be implemented from the Colonial Office, and less reliance would be placed upon the man on the spot, that is, the governor and his coterie of advisors and officials.[47] While this shift in authority and its consequences would not emerge fully until after the end of the war, the Moyne Commission emphasized the problems confronting Britain as an imperial power. It created an expectation of change. The outbreak of war, occurring between the end of the commission's hearings and the submission of the report of its findings and its recommendations, did little to reassure the colonial subjects that change would be rapid or far-reaching.

The pace of change began to assume a momentum which lay outside the control of the Colonial Office and that acceleration of pace reflected the growing influence of the United States in the region. Before 1940, American interest in these territories had been minimal. Beyond the occasional call for these territories to be transferred to the United States in payment of British war debts, there was little effort to develop a systematic policy towards these territories by successive American administrations.[48] The reasons for this were not hard to find. There was very little trade between the British colonies and the United States since the American acquisition of its own overseas empire from the Spanish-American War of 1898. The Philippines, Puerto Rico, and Cuba (together with Hawaii) effectively became suppliers of tropical products for the American market with preferences granted to their exports. In becoming a part of the American mercantilist trading system, these colonies effectively displaced the British West Indies as suppliers to the American market. Save for chicle and timber from British Honduras and bauxite from British Guiana, the British colonies were hard-pressed to establish and/or maintain a niche for their exports in the American market because of the competition from these other producers who enjoyed preferential access to the American market.

The lack of access to the American market for British West Indian exports was obviated by the preferences accorded to British West Indian products in the imperial system. Canada supplanted the United States as a North American market, with preferences accorded to the British West Indian products, and London served as the other major outlet for West Indian produce. Thus, mercantilism on both sides, American and British, conspired to prevent the growth of United States-British West Indian commercial relationships despite their geographical proximity. British policymakers were also wary of foreign investment in the colonies, and this policy was a significant constraint upon the development of commercial ties between the United States and these territories. Thus, prior to 1940, the peaceful coexistence of American and British mercantilism in the Caribbean did not favor the development of commercial relations across empires.

While the imperatives of official policy did little to promote the growth of ties between the United States and the British West Indies, the same could not be said at a more informal level. The continuing crisis of West Indian economy from the late nineteenth century onward, and the outflow of labor that resulted from this perennial state of crisis created a large West Indian community in New York City.[49] Despite being a minority within the black American community, the West Indians constituted an influential force in black political activities in New York; their role was a source of tensions within the West Indian community and with the wider black community.[50] A significant factor in this high profile enjoyed by West Indians was that their level of educational achievement prior to their arrival in the United States, their enterprise as immigrants, and their willingness to challenge the status quo all propelled them to leadership positions in the black community.[51] In addition, New York offered them the opportunity to engage in political activity which they did not enjoy in their societies of origin. Thus, through a combination of West Indian aggressiveness and the existence of a context for them to assert themselves, New York City became a Mecca of sorts for West Indians. The city served as a point of entry into a society perceived as providing considerable opportunities for self-improvement. From this perspective, West Indians came to view the United States in a positive light prior to the outbreak of the war. It was both a haven of refuge from the economic plight of the British colonies and an avenue of opportunity for those inclined to exploit it.

Through correspondence to, and the circulation of published material in the islands, the United States was also a source of information and ideas to West Indians. Of particular importance was the growth of trade union activity and the political activities of the labor movement in the United States. For West Indians engaged in the struggle to create the institutional framework for labor organization in the British West Indies, the growing strength of the labor movement in the United States during the 1930s represented a development to be seriously examined.

Despite the lack of formal ties prior to 1940, the colonial subjects in the British West Indies were engaged in a process of building ties to the West Indian community in the United States.[52] They were looking to the United States as a source of ideas and inspiration, but this interest was not restricted only to events in the continental United States. Relations between the United States and its colonies in the Caribbean, and the existing framework through which the American colonies were granted an opportunity to influence metropolitan policy toward the colonies had begun to influence West Indian attitudes. Even the Moyne commission believed it important, not only to visit the American colonies, but also to refer to the existing system of consultation between Washington and its colonies as an issue worthy of consideration in imperial efforts to establish a new dispensation in the British West Indies. Implicitly there was the recognition that United States policy represented an advance upon the existing British system of colonial administration.[53]

As a consequence, prior to 1940, the American presence within the British West Indies, while intangible was nonetheless real. For West Indians, the United States represented an alternative to their existing condition and an avenue of opportunity. Just as important, it represented a source of ideas and of experiences that could be useful to the elaboration of a new political dispensation in the British West Indies. Inevitably the American factor in the British West Indies had become an issue for consideration in the minds of both West Indians and the British.

The decision to allow the establishment of American bases in the British West Indies in 1940 transformed the strategic context of these colonies. It also opened the door for West Indians in the United States to assume a much more active role in American policy on behalf of these colonies.[54] These developments pushed the search for a new dispensation in the British West Indies in a direction that would have longer-term consequences for the British empire.

NOTES

1. In 1935, there was unrest in St. Kitts, Trinidad, British Guiana, St.Vincent, and St. Lucia. In 1937, strikes took place broke out in Barbados, British Guiana, and St. Lucia. In 1938, disturbances in Jamaica in January came to a head in May with widespread rioting throughout most of that month.

2. From a price of £23.10s per ton in 1923, sugar dropped to £5 in 1934. See John Mordecai, *The West Indies: The Federal Negotiations* (London: George Allen and Unwin, 1968), 21.

3. F. V. Meyer. *Britain's Colonies in World Trade* (London: Oxford University Press, 1948), 15-16.

4. *West India Royal Commission Report, 1945* CMD 6607 (London: HMSO, 1945), 17-24.

5. For a comprehensive discussion of the role of plantations in the Western Hemisphere and their role in perpetuating certain patterns of economic and political organization, see George L. Beckford, *Persistent Poverty: Underdevelopment in Plantation Economies of the Third World* (New York: Oxford University Press, 1972).

6. For a discussion of the shift in official attitudes to the peasantry in the British West Indian colonies, see Richard A. Lobdell, "British Officials and the West Indian Peasantry," in Malcolm Cross and Gad Heuman (eds.), *Labour in the Caribbean* (London: Macmillan, 1992), 195-207.

7. *West India Royal Commission Report*, 1945, 440-44.

8. Ibid., 20-21.

9. Ibid., 18-19.

10. Ibid., 22-23.

11. Ibid.

12. Ibid., 6.

13. The West India Royal Commission Report represented the first really comprehensive effort by the imperial government to deal with the problems of the West Indian colonies which had been accumulating since the end of slavery. Despite the outbreak of riots in St. Kitts in 1935 and the publication of W. M. Macmillan's

Warning from the West Indies in 1936, it was not until after the extensive riots in Jamaica in 1938 that the colonial office sought to lay the basis for a major effort to address those problems. See Howard Johnson, "The Political Uses of Commissions of Enquiry," *Social and Economic Studies* 27, no.3 (1978), 256-312.

14. See Judith Stein, *The World of Marcus Garvey: Race and Class in Modern Society* (Baton Rouge: Louisiana State University Press, 1986), passim.

15. *West India Royal Commission, 1945*, 10-11, and Roy S. Bryce-Laporte and Delores M. Mortimer, *Caribbean Immigration to the United States* (Washington, D.C.: Smithsonian Institution, 1983), 67.

16. *West Indian Royal Commission Report, 1945*, 8.

17. Ibid., 363

18. J. M. Lee, *Colonial Development and Good Government* (Oxford: Clarendon Press, 1967), 8.

19. It can be argued that whether the concept of government in the B.W.I. was law and order, or trusteeship, neither conceived of a role for the majority of the population who were not white. Thus, government was perceived as a preserve of whites, preferably from the Britain. For a discussion of the ethos of colonial administration in the B.W.I., see Gordon K. Lewis, *The Growth of the Modern West Indies* (London: MacGibbon & Kee, 1968), 101-110; and *West India Royal Commission Report, 1945*, 59-61.

20. Lewis, *The Modern West Indies*, 101-10.

21. Ibid.; and Lee, *Colonial Development and Good Government*, 5.

22. The decision to suppress the distribution of the Moyne Commission's Report after its publication in 1940 was a reflection of the Imperial Government's fear of its impact upon Britain's image.

23. For a discussion of the variety of West Indian labor systems after 1838, see O. Nigel Bolland, "Systems of Domination after Slavery: The Control of Land and Labor in British West Indies after 1838," *Comparative Studies in Society and History* 23, no. 4 (1981), 591-619.

24. For the evolution of British policy toward trade unions in the B.W.I., see Sahadeo Basdeo, "Colonial Policy and Labour Organization in the British Caribbean 1937-1939: An Issue in Political Sovereignty," *Boletin de Estudios Latinoamericanos y del Caribe* 31, 1981, 119-29; and Richard Hart, "Origin and development of the working class in the English-speaking Caribbean area 1897-1937," in Cross and Heumann, *Labour in the Caribbean*, 43-79.

25. Ibid. See also Sahadeo Basdeo, "The Role of the British Labour Movement in the Development of Labour organization in Trinidad 1929-1938". *Social and Economic Studies* 31, no. 1 (1982), 40-73; and Neal R. Malmsten "The British Labour Party and the West Indies" *Journal of Imperial and Commonwealth History*, 5, no. 2 (1977), 172-205.

26. Basdeo, "Colonial Policy and Labour Organization," 124-29.

27. *West India Royal Commission Report, 1945*, 372, 452-53. A fundamental problem, glossed over in the commission's report, was that the personnel recruited for service in the West Indies seemed to be less than competent. This view was expressed

by senior officials before 1939. See Basdeo, "Colonial Policy and Labour Organization," 119-20.

28. Ibid., 62.

29. T. S. Simey, *Welfare and Planning in the West Indies* (Oxford: Clarendon Press, 1946).

30. Elisabeth Wallace, *The British Caribbean: From the Decline of Colonialism to the End of Federation* (Toronto: University of Toronto Press, 1977), 24-5.

31. Even the Royal Commission's report offered little hope that this system would change. See *West India Royal Commission Report, 1945*, 55-66.

32. See *Trinidad and Tobago Disturbances, 1937: Report of Commission* (London: HMSO, 1938) for comments by the Governor revealing the extent of racial tensions in Trinidad prior to the outbreak of unrest.

33. *West India Royal Commission Report, 1945*, 59-61.

34. Ibid., 8.

35. The commission's members were divided with some supporting the immediate extension of universal suffrage throughout the B.W.I. and others opposed. It was unanimously agreed that universal suffrage should be the ultimate objective. See *West India Royal Commission Report, 1945*, 38.

36. For a discussion of the vitality of the West Indian middle class, see Simey, *Welfare and Planning in the West Indies*, 76-78.

37. Mordecai, *The West Indies*, 27.

38. See Patrick A. Lewis, *A Historical Analysis of the Development of the Union-Party System in the Commonwealth Caribbean, 1935-68*, Ph.D. diss., University of Cincinnati, 1974, passim; Caswell L. Johnson, "The Emergence of Political Unionism in Economies of British Colonial Origin: The Cases of Jamaica and Trinidad," *American Journal of Economics and Sociology*, 39, no. 2 (1980), 151-64 and no. 3 (1980), 237-48.

39. Norman Manley in Jamaica and Grantley Adams of Barbados were the earliest beneficiaries of this new alliance, but they established the model that most other nationalist movements would follow. For political developments in these colonies, see F. A. Hoyos, *Grantley Adams and the Social Revolution*, (London: Macmillan, 1988); and Trevor Munroe, *The Politics of Constitutional Decolonization*, (Jamaica: ISER, 1984).

40. See Lewis, *The Union-Party System*, 145-46.

41. For a discussion of the views of two leading West Indian intellectuals, see John Gaffar LaGuerre, *The Social and Political Thought of the Colonial Intelligentsia* (Jamaica: ISER, 1982), 51-126.

42. According to one source, copies of the report were removed from the desks of civil servants after it had been already distributed. See Mona Macmillan, "The Making of Warning from the West Indies." *Journal of Commonwealth and Comparative Politics* 18, no. 2 (1980), 218.

43. *West India Royal Commission Report, 1945*, 425-27.

44. Ibid.,451-53.

45. Ibid., 427-32.

47. This was part of the newly emerging approach to colonial policy of the late 1930s onward. See Lee, *Colonial Development and Good Government*, 78-99.

48. In June 1940, the U.S. consul in Barbados recommended that only Trinidad and Curacao-Aruba would be needed in addition to Puerto Rico and the U.S. Virgin Islands for the United States to ensure its security in the Caribbean. "If a change is necessary, I think the best solution would be for an independent Canada to have these islands. She now has no sugar cane and other tropical products, she is already established here and tied up with this region through the Canada-West Indies trade agreements and her Lady Boats. . . . .This scheme would be a lot cheaper for us and would eliminate the expense and worry of future maintenance and headaches over adjustments." This assessment was probably an accurate assessment of official American attitudes about the British West Indies. See 844c. 10/6-2440. Childs to Hickerson, June 24, 1940. Record Group 59, State Decimal Files, Box 4928.

49 Bryce-Laporte and Mortimer. *Caribbean Immigration to the United States*, 67.

50. See Ralph J. Bunche, *The Political Status of the Negro in the Age of FDR* (Chicago: University of Chicago Press, 1973), 599-604; and Denis Forsythe, "West Indian Radicalism in America: An Assessment of Ideologies" in Frances Henry (ed.) *Ethnicity in the Americas* (The Hague: Monton Publishers, 1976), 301-32.

51. Bryce-Laporte and Mortimer, *Caribbean Immigration to the United States*, 68-75; and Simey, *Welfare and Planning in the West Indies*, 75-78.

52. For a concrete example of how these links were operationalized in the case of Barbados where New York-based Hope Stevens helped to found the Barbados Labour Party (subsequently renamed the Barbados Progressive League and headed by Grantley Adams), see Hoyos, *Grantley Adams and the Social Revolution*, 81-83; and W. Burghardt Turner and Joyce Moore Turner (eds.), *Richard B. Moore: Caribbean Militant in Harlem* (Bloomington: Indiana University Press, 1988), 74-5.

53. *West India Royal Commission Report, 1945*, 382-83.

54. The offer of a new constitution to Jamaica in 1941 explicitly recognized the role of the Jamaican diaspora in the United States and elsewhere in forcing this change in British policy. See Ken Post, *Strike the Iron* (Atlantic Highlands, New Jersey: Humanities Press, 1981), 1, 154.

3

From the Bases-for-Destroyers Deal to the Caribbean Commission

Against a background of crisis in the British West Indies, events in Europe in 1940 forced a change in American-West Indian relations. It was a change that would bring sharply into focus the issue of the future of the British West Indies. The speed and spread of German military victories in the European campaigns of the spring and summer of 1940, and the rout of British forces on the European mainland, transformed the strategic situation in Europe. Not only was Germany the military victor but it had also become the effective arbiter of European affairs outside the borders of the Soviet Union and the United Kingdom. Britain's role as the pivot of the European balance had been usurped, and even its survival as an independent political and military force was in question by mid-1940. In this context, where Britain itself was confronted by victorious German armies, there were few viable options. Britain could either sue for peace with Germany or seek an alliance with the United States.[1] In mid-1940, however, conditions for the formalization of an Anglo-American alliance were not propitious.

For the British, the issue was simply to get the Americans to commit themselves to providing increased support for the war effort. For the Americans, the issue was not as straightforward. First, there were American concerns about the ability of Britain to survive the German onslaught. Second, the German occupation of the Netherlands, the rapid overrun of French defenses, and the threat to Britain itself, raised the necessity of preventing the transfer of the European colonies in the Americas to Germany. Such transfers, if effected, were likely to pose a direct threat to the security of the United States. Finally, 1940 was an election year in the United States. Roosevelt's desire to obtain an unprecedented third term as president implied caution in implementing any strategy of increasing aid to the British, as it could provoke a domestic backlash that could sabotage his chances at reelection.[2]

The effort to bridge the gap between British and American concerns led to a revaluation of the British colonies in the Western Hemisphere. They were transformed from the millstones of empire into the foundations upon which the Anglo-American alliance would be constructed. For both Britain and the United States, the immediate objective was to find a way for America to aid Britain to maintain its war effort in the face of the reversals of early 1940. For the two governments, however, the issue of how such assistance could be arranged without generating a domestic backlash in each country was of critical concern.

On May 15, 1940, Winston Churchill addressed a request to Roosevelt for destroyers, aircraft, antiaircraft equipment, ammunition, supplies of American steel, and the dispatch of American naval forces to Ireland and the Singapore area. On September 2, 1940, an exchange of notes between the two governments formalized the exchange of war materiel for bases in the Western Hemisphere. During that period between Churchill's initial request and the exchange of notes, there was an intense effort to devise the most acceptable formula and rationale for consummation of an alliance between a belligerent state and an ostensibly neutral power.

While the British focused on the terms of engagement for American support, the United States opted to pursue a two-track strategy. This dual-track strategy offered the United States both the opportunity for unilateral action in preventing the transfer of the European colonies, and a mechanism--that is, the Bases-for-Destroyers Agreement--for increasing aid to Britain. The first phase of this strategy was to establish the basis for unilateral action by instructing the War Department and the Navy to proceed with the development of plans for the military occupation of these colonies. In addition, the State Department was requested by the War Department to seek approval for the dispatch of American forces to these territories should it be deemed necessary. The second phase involved negotiations with the British to establish mutually acceptable terms for the transfer of the military equipment.

By the end of May 1940, the Navy and War departments submitted plans for military occupation of the area with the recommendation that the American government should assert its sovereignty over these territories in the event of a German demand for the cession of any of them.[3] Both the president and the State Department were opposed to the proposal for American annexation of these territories. Rather, they successfully sought congressional approval of a measure by which the United States would refuse to recognize any transfer of colonies from one non-American power to another. The measure also proposed American consultations with other hemispheric states on this issue, should Germany attempt to pursue such policies. Fortified by domestic political support, the State Department notified Germany and Italy on May 17, the day on which France requested an armistice, that the United States would not recognize any transfer of territories in the Western Hemisphere.[4]

Support for this policy from the other American states was sought through the convocation of a meeting of American foreign ministers in Havana from July 21 to July 27, 1940. The meeting drew up the Havana Convention authorizing the American states to establish a system of Pan-American trusteeships to administer the European colonies in the Western Hemisphere in the event that there was any attempt to transfer them to another European state.[5] A major concession to the United States was the agreement by the other states to allow it to act unilaterally in occupying the territories, should it determine that such action was necessary.[6] Despite a token nod toward the possibility of joint action on this issue, it was evident that the American effort to seek the endorsement of the other American republics for unilateral action had proved successful. The Roosevelt administration had won domestic and foreign support for its policy by carefully eschewing any assertion of sovereignty over these territories.

However, the effort to provide increased military aid to Britain had encountered several stumbling blocks. The British request of May 15 was rejected by the Roosevelt administration. The British War Cabinet had similarly rejected a suggestion from the British ambassador, Lord Lothian, that Britain should offer base rights in Bermuda, Newfoundland, and Trinidad to the United States. This preliminary impasse between the two governments created an opening for some active unofficial diplomacy by the Century Group, a New York-based private organization supportive of American assistance to Britain. The group linked the Churchill request and the Lothian proposal and actively sought to build support for the exchange of base rights for the transfer of war materials. In consultation with both the British Embassy and senior American officials, the Century Group drafted a version of the proposal that was submitted to the Roosevelt administration on August 1, just one day after a renewed request from Churchill for destroyers and other supplies.[7]

On August 2, the Roosevelt cabinet considered the entire problem of support for the British war effort. At that meeting, after discussion of the issue of support for the British and the option of American purchase of the British territories in the Western Hemisphere, it was agreed that the proposed exchange of destroyers for bases was necessary for the survival of Britain. To dampen potential congressional opposition to the exchange, it was decided to request from Britain a guarantee that, in the event of a German victory over the British Isles, the fleet would be sent to North America or other parts of the Empire where it might be of continued value to the war effort. The British War Cabinet subsequently provided the assurance. The endorsement of the proposed exchange by Wendell Willkie, the Republican presidential candidate, cleared the way for Roosevelt to proceed with the announcement of the exchange.[8] The formal agreement was consummated in an exchange of notes on September 2, 1940. For the Roosevelt administration which portrayed the exchange as the contemporary equivalent of the Louisiana Purchase, bipartisan support for and the lack of serious domestic opposition to the exchange were obviously welcome.[9]

For the British, the exchange was pregnant with possibilities and difficulties. At one level, it represented the desperately sought mechanism for obtaining increased American support for the British war effort. At another level, however, the grant of base rights in the British territories implied a derogation of sovereignty over parts of the empire. Nonetheless, from the perspective of late 1940, the exchange represented a major step in Anglo-American relations and, according to David Reynolds,

> the Prime Minister told his colleagues that such an unneutral act as the transfer of destroyers would be a long step towards U.S. entry into the war. And from various viewpoints, the Cabinet agreed that the proposal must be seen in a longer-term framework--as possibly the beginning of an Anglo-Saxon bloc, as the precursor of a new development for the Empire, or as the basis of a trusteeship principle which might stand Britain in good stead against anti-colonial pressures at the eventual peace conference.[10]

After 1940, these issues posed by the Bases-for-Destroyers Agreement became a fundamental problem afflicting the Anglo-American alliance. Even as it became Britain's closest ally, America was unable to overcome British unease about its previous advocacy of anticolonialism. Britain had become dependent upon the United States to underwrite its survival as a major international power and that dependence created a sensitivity to American criticism, particularly on issues affecting the empire. The American assumption of the role of guarantor of Britain's survival and its use of British colonies to ensure its own security were precedents for policy after 1945. The Bases-for-Destroyers Agreement foreshadowed America's increasing collaboration with the European colonial powers that would lead it to moderate its criticisms of European colonialism after 1945.

Nonetheless, both the United Kingdom and the United States had reason to be happy with the exchange of 1940. However, sentiment in the British West Indies was not exactly euphoric over the agreement between the two powers. While the grant of the bases to the Americans was seen as the West Indian contribution to the war effort, there were fears that the bases were the opening wedge of an American effort to secure the transfer of these colonies to the United States. For the majority of the population in the base territories, the coming of the Americans promised an easing of the economic crisis, the brunt of which had fallen upon their backs over the preceding decade. However, for the employer classes, the American presence threatened to disrupt their control over wage rates and the labor market. The fragility of that control had been revealed by the riots of the 1930s; the subsequent legitimation of trade union activity under the terms of the Colonial Development and Welfare Act of 1940 had further eroded their influence. Alternatively, there was the realization that the American military presence could be useful in containing any unrest and might prove useful as a buttress for the existing social order.[11]

To the colored population of the islands, the American presence raised the specter of the introduction into the colonies of the overt segregation and racism from the United States. Of particular concern were fears that the discrimination practiced in the Panama Canal Zone would be extended to the West Indian bases. For the middle-class colored population that enjoyed a measure of social prominence, there was special concern that American racial practices would be particularly threatening to their status. For the white communities in these societies, interacting with American whites would be inevitable given the situation, but sentiments ranged from a measure of acceptance through varying degrees of contempt to outright hostility, especially toward black Americans.[12] Finally, for the politically active elements in the territories there was caution about the coming of the Americans. The lack of consultation with which the exchange had been conducted generated some unease, particularly as it appeared to threaten efforts to introduce self-government. However, it was also given a measured welcome, as it opened the possibility that, in light of American anticolonial statement, the pursuit of self-government could receive a significant boost.[13] For all concerned, the major issue was how to use the American presence to fulfill their respective agendas.

Immediately after the exchange of notes on September 2, 1940, American attention began to focus upon the establishment of their military presence in the territories. However, there was also a recognition that American policymakers needed more information about the situation in the region. As early as September 8, 1940, Roosevelt held a conversation with Charles Taussig about the possibility of sending an American investigative mission to the British West Indies, an issue that Taussig had previously raised with Cordell Hull.[14] Taussig's concern with the situation in the Caribbean derived from his role as President of the American Molasses Company, which was engaged in the sugar trade in the Caribbean, and from his own personal observations of the depressing situation in the area during a visit in 1937. His visit led him to believe that the economic problems of the area had to be addressed to prevent the outbreak of further unrest. With the onset of the war and the uncertainty of the outcome of the 1940 campaign, his views began to assume a sense of greater immediacy and importance.

Charles Taussig's influence with Roosevelt and other members of the government arose from his long service on behalf of the administration. He was a member of Roosevelt's Brain Trust, which had served as a source of advice to the President. Taussig had also served as chairman of the National Youth Administration. As a result, he apparently developed a measure of personal intimacy with both Franklin D. Roosevelt and his wife, Eleanor. He also enjoyed access to Cordell Hull, Sumner Welles, and Adolf Berle at the State Department.[15] His personal knowledge of the Caribbean, coupled with his familiarity with leading figures in the Roosevelt administration, facilitated Taussig's emergence as the main figure in the development of American policy toward the British West Indies. His influence later extended to helping to shape the American response to the wider colonial issue.[16]

These preliminary discussions between Taussig and Hull, and Taussig and Roosevelt, resulted in the dispatch of a special mission to the British colonies by Hull and the departments of the Army and Navy. Under-secretary Welles, in recommending the mission to Roosevelt, cited the lack of consular officials in these territories as a reason for such a mission. In view of reports of restlessness among the population, American policymakers needed some insight into developments in the region.[17]

On October 30, Welles, Taussig, and representatives from the military departments met to discuss the planned mission. The mandate of the mission was to acquire information on the social and economic conditions in the territories with an eye to the implications of American occupation of the colonies in the event of a British defeat. A major concern was to determine the possibility of subversive activity and the establishment of contacts with both officials and local leaders who might become dangerous agitators. It was also decided to notify the British government of the mission but the mission itself would maintain a low profile.[18]

The British government approved the mission to be led by Taussig with a representative each from the departments of State, Army and Navy, on November 2. The mission departed in mid-November. However, very soon after its arrival in the Caribbean the British embassy in Washington indicated that the British government desired to have the Taussig mission aborted, on the grounds that the mission might sow confusion among the people of the islands.[19] Under-secretary Sumner Welles rejected the British request. He informed the British that the mission was economic, and that Roosevelt was unable to understand the United Kingdom's reversal of its position since the Moyne Commission had been allowed to visit the American colonies in the Caribbean.[20] Faced with the American refusal, the British demurred and accepted the American assurances about the nature of the mission. In addition, the British suggested a meeting of the mission with Sir Frank Stockdale, the recently appointed Comptroller for Development and Welfare in the West Indies.[21] This contretemps surrounding the Taussig mission was a reflection of British unwillingness to court American displeasure. Despite the fear of the growth of American influence in the West Indies, London was wary of a confrontation with the Roosevelt administration.

That fear of American influence was well founded. Prior to his departure, Taussig had discussions with Ira De A. Reid, a professor at Atlanta University, on issues of concern to local leaders in the Caribbean. Reid provided Taussig with letters of introduction to local leaders in the various territories. The report of the mission explicitly credited these letters of introduction with providing a measure of credibility to Taussig. He was able to obtain views from local leaders that would probably not have otherwise been forthcoming.[22] The standing thus derived from his access to these local leaders further strengthened Taussig's influence over American policy. He became an interlocutor on behalf of West Indian groups and individuals in dealing with the British government. The mission's access to these local leaders offered insights into colonial society that could be used to contrast the views of officialdom and the white colonial elite. By developing its own access to these unofficial leaders, the Taussig mission was demonstrating its willingness to go outside of officialdom to gain insights into the problems afflicting these territories.

Despite the concerns of London about the impact of the visit of American officials, the mission discovered that both the officials and the colonial subjects were not so constrained. The mission's report remarked upon the wide cross-section of views to which they were exposed in varying contexts, formal and informal. Governors were willing to speak off the record and they wanted to bypass the Colonial Office to deal directly with the Americans. The mission attended meetings of the legislatures and executive councils in various territories. They also arranged meetings with local leaders from which officials were excluded. British colonial security officials provided information on links between West Indian political and labor activists and their counterparts in the United States, especially those with a leftist orientation.[23]

The level of access provided to the Taussig mission was exceeded perhaps only by that enjoyed by the Moyne Commission. These parallel experiences resulted in a report that confirmed the findings of the Moyne Commission and its report borrowed liberally from the latter's own report.

As outsiders viewing West Indian colonial society, the Taussig Commission also provided some useful insights into that society in late 1940 in a way that the Moyne Commission probably could not have done. First, it reported the element of fear and uncertainty that shaped the response of the white social, commercial and political elites to the emerging nonwhite political and labor leadership, several of whom had been educated in the United States. Second, it was obvious that ideologies of the left, or socialism in its various contexts, enjoyed considerable popularity among these emergent leaders. Third, the white elites were unwilling to surrender their traditional control over West Indian society and the governors, whatever may have been their personal sentiments, remained hostage to these elites. Fourth, there was widespread support for the idea of greater self-government for the West Indies, with no clear definition of whether such self-government would constitute either complete independence, or dominion status within the British Empire.

Fifth, despite the promise of metropolitan subsidies for colonial reform held out under the Colonial Development and Welfare Act of 1940, the financial allocations were inadequate to deal with the immediate problems of the West Indies. In addition, several of the colonies had sent a part of their accumulated Treasury surpluses to help the imperial government's prosecution of the war. It was a paradox of the colonies helping to finance the war effort with sorely needed funds, at a time when the war had forced the imperial government to accept the necessity of subsidizing colonial reform. And finally, the mission reported that racial tensions underlying the West Indian colonial order had not been forced into the background either by the war, or by the implementation of the new metropolitan policy. Rather, it recommended that the American entry into the West Indies should be attentive to the local context in order not to provoke unrest through the display of a lack of sensitivity on the part of incoming Americans.[24] In addition to fulfilling its mandate to acquire information on the conditions in the British colonies, the Taussig Commission also promoted the concept of Anglo-American cooperation to address the problems afflicting the colonies of both nations in the Caribbean. British colonial officials, including the newly appointed comptroller of the West Indian Development and Welfare Organization, Sir Frank Stockdale, were receptive to the idea.

During the visit of President Roosevelt to the British West Indies in December 1940 to acquaint himself with the base sites chosen by the American military, these proposals from the Taussig mission were endorsed by the president. The president met with British colonial officials and stressed to them that the United States was not interested in acquiring the West Indian colonies. Rather, he emphasized that the United States was seeking Anglo-American cooperation and not the usurpation of British sovereignty. However, Roosevelt indicated that the United States would insist on American jurisdiction over American personnel in the base territories, as he was not prepared to accept local (read nonwhite) jurisdiction over American soldiers.[25]

The evidence of American insistence on Anglo-American cooperation, implying a strong American presence in the West Indies, was not received with general equanimity by either colonial officials or the Colonial Office in London. Two colonies in particular, Bermuda and Trinidad, were particularly concerned about the American presence. In both colonies, American military requirements were so large that it provoked a severe reaction from the local authorities. However, the metropolitan government overrode their objections to the American demands, stressing the necessity of not antagonizing the Americans.[26] The governor of Trinidad was later forced to resign because of his reluctant cooperation with the Americans, starting from the dispute over the site of the American base in Trinidad.[27]

This willingness to accommodate American demands was reinforced in late December 1940 when Lord Lloyd, on behalf of the Colonial Office, submitted to the War Cabinet a memorandum documenting areas of Anglo-American friction. The issues raised by the memorandum covered a wide range of tensions between the two countries: the areas claimed for base sites in Bermuda and Trinidad; American claims for jurisdiction in the base colonies that would compromise British sovereignty; the unilateral decision of the United States to offer use of the base facilities in the British territories to the

Latin American states but not to Britain; American claims to British islands in the Pacific; and the American desire to have the conference on the leases for the bases held in Washington rather than in London.

The position adopted by the War Cabinet on the Lloyd memorandum was unambiguous. Despite the perceived American threat to British sovereignty in these Caribbean territories, the United Kingdom could not afford to provoke a conflict with the United States in light of British dependence on the latter's assistance to the war effort. With regard to the American effort to host the conference on the leases for the bases, the War Cabinet's response was to instruct its Washington embassy to push for the conference to be held in London, though this proposal "should not be put as high as a sine qua non." By the end of 1940, British willingness to accommodate the United States had become the major factor shaping policy.[28]

The subsequent negotiations over the leases for the bases in early 1941 confirmed this trend in Anglo-American relations. While Roosevelt accepted Churchill's request that the discussions be held in London, the outcome of the negotiations revealed the increasing disparity of power between the allies. Even with the inclusion of representatives from the various colonies, usually the governor, the American demands for extensive authority and jurisdiction over the areas granted to them were largely accepted by the imperial government. The British capitulated and sought to portray the concessions in the public media as the strengthening of Anglo-American ties.[29] For the Americans, there was some joy at their ability to inflict their will upon the hapless British.[30] The willingness of the Imperial Government to sacrifice its authority in the colonies must have been disheartening for the colonial officials involved in the negotiations, and for the Colonial Office which continued to resent the American intrusion.[31]

The subsequent agreement by the imperial government to transfer the responsibility for the defense of the West Indian colonies to American forces was a further indication of the extent of British accommodation of American demands in the Caribbean. In effect, both in London and in the Caribbean colonies, the exercise of British authority in these colonies was constrained by the American presence and by British dependence on American military forces to underwrite the safety of these colonies. As a result, there was a rapid implementation of the strategy of "duality of control" without the "abrogation of sovereignty" proposed by Roosevelt during his visit in December 1940. Both the Colonial Office and colonial officials in the West Indies were wary of this development. For the rest of the war they consistently sought to contain the growth of American influence in the region.

This attitude on the part of the Colonial Office, and officials in the colonies, was revealed in the deliberations over the establishment of the Anglo-American Caribbean Commission. The commission was mandated to institutionalize Anglo-American cooperation in the Caribbean and originated in American suggestions for collaboration. The Taussig Commission's report had recommended the establishment of a joint British and American committee to collaborate on research into the problems of the Caribbean, and for the sharing of information that would be helpful in dealing with these problems. Another recommendation had been to create a Caribbean section in the Department of State that would deal with matters pertaining to the European colonies, Puerto Rico, the Virgin Islands, and the Caribbean countries.

In early 1941, the American initiative to institutionalize Anglo-American cooperation in the Caribbean began to take shape. On April 10, 1941, Lord Halifax, the British ambassador in Washington, sent a memorandum from the Department of State to Churchill. The memorandum formally advanced the proposal for Anglo-American cooperation in the Caribbean. According to the memorandum:

> It is suggested that the United States Advisory Committee and the British Welfare Fund initiate co-operative research and exchange of information in the fields of agriculture, labor, economics and social services. There is at present considerable duplication of efforts in these fields by the two governments, particularly in tropical agriculture, health and housing. Any effective means that might be worked out by these two governments to prevent duplication of effort would increase their efficiency and effect economies. To effect this purpose, it is suggested that a joint committee be set up by the two governments to consist of not more than six members. The Chairman of the United States Advisory Committee and the Chairman of the British Fund for Development and Welfare in the West Indies might be co-chairmen of the joint Advisory Committee.[32]

The proposals in the memorandum seemed innocuous. However, in a private letter to Sir Alexander Cadogan, to which was attached copies of the American memorandum and his letter to Churchill, Ambassador Halifax indicated that Roosevelt had engaged him in a lengthy discussion about the issue and the general future of the Caribbean. Halifax subsequently inquired of Welles the reasons for the American interest in the entire project and received an instructive reply. Welles said that the United States feared that disorder, resulting from the economic conditions in the British West Indies, might trigger an adverse reaction in the black population in New York. Halifax went on to offer his personal advice that the proposed collaboration should be endorsed by the Colonial Office and British government, as it could have an adverse impact on Anglo-American relations if Britain rejected this initiative. He also indicated that based on his visit to the West Indies twenty years before, he was of the opinion that cooperation with the Americans represented the only possibility of improving the situation in these colonies.[33]

This letter from Halifax to Churchill coincided with a visit to Washington by Sir Frank Stockdale. The visit was undertaken, with the knowledge of the Colonial Office, to hold exploratory discussions with American officials about the American proposals for collaboration. At a meeting at the Department of

State held on April 18, 1941, Stockdale met with Taussig, Bonsal of the Department of State's American Republics section, and Atherton of the European section. Arrangements were made for an exchange of the reports of the Moyne and Taussig commissions and it was agreed that only Britain and the United States would participate in this collaboration. The other colonial powers and the independent Caribbean states would not be invited to participate. Taussig outlined his thinking on areas of collaboration in agricultural research, the need to prevent duplication through the sharing of information, and the allocation of areas of research to each country that would then share its findings with the other. Other areas of potential cooperation in housing, health, labor, reform of land-tenure systems, and crop diversification were raised as well as the organization of meetings of the proposed joint commission. Stockdale indicated that he had no executive authority in the British West Indies and could not determine policy. This information undoubtedly contributed to the decision at the close of the meeting to await a formal response from the British government to the principle of collaboration, before attempting to establish an agenda for such collaboration.[34]

On May 5, the Colonial Office requested the governors in the colonies to respond to the American proposals as it sought to devise a response. The governors were generally favorable to the proposals for collaboration, though the governor of the Windward Islands raised the fear of American penetration of the region. The governor of Barbados queried whether the imperial government would be able or willing to undertake the financial implications of such collaboration, especially in light of the American government's largesse in financing reform in its own colonies.[35] After further consultation with Canada about the proposed Anglo-American collaboration, the British government indicated its approval of the project to the State Department. However, the Colonial Office stipulated, to the Foreign Office and the British embassy in Washington, that it conceived of the AACC as an advisory organization. Furthermore, the Colonial Office insisted that expansion of the commission should be subject to a British veto and that representation on the commission should be restricted to officials of the respective governments.[36] These restrictions on the membership and role of the proposed joint commission were undoubtedly aimed at preventing the commission from emerging as an entity with independence from the Colonial Office. In effect, the Colonial Office remained fearful of the growth of American influence in these territories and the potential of the AACC to promote such growth.

While Under Secretary Welles displayed little willingness to challenge the restrictions placed upon the joint commission by the Colonial Office, he suggested that a non-official might at some time in the future be considered for membership on the committee.[37] The Washington embassy was unclear about the nature of the response that should be made to the suggestion from Welles. The Colonial Office displayed little enthusiasm for the idea. It was of the view that the ability of a single individual to represent the entire range of colonies would be questioned and detract from the work of the joint commission.[38]

Welles's initiative to solicit nonofficial representation on the proposed commission was significant within the context of events in the West Indies in 1941. In June 1941 the Jamaican government had detained Wilfred Domingo, a founding member of the Jamaica Progressive League in New York and a long-time political activist in New York politics. Domingo had decided to return to Jamaica to work for the newly established People's National Party (PNP) and was arrested upon his arrival in Kingston. This action unleashed criticism of the governor in Jamaica and his superiors in London. The West Indies National Council (WINC) of New York immediately contacted the National Association for the Advancement of Colored People (NAACP) for support.[39] Walter White, the president of the NAACP, wrote to Taussig requesting information on the matter and opined that the arrest was stupid and likely to raise questions about British objectives.[40] Subsequently, White informed the Department of State that the NAACP was expressing concern about the fate of Domingo, even though he was not an American citizen, because American citizens were concerned about the action by the British authorities.[41] Given Welles's views, as explained by Halifax, about the potential for unrest in the British West Indies affecting the black community in New York, it would have been surprising if Welles and Taussig were not apprehensive about the action by the Jamaican government.

The NAACP action on the Domingo case was followed by a letter from White to Taussig about the need to have a black member on the proposed Anglo-American joint commission. White argued that this would do much to remove the image of white philanthropy.[42] This letter followed upon others sent by the NAACP to the Department of State in 1941 raising questions about American activities and policies in the West Indies, including whether the United States had deferred to British pressures to prevent black Americans from working on the base sites in the West Indies.[43] White had also written to Nelson Rockefeller suggesting that the United States should appoint more blacks to diplomatic and consular posts in Latin America and the Caribbean, to improve foreign images of American treatment of nonwhites.[44] In addition, at the end of July, Ira De A. Reid wrote Taussig, complaining about the lack of attention by the government to problems in the Caribbean.[45] The actions of the Jamaican government in arresting Domingo and the questioning of American policy in the West Indies by black Americans were undoubtedly among the influences upon Welles's demarche on nonofficial representation on the commission.

British unwillingness to have nonofficial representation on the joint commission in mid-1941 can be construed as an indication of fear at both the level of the West Indian governments and London, and of the American connection to these colonies. It was a fear that continued to manifest itself in foot-dragging on the formal establishment of the joint commission. With agreement in principle on the need for Anglo-American collaboration reached, the Americans proceeded to establish an institutional structure to formulate policy. Taussig, in early September, wrote Eleanor Roosevelt expressing his concern about conditions in the Caribbean and requesting her to arrange a meeting with the president.[46] In late October, the Department of State approved a survey trip through the Caribbean for Taussig, Edward A. Pierce, and Coert duBois.[47] In addition, a Caribbean office in the Department of State under Welles' supervision was created. Welles also began to identify individuals to serve on the proposed joint commission and on a Caribbean Advisory Committee that would report to the president.[48]

While the Americans were thus continuing their efforts to promote Anglo-American collaboration in the Caribbean, the pace on the other side of the Atlantic was decidedly more leisurely. According to Morgan, in late 1941, the Under Secretary was still puzzled about the American interest though the Colonial Office was fearful of appearing reluctant to engage in collaboration with the United States.[49] However, a Foreign Office memorandum in late December 1941 gave a different interpretation for the lack of enthusiasm displayed by the Colonial Office. According to the memorandum, on December 21, Welles had a discussion with Halifax in which the former indicated that there were reports of the food situation in the West Indies becoming difficult. He expressed the view that the early establishment of the joint commission would facilitate Anglo-American coordination in addressing the problem. The Colonial Office's explanation for its hesitant response to the American intiative was that the American conception of the commission was too broad. The suggestion that the agency would engage itself in relief work was just as worrisome.[50]

The Foreign Office memorandum continued with an assessment of the price of the dilatoriness of the Colonial Office. First, First, it argued that given conditions in the Caribbean, the United Kingdom would have a problem if it rejected Anglo-American cooperation. Second, it was of the view that American efforts to introduce reform in its own colonies in the Caribbean, without a parallel British effort, would not help the situation when the comparison came to be made between the state of British and American colonies. As the memorandum argued, "This is not likely to help either the loyalty or the satisfaction of our own subjects in this area." Further, given the importance of the Caribbean to the United States, failure to "collaborate in a generous spirit on Caribbean affairs can only result in the United States strengthening her influence in this region at our expense." The memorandum continued:

> The Prime Minister and others have expressed their hope, and indeed, their belief, that British and American affairs will be increasingly interlocked as time goes on. It is widely believed in Britain that no other course would offer us reasonable security for the future. The present proposal by the U.S.G. to collaborate with us in the

rehabilitation of the Caribbean islands would seem to present an excellent and particularly favourable occasion for promoting closer relations between the two nations at any rate, this is the conclusion which the Americans would be likely to draw, and we must not be surprised if this has its repercussions in America's postwar actions.[51]

The memorandum revealed, in essence, the nature of the consensus in the wartime government. Britain's most important relationship lay in the Anglo-American alliance, and collaboration on colonial reform in the Caribbean would contribute greatly to the development of that alliance during the war and after. In view of the psychological importance of the Caribbean to American political culture, its geographic proximity to the United States, and the need to introduce colonial reform in the area to match American initiatives in its own colonies, the Colonial Office found itself confronting pressures from the War Cabinet, from the colonies, and from the Americans to advance the pace of collaboration with the United States.

The American entry into the war in December 1941 and the pace of events in 1942, particularly in Asia and the Caribbean, led to heightened American criticism of British colonial policy. By early 1942, there was even greater pressure on the Colonial Office to move toward collaboration with the Americans in the Caribbean and to address the issue of colonial reform in the region. The American entry into the war in December 1941 resulted in the operational transfer of responsibility for defense of the British colonies to the United States. British officials in the colonies were reminded of this policy in early 1942, after some friction in the area was brought to the attention of the War Cabinet. Defense against both external and internal threats to the Caribbean was an American responsibility, and British officials had to operate within this framework.[52] The rapid Japanese advances in December 1941 and early 1942 with the capture of Singapore in mid-February was both a stunning blow to British morale and a catalyst for vehement American criticism of British colonial policy. The rapidity of the Japanese advance throughout Asia was held by American public opinion and influential Americans to be due to the resentment of British and, more generally, European rule. The lack of enlightenment in European colonial policy was held to be the reason for the failure of prolonged resistance to Japanese advances.

Roosevelt's efforts to induce British acceptance of the applicability of the Atlantic Charter to the world outside of Europe, and the crisis over India's future where the Roosevelt administration tried to play a broker's role in the conflict between the British and the Indian National Congress, reflected the problem posed by the colonial issue to Anglo-American relations. As Robert Dallek has argued, Roosevelt's policy on India had to navigate between domestic sentiment critical of Britain and its imperial record and his desire to consolidate the Anglo-American alliance at this critical phase of the war.[53] In the Caribbean in early 1942, however, the British were moving with relative alacrity to institutionalize collaboration with the United States. Undoubtedly, having found itself isolated within the government through its resistance to the idea of Anglo-American collaboration in the Caribbean and traumatized by the pace of events in Asia, the Colonial Office moved to establish the Anglo-American Caribbean Commission in early 1942.

On March 9, 1942, the two governments issued a joint communique announcing the establishment of the AACC: "For the purpose of encouraging and strengthening social and economic co-operation between the United States of America and its possessions and bases in the area known geographically and politically as the Caribbean, and the United Kingdom and the British colonies in the same area."[54] The announcement of the creation of the AACC was accompanied by a clear public statement that the United States was not seeking the transfer of sovereignty over the West Indies to the United States. The promise of this statement had been given by Roosevelt to Churchill at the latter's request, responding to both Colonial Office concerns and sentiment within the British colonies.[55]

The American representatives named to the AACC were Taussig, designated as American co-chairman (his British counterpart was Sir Frank Stockdale); Rexford G. Tugwell, governor of Puerto Rico; and Coert du Bois, chief of the Caribbean Office of the Department of State. In addition, Roosevelt also appointed a Caribbean Advisory Committee directly responsible to him, comprising Taussig as chairman; Tugwell; Martin Travieso, a justice of the supreme court in Puerto Rico; William H. Hastie, a black aide to the secretary of war; and a former president of the Commodity Credit Corporation, Carl Robbins. This Caribbean Advisory Committee was charged with preparing a study of conditions in the Caribbean. While, as in the original proposal for Anglo-American collaboration, the announcement of the AACC was couched in banal language, the American government was already moving toward greater activism for which the British were not prepared. American policy assumed an urgency directed at ensuring that the Caribbean would not become a trouble spot as the country was putting itself on a war footing.

The urgency was reflected in a meeting of Roosevelt, Taussig, and du Bois in March 1942, within two weeks of the issue of the joint communique. At the meeting, Roosevelt indicated that the food situation in the West Indies needed to be remedied through the creation of an emergency stock of supplies. Taussig's response was to affirm that it would be the primary objective of the newly established AACC. Roosevelt was also insistent that the British should be pressured into increasing the production of food crops and introducing land reform through breaking up the plantations. According to the report of the meeting: "He practically instructed us to withdraw all support if the British definitely refused to make any material program along this particular line." Roosevelt also raised the issue that there was need for coordination of national policies to promote economic diversification and intra-Caribbean trade, thus reorienting the economies of these territories away from a reliance on sugar, and the persistent overproduction of this commodity.[56]

As outlined in the meeting, Roosevelt's conception of the AACC varied considerably from that held by the Colonial Office. The latter's hope that through collaboration with the United States it would be able to contain the growth of American influence in the West Indies appeared to be very naive. In 1941, Taussig had also advocated economic and land reform in the West Indies, emphasizing the need to diversify away from sugar and the plantation system.[57] This similarity in thinking between Taussig and Roosevelt was a sign that the British were underestimating the American conceptions of change in the region.

The first meeting of the commission in Trinidad, March 26-31, 1942, focused upon the crisis affecting supplies in the area. Submarine attacks were on the increase, disrupting shipping throughout the Caribbean. The two delegations were agreed on the establishment of a stock of emergency supplies, and on the importance of anticipatory measures to offset the impact of the shipping situation. After this initial meeting, the British sought the intervention of their embassy in Washington to brake the enthusiasm and activism of the American representatives of the AACC.[58]

The deteriorating shipping situation throughout 1942, particularly in the first half of the year, was accompanied by reports of potential unrest from American consular officials in the territories. The growing sense of crisis led to increased activism by West Indian-Americans and their allies in New York to influence American policy in the region. In turn, American pressure and frequent reports by British diplomats that Roosevelt's policy in the West Indies and on the colonial issue in general were a response to militancy in the black American communities pushed the British into introducing far-reaching reform in the West Indies. British dependence upon American goodwill and material support and the War Cabinet's recognition of that vulnerability provided the incentives for the Colonial Office to accelerate the pace of reform in the Caribbean.

The deterioration in the shipping situation in the region during 1942 was directly attributable to the increase in submarine warfare waged by Germany. From early 1942, German submarines attacked shipping in an effort to disrupt both shipping across the Atlantic and shipping from the Caribbean carrying petroleum and bauxite supplies to the United States.[59] For these colonies, producing sugar beyond their requirements and largely dependent on imported food and other inputs, shipping was an absolute necessity. The German campaign forced the introduction of rationing and provoked spiraling inflation. Given the reluctance of the business sector, particularly the sugar industry, to concede large-scale wage increases to cope with the inflation and the winding down of construction activity on the base territories, the specter of labor unrest loomed large in the minds of American officials. This uneasiness about the situation in the Caribbean was strengthened by Taussig's trip through the region after the first meeting of the AACC. In a telegram to Roosevelt, he indicated that food and fuel supplies in the Caribbean were inadequate for the emergency. There had been little effort to increase food production in the territories.[60]

In a later message, he informed Welles that the imperial government had specifically requested that sugar production should not be curtailed in favor of increasing food production. He further elaborated that in Jamaica a law had been enacted to provide for a percentage of land to be cultivated in food. There was a flat refusal to comply with the law by a large number of landowners.[61] In view of increasing submarine activity and a consequent rise in the tonnage of shipping lost, there seems to have been little foresight operating at the level of the imperial government and among the local landowners. The local governments were demonstrating a greater sensitivity to the evolving wartime situation. The reality of the pre-war impasse--a colonial government trapped between the desires of the local landholding classes and the dictates of policy set in London--continued to operate during the war. The welfare of the subjects of colonial rule remained the lowest priority in the imperial scheme.

While the shipping and supply situation was deteriorating, there was no end to the political activity or demands for a new dispensation. According to Taussig, the demands for change were best articulated in Jamaica, where the new constitution introducing universal suffrage and a simultaneous increase in the Governor's reserve powers was rejected by the elected members of the legislature. Political groups in the colony leaned to the view that the imperial government's initiatives were inadequate. Further, opinion remained strongly in favor of ending colonial status. William Hastie, who had remained in Jamaica for consultations with local leaders, reported that popular sentiment was that London had to offer substantially greater self-government in Jamaica for the war to have meaning to Jamaicans. Developments in India were being followed with keen attention in both the West Indies and Puerto Rico. According to Taussig, voluntary changes were necessary to prevent change being achieved "at the point of a figurative or literal gun."[62] This assessment could only reinforce the American view that maintenance of loyalty of colonial subjects and the reform of colonial rule were inextricably intertwined. Events in Asia were being paralleled by developments in the Caribbean. Finally, Taussig reported that the inclusion of Hastie on the president's Caribbean Advisory Committee had done much to bolster American esteem in West Indian eyes and put pressure on the British to find a counterpart.

American consular officials in the British colonies, confirmed the view of a deteriorating situation in the region in July 1942 in response to a State Department request for information.[63] These reports followed upon the use of American troops to put down unrest in St. Lucia and the Bahamas. The governor of the Bahamas, the duke of Windsor (the former king), had to interrupt a visit to the United States and requested the dispatch of American military forces to put down the unrest.[64] In Jamaica, there were fears that Japanese propaganda was linked to the deteriorating situation. In British Guiana, discontent with working conditions on the sugar estates, and reports on developments in the Far East, were reportedly creating unrest in that colony among the sugar workers of Indian origin.[65]

These developments in the Caribbean did not escape the attention of the West Indian lobby in New York City that engaged in an active campaign to win the interest of American policymakers. Through the efforts of Adam Clayton Powell, Jr., who was engaged in building his political base in New York, a meeting was arranged with Taussig and Hastie at the State Department.[66] The activism by the West Indian lobby in New York was only one part of a growing militancy in the black American community during 1942. As in the European colonies, the black American community began to argue that their rights had to be addressed as part of the war effort--democracy had to be fought for abroad as well as at home.[67] The shift in allegiance of black Americans (or the majority of those able to vote) from the Republican to the Democratic party over the previous decade had resulted in a situation where, by 1940, black votes in the northern states were more important to Democratic control over the White House than southern white votes.[68] The latter remained critical to control over the Congress, and Roosevelt's ability to maintain the coalition that had supported him in the presidential elections.

The Republican party, however, was not inclined to accept that the transfer of loyalty by the black community was permanent. Rhetoric by both Wendell Willkie, the Republican presidential candidate in 1940, and administration spokesmen in 1942 about the need to end European colonialism and Negro rights reflected the interparty competition over the black vote.[69] In addition, the British embassy reported Republican efforts to have the poll-tax abolished in 1942 was directed at dividing the Democratic party on racial issues and thus strengthening the electoral fortunes of the Republicans.[70] Race and the colonial issue formed a potent amalgam in the domestic and foreign policies of the United States.

This linkage between domestic and foreign policy, where the Roosevelt administration articulated a progressive stance on colonialism as a means of winning support from the black community, was further complicated by the fact that the newspapers targeted at the black community were consistently hostile to British imperialism. This hostility was undoubtedly the result of the West Indian presence, the relatively easy access to information about the British Empire published in English, and the India crisis of 1942.

In the case of the West Indies, Lord Halifax, in a meeting at the Colonial Office in July 1942 reiterated his earlier assessment that American policy was shaped by concerns about the domestic repercussions of unrest in the West Indian colonies.[71] A member of the British mission in Washington confirmed the accuracy of Halifax's views in a report of a conversation with President Roosevelt. After disclaiming any interest in acquiring the West Indies,Roosevelt expressed the view that the territories "were in a bad way economically and we had moreover to keep troops in Jamaica and other places to keep order. He didn't want to have to do this, especially in view of his own

Negro population."[72] Both Halifax and Campbell emphasized that Americans considered the West Indies, and the British image therein, to be in dire need of improvement.

American views of the situation in the British colonies showed signs of hardening in late July 1942. Secretary of State Hull cabled Ambassador Winant in London instructing him to transmit the administration's views on the urgent necessity for addressing the problems in the West Indies, especially in Jamaica where trouble was expected by both the local government and American officials. Referring to the fact that American forces had to be used to suppress unrest in St. Lucia and the Bahamas, Hull suggested that Britain and the United States should work to reduce unemployment and introduce "remedial action in social, economic and political fields." Toward this end, Hull invited the United Kingdom to send "someone with vision and authority to Washington to confer with us . . . with a view to prompt action."[73] Winant, in communicating Hull's views to the British, also informed them that a recent survey of opinion in the United States had shown that " a principal reason for anti-British sentiment, apart from anything due to the racial origin of the section concerned, is a vague hostility to alleged British `Colonial Policy'." Winant's view was that the British had an opportunity in the British Caribbean to demonstrate enlightened and progressive vision of colonial administration and thus remove the impression that Britain was "a reactionary and incompetent imperialist power." Winant was particularly concerned that a further outbreak of unrest and the use of American troops to put down that unrest would have serious consequences. He reportedly used the phrase *you have been warned* to demonstrate the gravity of the issue in his conversations with British officials.[74] In a public address to a luncheon meeting of the Royal Empire Society, Winant reiterated his argument that Anglo-American cooperation in the Caribbean would serve as a symbol of enlightenment in British colonial policy and assuage American concerns.[75]

Reports from the embassy in Washington provided further evidence of the jaundiced American views of the situation in the Caribbean. In August, Campbell at the British embassy in Washington minuted that the United States perceived the white elite in the West Indies as reactionary, and that American perceptions of events in the West Indies would be likely to correspond to those in the East Indies. He further argued that American concern focused on the need to introduce greater democracy in the British colonies.[76] Richard Law, in a meeting with Taussig confirmed the thrust of American policy. According to Law, Taussig emphasized that the United States had both a defense responsibility for and an interest in the stability of the West Indies. Taussig argued that greater representation for the colonial subjects was necessary in the West Indies and that constitutional reform would provide a basis for enhancing stability. Law also indicated that Taussig was not advocating complete independence for the West Indies.[77] The Foreign Office itself added further pressure upon the Colonial Office to establish an entente with the United States over the West Indies. In response to Cranborne's complaints about American interference in the West Indies, Eden indicated that

> the plain fact, as it seems to me, is that unless all possible steps are taken to make our colonies in the Caribbean good examples of our Imperial work, we shall infallibly not only contribute to the present disparagement of that work and the indifference to it, but also continue to have trouble from the fact that these territories are in close proximity to the United States.[78]

Despite the residual reluctance to collaborate with the United States in the Caribbean, the Colonial Office began to shift ground in response to the exigencies of the situation. By the end of the second meeting of the AACC in Washington in early June 1942, the British representative, Sidney Caine, returned to London and advocated that the AACC should operate along the lines suggested by the Americans. In his view, this strategy was best for reasons of administrative efficiency and political expediency. The Colonial Office also appointed Sir George Huggins to the British Supply Mission in Washington and as a British representative on the AACC.[79] This appointment was made at the suggestion of Ambassador Halifax that the Colonial Office should have a representative in Washington. These initial steps were followed by the decision to send Sir George Gater, the under secretary in the Colonial Office, to Washington in the wake of Winant's discussions with British officials and his speech to the Royal Empire Society. This was followed by an invitation to Taussig, extended during Gater's visit to Washington, to visit London for further discussions on Anglo-American cooperation in the Caribbean.

Gater's visit to Washington, while exploratory, was expected to focus on the West Indies with special attention to Jamaica. However, his report on the visit revealed the widespread view in the Roosevelt administration that colonial reform, and the extension of suffrage particularly, was a necessity in the Caribbean. As he indicated in his report, he did not have the sense of being pressured but there was widespread consensus among his American hosts that constitutional reform in the colonies was a necessity. This consensus implied that British colonial policy could not afford to ignore the American perceptions. His American hosts also revealed that they had delayed the announcement of an elective governorship for Puerto Rico out of deference to British sensibilities. They felt such an announcement should be coordinated with a parallel announcement on a new dispensation in the West Indies by the British. This decision, and the thinking surrounding it, reflected the continuing dilemma for the Colonial Office--either coordinate policy with the United States or run the risk of American unilateral action that would place Britain in an unfavorable light.

Despite his efforts to convince his hosts that the AACC should remain advisory, Gater's report testified to the urgency which shaped American attitudes toward the situation in the Caribbean and the need for an effective British response. In his meeting with President Roosevelt, the latter made it clear that land reform, economic diversification, increased intra-Caribbean trade, universal suffrage (to be implemented during the war), and eventually the combination of all the disparate Caribbean units into a federal entity were all policies that might be considered for redressing the problems of the region. Gater responded that the only federation project under consideration was the one to unite the British Leeward and Windward Islands. On the suffrage issue, Gater indicated that Britain was awaiting the reports of the franchise commissions appointed to consider the issue in the various colonies. He also ventured that the sensibilities of the Bahamas, Barbados, and Bermuda, which all enjoyed a degree of autonomy from the Colonial Office, would have to be taken into account in any decision to expand the electorate in the colonies. His hosts left him in no doubt that these three colonies were constitutional anachronisms that had to be brought into the mainstream of the changing Caribbean. With regard to suggestions for the economic reorganization of the West Indies, Gater expressed the view that the seeds of future Anglo-American conflict lay in divergent perceptions of the wartime situation. While the British were willing to accept some economic reorganization as a wartime expedient, the Americans perceived it as a path to self-sufficiency upon which the territories could be launched, using the crisis situation to full advantage. The British preferred to consider the general economic situation after the war before attempting to deal with economic diversification away from sugar in the West Indies.[80]

Gater's visit to the United States provided the Colonial Office with an insight into American thinking on the West Indies and on the Caribbean generally. Of even greater importance, it confirmed the influence that Taussig enjoyed in the Roosevelt administration and Roosevelt's personal endorsement of far-reaching changes in the political and economic landscape in the Caribbean. The invitation for Taussig to visit London signaled the British interest in securing an agreement with the Americans that would minimize frictions over the problems confronting the Caribbean in 1942.

In the interim between Gater's return to Britain and Taussig's arrival in London in December 1942, Oliver Stanley was appointed to replace Lord Cranborne as secretary for the colonies. Given Cranborne's defensiveness about the Americans, his departure may have set the stage for a new tone in Anglo-American relations on the colonial issue. However, the initial American response to Stanley was not enthusiastic. Welles displayed considerable skepticism about Stanley's views and perceived the latter's appointment as a stumbling block to colonial reform. He referred to Stanley as "a narrow, bigoted reactionary." Welles also indicated that Taussig should not make any official proposals during his visit. Taussig's responded that he would seek to get a British commitment to implement the findings of the Moyne Commission and to spend more money in the islands.[81]

Notwithstanding Welles's pessimism, Taussig's trip to Britain provided him with the opportunity to meet with a wide cross-section of officials including Churchill. Further, in the actual discussions the British seemed to be prepared to go much further in meeting American concerns than Welles had foreseen.

By the end of Taussig's visit, the British had committed themselves to a wide range of initiatives aimed at overcoming the problems confronting these territories. Among the areas in which Taussig reached agreement with his hosts were (1) the need to end monoculture in the Caribbean; (2) a regional approach to the economic problems of the Caribbean; (3) the development of interisland trade; (4) investigating the possibility of industrial development in these territories; (5) developing local fisheries; (6) introducing vocational education; (7) introducing housing and sanitation improvements and a school-building program; (8) accepting the need to improve transport within and to the Caribbean; (9) engaging in a survey of the tourism potential of the territories; (10) accepting an investigation by the AACC of the possibility of establishing a feeding program for school children in the region.[82] In addition, the British agreed to the establishment of a system of West Indian conferences under the auspices of the AACC. Representatives and officials from the various colonies would play an initial advisory role in these conferences and later, hopefully, would assume responsibility for supervision over common services in the region.

On paper, at least, it would seem that the Colonial Office and the British government were prepared to go considerably beyond the recommendations of the Moyne Commission. Certainly their agreement to promote the economic restructuring and diversification of the West Indian economy, including the development of industries, was a shift away from their pre-1940 stance. Equally important, the British government agreed to begin the process of social, economic and political reform during the war. It also decided to allocate £6 million over the period 1943-44 for public works and unemployment relief in the West Indies.

Many of Taussig's discussions with senior British officials excluded his counterpart, Stockdale, who had returned to England to attend the meetings between the Colonial Office and Taussig. It was in the course of these outside discussions that the extent of British accommodation revealed itself. Churchill's discussion with Taussig ranged from acknowledgment that British and American interests were intermingled in the Caribbean, through the refusal to extend the Atlantic Charter to the colonies. He was also against the ending of white privilege in Africa and referred to his discussions with Stalin. Taussig took the occasion to inform Churchill that developments in the British West Indies had implications for American domestic politics.[83] Taussig also raised with British officials the issue of the release from detention of W. A. Domingo, the Jamaican nationalist. In his report, he indicated that his conversations with the new colonial secretary, revealed that the British were cognizant of the fact that "social and political unrest in the British West Indies has important and unpleasant repercussions within the United States, particularly among our Negro citizens."[84]

Undoubtedly, the British willingness to accommodate American pressures in the West Indies was linked to this intermingling of British imperial and American domestic politics. Stanley revealed that the new constitution for Jamaica, including universal suffrage and the curtailment of the governor's reserve powers, was seen as opening the way for constitutional reform throughout the West Indian colonies, including the three B's--Barbados, the Bahamas, and Bermuda. Stanley also intimated that the recall of Sir Arthur Richards, the governor of Jamaica, was being discussed in the Colonial Office. He further indicated that an invitation for Manley to visit London was under consideration.[85] The importance of the subsequent transfer of Richards to Nigeria cannot be underestimated in assessing the shift in Colonial Office policy. Richards had been instrumental, through his efforts to use the wartime situation in Jamaica to increase his own powers and to foment a split among the nationalist leadership, in provoking the crisis in Jamaica throughout 1942. Further, in an interview with an American correspondent, he had contemptuously dismissed the idea that a new political dispensation, including greater self-government, was needed in the West Indies.[86] Given American pressures and the shift in Colonial Office policy in late 1942, it was obvious that Richards, as a symbol of an anachronistic order, had to depart.

In addition, Stanley expressed an interest in visiting the United States. Taussig responded by indicating that such a visit should be timed with the announcement of a new constitution for Jamaica. In a subsequent meeting with Sir Stafford Cripps, who had acted as an intermediary between Manley and Lord Cranborne to resolve the dispute over the new constitution for Jamaica, Taussig went further in establishing the conditions for a possible visit by Stanley to the United States. He stipulated that a major shift in British colonial policy would be necessary for such a visit to have an impact and he "further stated that a mere repetition of the ultimate objective of Great Britain to grant self-government would not make such a visit useful."[87] Finally, Taussig rounded off his visit by negotiating an Anglo-American understanding that British restrictions on efforts by Pan American Airlines to develop an air route in the West Indies were a wartime measure. It was agreed that they would be lifted after the war and that the development of such a route would then be organized under the principle of equality of commercial opportunity. Even as he was promoting political reform for the British colonies, Taussig was seeking to ensure that American commercial interests in the region were safeguarded.

Taussig's visit to London marked a decisive shift in British colonial policy in the West Indies. American pressure had helped to create the context in which this shift would occur. However, more important was the fact that wartime conditions had aggravated the prewar crisis of the colonial order and forced the Colonial Office to introduce a new political dispensation in the area. In effect, the prewar crisis, the dislocation caused by the war, American pressure during 1942, and the growing demand in the colonies for a new dispensation had forced the Colonial Office to enact reform during the war. It was a shift that implied devolution of authority within the empire, and was one for which the Colonial Office had been largely unprepared. In the wake of Taussig's visit, the Colonial Office began to implement some of the changes that it had endorsed.

Early in 1943, the Colonial Office transmitted the proposed constitutional changes to the government in Jamaica. Sir Arthur Richards was recalled from Jamaica and transferred to Nigeria. His replacement, Sir George Huggins, was considered friendly to the United States by Taussig. W. A. Domingo and other PNP activists were subsequently released. All of these initiatives undertaken in 1943 had a stabilizing effect on the colony. These changes in Jamaica were accompanied by the colonial secretary's decision to introduce the system of West Indian conferences under the aegis of the AACC. Opposition to the project was registered by the Governors but the colonial secretary reassured them that the conferences would remain advisory.[88] The fear of a West Indian conference undoubtedly arose from the belief among the colonial administrators that their authority would be undermined by an organization representing their subjects, and an institutionalized American presence. Despite the process of constitutional devolution inaugurated by the Colonial Office, it was not evident that officials in these territories were in agreement with the pace and direction of the changes.

The decline of German submarine activity in the Caribbean in 1943 and for the rest of the war transformed the region into a postwar zone. The sense of urgency that had motivated action in 1942 diminished as the threat to shipping receded. In addition, both governments undertook measures to stabilize the economic and employment situation in the region. Stockpiling of sugar or deliberate wasting of production kept employment up and reduced the pressure on shipping. With the full American conversion to a war economy by 1943, West Indian laborers were recruited to work on a seasonal basis on American farms. These policies effectively reduced the pressure of unemployment that had loomed large in 1942.[89]

In addition, changes had occurred or were occurring in the United States that had consequences upon American policy toward the colonies. The concentration upon the invasion of Europe, and military successes in the Mediterranean began to shift American attention away from safeguarding the Western Hemisphere. As Anglo-American collaboration increased, there was a growing convergence of views, especially on the maintenance of the British Empire as an ally in the anticipated conflict with the Soviet Union after the war. Further, as was evidenced by the negotiations over the Colonial Charter, American views from 1943 onward reflected little effort to incorporate some of the more strident rhetoric of 1942.[90] This was both a reflection of deference to

British views, and the changed political climate within the United States where the November 1942 elections had resulted in a Congress controlled by southern Democrats who had little tolerance for Roosevelt's tepid efforts to conciliate domestic black opinion. A decline in black militancy from 1943 onwards also decreased the pressure on Roosevelt, thus facilitating the dampening of American pressure on anticolonial issues.[91]

The turn in military fortunes from 1943 onward and the ability of the British War Cabinet to withstand American pressure on the issue of India in 1942 undoubtedly strengthened the latter's hand in negotiations with the Americans. Having made concessions in the West Indies to American pressure and local sentiment, the British government undoubtedly felt that it could effectively insulate the rest of the empire from American anticolonial pressures. The convergence of Anglo-American security interests offered Britain the opportunity to strengthen its grip on the rest of the empire. The context in which American policy toward the West Indies was shaped changed radically after 1942. As a consequence, American policy lacked its previous urgency following upon the changes in conditions in the Caribbean, in the United States, and in Britain.

The shift in American policy was most marked on the issue of the economic reorganization of the West Indies. Gater's visit to Washington in 1942 had placed the issue on the agenda of Anglo-American relations. The Americans had conjured up visions of a complete reorientation of the economies of the Caribbean through economic diversification and promotion of intra-Caribbean trading ties. The wartime situation was seen as a good opportunity to undertake this process. The British, however, while desirous of promoting the diversification of the economies of these territories and reducing the preferences accorded to sugar, preferred to wait until after the war. The reasons for this British decision were secretly transmitted to Stockdale by the colonial secretary late in 1943:

> Future of world sugar industry is still most uncertain. For one and probably two years after the end of war in Europe there will be world shortage of sugar and clearly there can be no question of discouraging production during that period. What happens after that entirely depends on the extent to which countries intemperate climes can be induced to cut down their highly protected beet industries and this in its turn depends on the possibility of working out a new economic structure for Europe and the world at large.[92]

British policy in the West Indies was directly opposed to American schemes for economic reorganization in the Caribbean during, and immediately after, the war.

These conflicting perspectives on the future of the Caribbean came out into the open during the first West Indian Conference held in Barbados in 1944. The American delegation pressed for far-reaching proposals for economic diversification, particularly in the introduction of new crops and changes in land tenure that would result in the break-up of plantation holdings. The British delegation, led by Stockwell, successfully resisted these efforts.[93] This resistance by the imperial government to economic reorganization in the West Indies was facilitated by opposition within the colonies from the sugar interests, aided undoubtedly by their allies in London. Another factor was the inability of the colonial governments to improve on the record of poor performance that had been evoked by the Moyne Commission. Despite the December 1942 agreement between Britain and the United States that British requests for materials and supplies for public works projects in the Caribbean would receive priority treatment, the colonial administrations proved themselves incapable of rapidly preparing the requests.[94] The first formal request did not arrive until early 1944, and the delays in starting up projects were attributed to the difficulties in getting supplies.[95] The cconomic adviser to the commissioner for development and welfare later referred to colonial administration in the West Indies as "mediocre at best to culpably negligent at worst." He also criticized the Colonial Office for its failure to reduce the power of expatriate commercial interests and improve the administration of these territories.[96] Consequently, through both design and default, economic transformation in the West Indies was hindered by colonial policy.

This situation was not helped by the fact that political reform and the extension of greater self-government remained high on the agenda of West Indian political activists. The introduction of the new constitution in Jamaica in late 1944, and the holding of elections under universal suffrage in December of the same year contributed greatly to this focus on the issues of constitutional reform and greater self-government. The Colonial Development and Welfare Organization was viewed as charity from the British government and there was the sentiment that greater self-government would obviate the need for such munificence. More critical wits in the colonies referred to the organization as the Stockdale Circus.[97] There was little opinion favorable to further metropolitan direction and guidance in the affairs of the West Indies. This criticism of external influences seeking to shape the future of the colonies was extended to the American presence in the region. By early 1944, there were calls by political activists in the various territories for an end to the American military presence and bases. There was considerable sentiment that the bases represented a barrier to the development of self-government in the region. The American presence during the war had brought with it several disruptive influences including the growth of prostitution in the base territories and efforts to introduce the blatant racism and segregation that was part and parcel of American culture. By 1944 and early 1945, the American presence was viewed with considerably less enthusiasm than had been the case in 1941 and 1942.[98]

The growing influence of the State Department over American policy toward colonial areas was also a critical factor in shifting the focus away from the economic reorganization of the West Indies. By early 1944, both the Interior and State departments were increasingly inclined toward the view that a regional economic grouping would facilitate Puerto Rico's industrialization and reduce its financial dependence on the United States. However, there were also fears that American business interests would be opposed to any preferential treatment accorded to Puerto Rico in a regional economic grouping.[99] Later in the year, Dean Acheson requested the American Consulate in Jamaica to establish whether trade restrictions in Jamaica were discriminatory against imports from America, as businessmen were complaining about the effects of such restrictions on their exports to the West Indies.[100] Similarly, from 1943 onward, the State Department lent its active support to the Reynolds Metals Company to acquire concessions to exploit bauxite resources in Jamaica.[101] As in the earlier negotiations over Pan American Airlines rights to develop a civilian route in the British West Indies, the State Department was interested in securing equality of access for American commercial interests in the British Empire.

This shift in emphasis in American policy toward commercial concerns resulted in the decision to refer American policy toward the colonial Caribbean to the Executive Committee on Economic Foreign Policy (ECEFP). In September, a Committee on Recommendations of the West Indian Conference, chaired by the State Department, was established under the ECEFP. Its terms of reference were:

> 1. To examine the economic recommendations of the West Indian Conference, with special consideration to the questions of diversification of the economy, and of increasing employment and standards of living, with special emphasis on inter-island trade and transportation, 2. To make recommendations with respect to policies which should be followed in carrying out the economic objectives outlined by the Conference, *bearing in mind the relation of such recommendations to the economic objectives set forth in the Atlantic Charter and Article VII of the Mutual Aid Agreements.* (Emphasis added) [102]

By late 1944, American policy to the British colonies was becoming a part of the policy advocating the liberal economic trading order envisaged by the State Department for the postwar era. In May 1945, the Committee on Recommendations of West Indian Conference submitted its report, endorsing the objectives of economic reorganization through increasing financial aid to the colonies. However, it adamantly opposed a regional economic arrangement or customs union. According to the report:

> Rather than instituting additional preferential tariff arrangements or an area-wide customs union, there should be international collaboration towards the solution of the trade problems of the area. *Such programs would be consistent with the objective of*

developing the economy of the area and would at the same time be consistent with the trade policies now being advocated by this Government. (Emphasis added) [103]

The extent of the American shift was revealed in meetings between State Department officials and Sir Sydney Caine and Sir John Macpherson (the newly appointed successor to Sir Frank Stockdale) in July and August of 1945. According to the British officials, the Americans had explicitly repudiated the earlier visions of Caribbean self-sufficiency and progressive agricultural diversification, as well as the proposed customs union. In addition, the Americans revealed themselves to be pessimistic about rapid economic progress and were emphatic about the advisory nature of the AACC.[104]

This new emphasis in American policy mirrored the larger shift in its policy toward the European colonial powers, particularly Britain, since 1943. The establishment of the Caribbean Commission in 1946, with France and the Netherlands joining Britain and the United States in establishing an agency to succeed the AACC, testified to this new direction in American policy. American interests were oriented toward collaboration with the European colonial powers in the process of reassertion of empire under the banner of colonial reform. The decision to accept the European position in San Francisco on their right to chart the future of their own empires was institutionalized in this new regional grouping, the Caribbean Commission. The end of the war saw a change in American policy toward the West Indies. There was a retreat from the high profile and activist policy of 1940 to 1942. By 1945, the strategic value of the West Indies and their role as a bridge between the United States and Britain had declined in importance. The new alignments of power in the international system had shifted the primary axis of Anglo-American collaboration to Western and Central Europe. With the British Empire seen as a pillar of American security after 1945, American policy in the West Indies shifted to accommodate Britain's efforts to reshape the imperial bonds.

NOTES

1. For a discussion of the evolution of British thinking about seeking U.S. support, see David Reynolds, T*he Creation of the Anglo-American Alliance 1937-41* (London: Europa Publications, 1981), 88-120.

2. See Robert Dallek, *Franklin D. Roosevelt and American Foreign Policy, 1932-1945* (New York: Oxford University Press, 1979), 243-251.

3. Ibid., 234-35; and Stetson Conn and Byron Fairchild, *United States Army in World War II: The Western Hemisphere*, (Washington, D.C.: Office of the Chief of Military History, Department of the Army, 1960), 1: 47-48.

4. Ibid.

5. Argentina played a leading role in getting the conference to accept the need for a referendum to determine the wishes of the people of the territories before their final disposition. The West Indian community in New York sent an unofficial, and uninvited, delegation to the conference. They played a critical role in winning Argentine support for the views of the West Indians. See Charles Petioni, "West Indian View," Letter to the Editor, *New York Times*, January 19, 1941; and 844.00B/3, FBI Internal Security Report, "West Indies National Council, Subversive Activities in the West Indies", April 11, 1942. R.G.59, State Decimal File; and W. Burghardt Turner and Joyce Moore Turner (eds.), *Richard B. Moore: Caribbean Militant in Harlem* (Bloomington: Indiana University Press, 1988), 75-76.

6. Conn and Fairchild, *United States Army*, 48-49; William L. Langer and S. Everett Gleason, *The Challenge to Isolation 1937-1940* (New York: Council on Foreign Relations, 1952), 697.

7. Conn and Fairchild, *United States Army*, 53.

8. Langer and Gleason, *The Challenge to Isolation*, 758; and Cordell Hull, *The Memoirs of Cordell Hull* (New York: Macmillan, 1948) 1: 833.

9. Rexford Tugwell provided an interesting account of the interaction on this agreement between Churchill and Roosevelt: "Franklin was anxious to represent it to the country as a bargain, advantageous to the United States, and not as a gift to the British. Churchill thought and said that this was a rather low level of international dealing. He urged Franklin to be high-minded; he wanted to show his British people, who were inclined to think the worst of Americans that Yankees could be generous. The two statesmen could not agree. So what actually happened was that the destroyers were traded for certain bases; but Churchill, to shame Franklin, made a gift of others." Rexford G. Tugwell, *The Democratic Roosevelt* (New York: Doubleday, 1957) 541.

10. Reynolds, *Anglo-American Alliance*, 128-29.

11. Annette Palmer, "The United States and the Commonwealth Caribbean, 1940-45" (Ph.D. diss., Fordham University, 1979), 76-77.

12. For an account of some of the reactions to the American military presence, see Annette Palmer, "Black American Soldiers in Trinidad, 1942-44: Wartime Politics in a Colonial Society," *Journal of Imperial and Commonwealth History* 14, no. 3 (1986) 203-18.

13. Report of the United States Commission to Study Social and Economic Conditions in the British West Indies, Appointed by the President of the United States on November 13, 1940. Taussig Caribbean Files, Box 35, 68-69 (hereafter referred to as Taussig Report, 1940).

14. Howard Johnson, "The United States and the Establishment of the Anglo-American Commission," *Journal of Caribbean History* 19, no.1 (1984), 27.

15. Rexford Tugwell provided an interesting assessment of Taussig's relationship with Hull: "Cordell Hull was an old and experienced politician, and I, at least, listened to him with deference. He took some pains with me because of my obvious respect--usually in company with Charles Taussig, who regarded him as a prophet and haunted his office for years." Tugwell, *The Democratic Roosevelt*, 221.

16. For a contemporary view of Taussig's role, see "An Analysis of the Operation of the Anglo-American Caribbean Commission." December 15, 1944, Box 34, Taussig Papers.

17. Letter, Welles to Roosevelt, October 8, 1940. Official File 4318 , Folder "Taussig, Charles W.; 1937-42." FDRL.

18. 811.34544/296, Memorandum of Conversation, participants: Under-secretary Welles, C. W. Taussig, Lieutenant-Colonel A. F. Kebler, Lieutenant-Commander W. S. Campbell, and Mr. Orme-Wilson. October 30, 1940. R.G. 59, State Decimal File, Box 3648.

19. 811.34544/371, Memorandum of Conversation, participants: N. Butler and Sumner Welles, November 19, 1940. R.G. 59, State Decimal File, Box 3648.

20. Ibid.

21. 811.34544/281. Telegram, Welles to Taussig, November 23, 1940. R.G. 59, State Decimal File, Box 3648.

22. Taussig Report 1940, 4-5.

23. Ibid.

24. Ibid., passim.

25. F0371/26155. A 541/20/45. Record of Conversation between President Roosevelt and the Governor of the Leeward Islands in Washington on January 23, 1941, at which Mr. Butler was present. "He (Roosevelt) went into certain matters of detail, such as disciplinary action which might be necessary vis-à-vis United States enlisted men, the undesirability of their having to go before courts on which sat coloured Magistrates or Judges, and of arrests being made by negro police. This could be met better by the use of United States military police, and disciplinary action being taken in United States military court."

26. F0371/26152. A57/20/45. Telegram, Colonial Office to Governor Bermuda, 7 January, 1941. "U.S. authorities attach greatest importance to establishment of seaplane base on Morgan's and Tucker's islands and. . . refusal to lease these islands might have most serious consequences on assistance from United States, e.g. munitions and finance, importance of which at present juncture cannot be exaggerated."

27. 844.00/43. Telegram, Taussig to Welles, March 28, 1942. R.G. 59, State Decimal File, Box 708.

28. The financial predicament of the British in late 1940 was a critical factor in creating this dependence. See Alan P. Dobson, *U.S. Wartime Aid to Britain, 1940-46* (London: Croom Helm, 1986), 19-24.

29. F0371/26159. A 2139/20/45. Memorandum "United States Bases Agreement," Mayle, Colonial Office, to Randall, March 21, 1941; and Reynolds, *Anglo-American Alliance*, 174.

30. 811.34544/1037. Letter, Ted(?), London to Hickerson, April 10, 1941. R.G. 59, State Decimal File, Box 3256. The following quote from this letter revealed the American glee: "H.M.G. is not used to having its back teeth extracted and the boys had to do quite a bit of pulling. Your pet term for the British from Trade Agreement days often seemed appropriate but it was good clean fun and enjoyed by all."

31. Anthony Eden, the Foreign Secretary, recognized that British authority in the Caribbean had been compromised by the grant of base rights to the Americans but felt that Britain was powerless to do otherwise. The Admiralty also shared this view. See Reynolds, *Anglo-American Alliance*, 170-71.

32. F0371/26175. A 3316/67/45. Letter, Halifax to Prime Minister, April 10, 1941. U.S. memorandum attached to letter.

33. Ibid.

34. F0371/26175. A 3376/67/45. Report of Meeting between Sir Frank Stockdale and U.S. officials in Washington, April 18, 1941; and, 844c. 50/13, Memorandum of Conversation, participants: Taussig, Stockdale, Jopson, Bonsal, and Atherton, April 18, 1941. R.G. 59, State Decimal File, Box 4928.

35. F0371/26175. A 3376/67/45. Telegram, Secretary of State/Colonies to Governors in the B.W.I., Bermuda and Bahamas. May 5, 1941. For the response of the various Governors, see F0371/26175. A 3390/67/45 and F0371/26175. A3542/67/45.

36. F0371/26175. A 3341/67/45, Letter, Under Secretary of State for the Colonies to the Under Secretary of State for the Foreign Office, May 21, 1941.

37. 0371/26175, A 6198/67/45. Telegram, Halifax to Foreign Office, August 4, 1941.

38. F0371/26175, A 6467/67/45. Letter, Downie C.O. to Balfour, August 15, 1941.

39. Letter, Walter White to Taussig, July 14, 1941. Taussig Caribbean Files, Box 36, FDRL.

40. Ibid.

41. Letter, Walter White to Green H. Hackworth, July 28, 1941. Taussig Caribbean File, Box 36, FDRL.

42. Letter, Walter White to Taussig, July 17, 1941. Taussig Caribbean Files, Box 36, FDRL.

43. 811.34544/927. Letter, Walter White to Secretary of State, April 23, 1941.

44. Memorandum, Walter White to Nelson Rockefeller, April 28, 1941. Taussig Caribbean Files, Box 36, FDRL. "The mere selection of such persons would do infinite good in tangible demonstration that lynching is not the sole manifestation of the American white attitude toward those who are not white."

45. Letter, Ira De A. Reid to Taussig, July 31, 1941. Taussig Caribbean Files, Box 36, FDRL.

46. Letter, Taussig to Mrs. Franklin D. Roosevelt, September 3, 1941. PPF 1643-PPF 1661, FDRL.

47. 844.00/5A. Letter, G. Howland Shaw, DOS to C. W. Taussig, October 27, 1941. R. G. 59 State Decimal File, Box 4525.

48. 844.00/6A. Letter, Welles to the President, October 29, 1941. R.G. 59, State Decimal File, Box 4526.

49. D. J. Morgan, *The Origins of British Aid Policy 1942-45*, vol. 1 of *The Official History of Colonial Development* (London: Macmillan , 1980), 158

50. F0371/30673. A 431/431/45. Foreign Office Memorandum, prepared by Mr. Whitehead, "Anglo-American Co-operation in the Caribbean."

51. Ibid.

52. F0371/30637. A 459/10/45. Draft Minutes of Meeting at the Colonial Office on January 20, 1942: "Article II of the original Bases Agreement gives the United States rights, power and authority as may be necessary for conducting military operations deemed desirable by the United States in the territories and surrounding waters or airspaces. This sweeping but necessary authority is not abated by the defence agreement but rather is supplemented, and it was agreed that it must override any limiting consideration contained in the defence agreement." See also, F0371/30639. A 1588/10/45. Telegram, British Joint Staff Mission Washington to War Office, February 12, 1942: "Such difficulties as may have arisen in the working of the leased bases agreement have been largely through failure by British officials to realize that defence of the Caribbean area is now whether they like it or not an American responsibility."

53. Dallek, *FDR and American Foreign Policy, 1932-1945*, 327.

54. Joint Communique, March 9, 1942 Taussig Caribbean Files, Box 35.

55. Ibid.; a factor in Roosevelt's rejection of the acquisition of the B.W.I. was the concern about increasing the number of nonwhite American citizens. See Lowell T. Young, "Franklin D. Roosevelt and America's Islets: Acquisition of Territory in the Caribbean and in the Pacific," *The Historian* 35, no.2 (1972-73), 211.

56. Memorandum "Interview with the President, March 19, 1942." Taussig Caribbean Files, Box 36.

57. F0371/26175. A 5890/67/45. "Some Aspects of the Caribbean Problem." Speech given by Mr. Charles William Taussig to the Institute of Public Affairs, University of Virginia, Charlottesville, July 1, 1941.

58. Morgan, *The Origins of British Aid Policy*, 169; and F0371/30673. A 4740/431/45. Memorandum, H. F. Downie C.O. to Evans, May 15, 1942.

59. Alfred E. Eckes, Jr., *The United States and the Global Struggle for Minerals* (Austin: University of Texas Press, 1979), 107.

60. Letter, Taussig to the President, re: Observations made while in Barbados, St. Lucia, Antigua, British Guiana, Bahamas, etc., April 22, 1942. Taussig Caribbean Files, Box 34, FDRL.

61. 844D. 6135/3. Telegram, Taussig to Welles, May 14, 1942. R.G. 59, State Decimal File, Box 4929.

62. Letter, Taussig to the President, April 22, 1942.

63. 844C. 50/14. Memorandum, "Economic Situation in Jamaica, B.W.I." J. Edgar Hoover to Adolf A. Berle, Jr., June 6, 1942. R.G. 59, State Decimal File, Box 4928; 844. 00/99, Funk to Secretary of State, July 3, 1942; 844. 00/101, Schuler to Secretary of State, July 3, 1942; 844. 00/104, Dye to Secretary of State, July 3, 1942; Only in Trinidad where the largest U.S. base existed was there relative calm. See 844. 00/100, Hall to Secretary of State, July 3, 1942; R.G. 59, State Decimal File, Box 4525.

64. F0371/30644. A 5263/10/45. Telegram, Halifax to Foreign Office, June 2, 1942.

65. 844. 00/105, Telegram, Hurst to Secretary of State, July 7, 1942. R.G. 59 State Decimal File, Box 4525.

66. 844. 00/148. F.B.I. Internal Security Report, "American West Indian Association on Caribbean Affairs," March 30, 1943. R.G. 59, State Decimal File, Box 4525; and 844. 00/95, Telegram, Ochtree to J. C. Morris, June 16, 1942. R.G. 59 State Decimal File, Box 4525.

67. For accounts of black American political activity during World War II, particularly the increasing militancy of this group in 1942, see Richard M. Dalfiume, "The `Forgotten Years' of the Negro Revolution," *Journal of American History*, 55, no.2 (1968), 90-106; Maurice Davie, *Negroes in American Society* (New York: McGraw-Hill, 1949); James A. Nuechterlein, "The Politics of Civil Rights: The FEPC 1941-46," *Prologue*, 10, no. 3 (1978), 171-91; Harvard Sitkoff, "Racial Militancy and Interracial Violence in the Second World War," *Journal of American History* 58, no. 3 (1971), 661-81; and Patrick S. Washburn, *A Question of Sedition: The Federal Government's Investigation of the Black Press during World War II* (New York: Oxford University Press, 1986).

68. In an analysis of the importance of the black vote to the 1944 presidential election, the British Embassy in Washington reported that: "Negro vote seems really vital since, as a writer in *New York Times* on July 9 put it, President might have won in 1940 even if he had lost the entire electoral vote of solid South, but could not have won even with the South if he had lost Negro votes of crucial Midwestern and Eastern states with their large electoral votes, since Negro votes tipped the balance precisely." See H.G. Nicholas, *Washington Dispatches 1941-1945: Weekly Political Reports from the British Embassy* (Chicago: University of Chicago Press, 1981), 386.

69. According to the British Embassy, "The Negroes continue to be a source of anxiety to the administration. Paul McNutt, doubtless with one eye on the presidential election of 1944, has delivered an address out-doing Willkie in rhetorical appeal to a Harlem audience. A pro-Negro plank is evidently a sine qua non in the presidential platform and the Democrats are making every effort to prevent the Republicans from profiting by the attitude of the South." Ibid., 53.

70. Ibid., 75-76.

71. Morgan, *The Origins of British Aid Policy*, 161. In November 1942, this theme was again repeated by the British embassy in a dispatch to London: "It is, too, not impossible that the Administration's interest in the Caribbean has as one of its motives a desire to show interest in Negro welfare while diverting attention to an area outside the Union but near enough to secure some credit from Negroes of the United States of America." See Nicholas, *Wahington Dispatches 1941-1945*, 103.

72. F0371/30695. A 7635/3760/45, Letter, Campbell to Cadogan, August 6, 1942.

73. 844. 00/107A. Telegram, Hull to Winant, July 22, 1942. R.G. 59, State Decimal File, Box 4525.

74. F0371/30674. A 7506/431/45. Memorandum, "Anglo-United States Cooperation in the Caribbean Islands," Major Morton to Lawford, August 7, 1942.

75. Telegram, Winant to Secretary of State, July 29, 1942. Text of speech given by Winant to Royal Empire Society on July 28, 1942. Taussig Caribbean Files, Box 36. FDRL.

76. F0371/30674. 76408, Minute, Campbell, August 29, 1942.

77. F0371/30674. A 8849/431/45, Memorandum, R. K. Law, September 4, 1942.

78. F0371/30718. A 9765/8843/45. Letter, Eden to Cranborne, November 13, 1942.

79. F0371/30674. A 5367/431/45. Telegram, Halifax to Foreign Office, June 6, 1942; and, F0371/30718. A 8843/45, Colonial Office Memorandum, "U.S. Views on British West Indies," September 16, 1942.

80. Morgan, *The Origins of British Aid Policy*, 165.

81. Resume of Conversations between Welles and Taussig, November 30, 1942. Taussig Caribbean Files, Box 35, FDRL.

82. F0371/34132. A 52/52/45, Report on visit of Mr. Taussig and Mr. de la Rue to the United Kingdom; and Morgan, *The Origins of British Aid Policy*, 165-66.

83. See "Luncheon with Winston Churchill at 10 Downing Street, December 17, 1942." Report of the visit of Charles W. Taussig, United States Chairman of the Anglo-American Caribbean Commission, accompanied by Sidney de la Rue, Chief of the Caribbean Office of Lend-Lease Administration, to London, December 9th to December 19th, 1942, inclusive. Taussig Caribbean Files, Box 35, FDRL.

84. Ibid., Summary.

85. Ibid., see "Discussion between Colonel Oliver Stanley, Secretary of State for the Colonies, and Charles W. Taussig on the Political Problems in the British West Indies."

86. *The Economist*, February 6, 1943, 168-69

87. "Conversation with Sir Stafford Cripps, Friday, December 13, 1942." Report of Taussig visit to London, Taussig Caribbean Files, Box 35, FDRL.

88. F0371/34133. A 4877/52/45. Telegram, Secretary of State for the Colonies to all Governors in the B.W.I., May 20, 1943.

89. Department of State Press Release, May 29, 1944. Taussig Caribbean Files, Box 35. According to this statement, in 1944, Barbados was expected to send 5,000 laborers to the United States; Jamaica, 16,000 and more if transportation were available; the Bahamas, 5,000; and, British Honduras, 1,200.

90. For discussion of the shift in U.S. policy see J. E. Williams, "The Joint Declaration on the Colonies: An Issue in Anglo-American Relations, 1942-1944," *British Journal of International Studies* 2, no. 3 (1976), 267-92; John Sbrega, *Anglo-American Relations and Colonialism in East Asia, 1941-1945* (New York: Garland Publishing, Inc., 1983), 124-53; and, William Roger Louis, *Imperialism at Bay* (Oxford: Oxford University Press, 1977), 567-68.

91. See Sitkoff, "Racial Militancy and Interracial Violence," 675-76.

92. F0371/34133. A 10665/52/45. Telegram, Secretary of State for the Colonies to Comptroller, Development and Welfare, November 11, 1943.

93. Report to the President and Secretary of State on the First West Indian Conference held in Barbados, B.W.I., March 21-30, 1944, under the auspices of the

Anglo-American Caribbean Commission, May 13, 1944, 21.; and, F0371/38561. AN 1559/35/45. Telegram, Stockdale to Secretary of State for the Colonies, April 12, 1944.

94. 844.00/151. Letter, Taussig to Hickerson, June 18, 1942. R.G. 59, State Decimal File, Box 4525. Taussig reported that Huggins of the British Supply Mission had shown him correspondence dealing with the problem. Taussig also sought to have Stockdale removed as co-chairman of the AACC, with the approval of Hull, because he considered Stockdale to be not forceful enough. Both Eden and Stanley rejected this initiative. See 844.00/152A. Telegram, Taussig to Winant, July 23, 1943; and, 844.00/154. Telegram, Winant to Taussig, August 6, 1943. R.G. 59 State Decimal File, Box 4525.

95. 844.00/7-844. Memorandum, Taussig to Hull, July 7, 1944. R.G. 59 State Decimal File, Box 4526.

96. D. J. Morgan, *Developing British Colonial Resources, 1945-1951*, vol.2 of *The Official History of Colonial Development* (London: Macmillan, 1980), 9-11.

97. 844.00/271. Dispatch, Christensen to Secretary of State, April 11, 1944. R.G. 59, State Decimal File, Box 4526.

98. 844.504/22. Dispatch, Hurst to Secretary of State, March 7, 1944. R.G. 59, State Decimal File, Box 4527. The U.S. Consul was reporting the passage of a resolution calling for ending the Anglo-American agreement on bases in the B.W.I. at the end of hostilities, at the British Guiana and West Indies Labor Conference; and 844C. 9111/10-2344. Telegram, Christensen to Secretary of State, October 25, 1944. R.G. 59, State Decimal File, Box 4928. Reports rejection of call by Senator Kenneth McKeller to have B.W.I. transferred to the United States.

99. 844.00/1-2944, Memorandum of Conversation, participants Fortas, Brophy, and S. de la Rue, January 28, 1944. R.G. 59, State Decimal File, Box 4526.

100. 844D. 24/15. Letter, Acheson to Lord, June 6, 1944. R.G. 59, State Decimal File, Box 4929.

101. See Ken Post, *Strike The Iron*. (Atlantic Highlands, New Jersey: Humanities Press, 1981), vol. 2, pp. 347-349; Ronald Graham, *The Aluminium Industry and the Third World* (London: Zed, 1982), pp. 33-39.

102. 844.00/9-2344. Letter, Hull to Ickes, September 23, 1944. R.G. 59, State Decimal File, Box 4526.

103. 844.00/5-1045. "Implementation of Recommendations of West Indian Conference." May 10, 1945, 2. R.G. 59, State Decimal File, Box 6060.

104. Morgan, *The Origins of British Aid Policy*, 174-75.

4

Imperial Reassertion, American Disengagement, and the Evolving Nationalist Challenge, 1945–52

The British colonies in the Caribbean continued to decline in importance to American foreign policy after 1945. The reasons were numerous and reflected the reorientation of the priorities of the United States, Britain, and the nationalist elites in the West Indian territories during this period. The transformation of the United States into the foremost economic and military power in the international system after 1945 shifted the horizons of its policymakers and focused their attention increasingly upon the issues of European and Asian recovery and stability. The focus upon Europe and Asia was facilitated by the fact that the United States was unchallenged in the Western Hemisphere, notwithstanding its continued problems with Juan Peron's regime in Argentina. There was no sense of threat to the United States in its historic sphere of influence which, combined with the urgency of postwar issues outside the hemisphere lessened American sensitivities to developments in the Caribbean.

The declining American concern with events in the Caribbean was evidenced by the decision to expand the AACC through the inclusion of France and the Netherlands. The new agency was renamed the Caribbean Commission and it provided a framework through which the United States could continue to monitor and possibly influence the policies of the various European powers in the Caribbean. This framework of collaboration with the other colonial powers provided for the institutionalization of an American presence in the colonial territories of the other powers. The continued stress upon the advisory nature of the commission reflected the willingness to accommodate the sensitivities of the European states and their desire to insulate their colonial administrations from American pressures.[1]

This framework of collaboration among the colonial powers in the Caribbean in which the United States participated reflected the broader trend in American foreign policy at the end of the war. American policymakers began to mute their criticism of European colonialism. Franklin D. Roosevelt had symbolized the commitment of the United States to an anticolonial platform in foreign policy. By early 1945, Roosevelt's acceptance of the French return to Indochina reflected a willingness to tolerate the continuation of European colonialism in Asia after 1945. His support of American acquisition of the Japanese-mandate territories in the Pacific also demonstrated his willingness to expand of America's own colonial frontiers. Roosevelt's endorsement of these policies set the stage for a return to collaboration in the colonial enterprise among the European colonial powers and the United States that his successors would find very difficult to manage.[2] This shift away from America's stance as a champion of anti-colonialism was demonstrated at the 1945 San Francisco Conference on the establishment of the United Nations Organization (UN). At the conference, Charles Taussig argued for American support for the inclusion of an express commitment in the UN Charter to the objective of independence for colonial territories. In advancing this argument, Taussig advocated that the United States should align itself with the position adopted by the Soviet Union and China as a means of defusing the popularity that the Soviet Union would derive among colonial peoples for its stand. However, opinion in the discussion was overwhelmingly opposed to an open espousal of independence in the face of British and French opposition to the inclusion of the term in the UN Charter. Taussig bowed before this opposition.[3] The American position at San Francisco reflected the ascendancy of collaboration with the colonial powers in American foreign policy and the abdication of the role of champion of anticolonialism.

The growing isolation of Taussig as the Truman administration moved into closer collaboration with the European colonial powers from 1945 onward was evident in a meeting in December 1945. Taussig presented a memorandum on the Caribbean area in which he suggested that

> consideration should be given to the policy proposal laid down by Secretary Hull, March 1943, providing for the announcement of time schedules for granting autonomy to non-self governing territories, and whether this should be supported as a desirable policy as regards European dependencies in the Western Hemisphere.[4]

Taussig's suggestion was challenged by E. T. Wailes of the British Commonwealth Division of the State Department who argued for greater emphasis on economic improvement over political independence. Taussig reminded Wailes that the statement was only reflecting upon the position held by the former secretary of state, Cordell Hull.[5] An intervention by the under secretary for the interior, Abe Fortas, another veteran of the Roosevelt administration, illustrated the issues at play in the discussion. Fortas observed that "a fundamental question was whether this Government was seeking the good will of the various peoples in the Caribbean islands or the good will of the governments which control their respective colonies. To do the latter would perhaps tend towards stability in the area."[6] Though Fortas expressed his preference for the former approach, an approach with which Taussig was probably in agreement, subsequent events in the Caribbean Commission and elsewhere demonstrated that American policy consistently sought "the good will of the governments which control their respective colonies."

The issues raised in this meeting paralleled developments in other areas, particularly Asia, in which there was the fundamental conflict over the priority to be accorded to European interests versus those of the subjects of colonial rule. As is shown later in this chapter, by 1948 the Europeanists in the Department of State had triumphed over those policymakers whose views tended to be sensitive to the concerns of colonial subjects.[7] This growing isolation within the Truman administration suffered by Taussig (and others of like mind) was due in part to the death of Roosevelt earlier in the year. But the departure of Hull in 1945, from the federal government undoubtedly helped to undermine the remnants of anticolonial policy and rhetoric that made the transition from Roosevelt to Truman. For Taussig, whose authority had derived largely from his personal relationship with Roosevelt, Hull, and Welles and who lacked an institutional base within the structure of the federal government, it was a crippling situation. The decline in relative importance of the Caribbean to American foreign policy was also a contributory factor to this isolation of Taussig within the Truman administration. By the end of 1945, Taussig's ability to influence the State Department and American policy was severely compromised, though he continued in his post as American co-chairman for the Caribbean Commission.

This reduction in Taussig's authority was accompanied by the shift in British colonial policy toward the West Indies in early 1945. In a speech before the new legislature in Jamaica in January 1945, Secretary of State for the Colonies Oliver Stanley indicated that the new constitution in Jamaica was an experiment that the Colonial Office would observe and use for implementing constitutional change and extending self-government throughout the empire. In March, Stanley sent a dispatch to all the governors in the Caribbean colonies indicating that the ultimate objective of British colonial policy was "to quicken the progress of all Colonial peoples towards the ultimate goal of self-government and I take this opportunity of reaffirming the basic aim in relation to the Caribbean area." In addition, Stanley indicated that a political federation of its Caribbean colonies, with full internal self-government within the British Commonwealth, was also part of the agenda of British policy in the Caribbean.[8] Though there was no immediate intention of imposing it upon the territories, the Colonial Office was awaiting a shift in public opinion to implement steps to establish the proposed federation. The argument for federation, from the Colonial Office's perspective, was skepticism about the ability of small units to achieve independence and the assumption that government could only be efficient or economical in larger units. Stanley also made it clear that financial stability, that is, the ability of the future federation to meet its obligations without requirement of recurrent financial assistance from external sources, was considered a critical indicator of preparedness for self-government. Further, his dispatch stipulated that a federal constitution would not be introduced nor imposed in the face of serious opposition from any significant groups in the colonies.[9]

By early 1945, the imperial government had committed itself to progressive constitutional reform and the extension of self-government as the objectives of British policy in the Caribbean colonies. While it was clear that constitutional reform would be implemented in the individual colonies, the larger political project of federation was held up as the ultimate objective, and the project had to be built upon a consensus arrived at by the Caribbean colonies themselves. The new dispensation did not extend to economic reform of these territories. Nonetheless, the imperial government had accepted two critical demands made by West Indian political activists before 1939--the goal of federation, and a commitment to introduce greater measures of self-government in the individual territories. By enunciating the new dispensation in 1945, the Colonial Office was also making concessions to the pressures exerted by the Roosevelt administration in 1942, at the height of American concern about the situation in the Caribbean.

The consequences of these initiatives by the imperial government had the paradoxical effect of reducing American influence in the political evolution of these territories. With the aims of federation and self-government clearly identified, energy became focused among the nationalists on building the political base necessary to survive and establish political credibility as successors to colonial government. Building such credibility, within competitive electoral systems based on universal suffrage, required the expenditure of time and energy to territorial concerns. With political legitimacy based on domestic constituencies, the new political leaders became the agents of demands for political change and were treated as such by London. There was little need for the role that American officials had played in 1942, a source of pressure on a reluctant, if not recalcitrant, imperial government.

For the Colonial Office, the focus of concern was managing the transition from colonial rule to self-government in such a way that British interests and influence were not compromised or jettisoned. For both sides in this process, the United States was not of central importance. The results of the December 1944 election in Jamaica, the first held under the new constitution also created uncertainty about the direction of political reform and self-government in the British Caribbean. The Jamaican Labour party (JLP), headed by Alexander Bustamante, the labor leader who leapt into prominence as a result of the riots of the late 1930s, won the election running on a platform that self-government would mean slavery. With the largest share (41%) of the votes, reflecting support from the white elite and the black working classes, the Jamaican Labour Party had emerged as a powerful political force within Jamaican politics. The Jamaican Democratic party (JDP), the electoral vehicle for the traditional elites, did not get 12 percent of the vote in any constituency in which it ran a candidate. In fact, of the total votes cast, it gained 5.1 percent. The JLP won twenty-two seats while the People's National party (PNP), led by Norman Manley, running on a platform of self-government and Fabian socialism, won only five seats with 23.5 percent of the votes. Independents won 30 percent of the vote and 5 seats in the new Legislature.[10] This first election under universal suffrage seemed to represent a rejection of the demands for self-government from the Jamaican nationalist leadership. An American observer sympathetic to Manley and the PNP noted that both the colonial government and local business circles were happy with the JLP victory. The source of joy for colonial officialdom may have been that the results of the election vindicated the strategy of releasing Bustamante in 1943, on the reported promise that the latter would lend his authority and energy to undermining the PNP, and slow the growth of PNP popularity that had pushed Jamaica into a crisis situation in 1942.

For the traditional elites and business circles, the PNP's espousal of socialism (centralized planning and nationalization of key sectors of the economy, though only after the acquisition of self-government) undoubtedly provoked tremors of fear among these groups. According to the American observer,

> The defeat of the PNP was partly due to its advocacy of socialism and its failure to explain adequately that it did not intend to take away the little man's house and donkey. The character of the attack on Manley by the island's press was similar to that directed against Tugwell and the Popular Democratic party in Puerto Rico; and God, communism and the British Empire were all dragged in for the final assault.[11]

The election of 1944, set in train a process of realignment within Jamaican society that showed how little consensus existed on the future development of the society. The absolute rout of the JDP in the elections showed that the days of government by whites was over and that there was a widespread wariness of socialism. But beyond these two trends, little else seemed to be clear. Nonetheless, the loss of Manley and the PNP made it evident that the new political dispensation was not without its problems and its direction was still unclear.

The subsequent victory of the British Labour Party in the 1945 general election was welcomed by the progressive factions in the British West Indies, reflecting their historic ties with the Labour party, and their belief that a Labour Party government would be more sympathetic to demands for the extension of self-government to the colonies. In 1945, there was an unusual context of the elections in Jamaica producing a majority party opposed to self-government, while in Britain the British Labour government came into office with a secretary of state for the colonies coming from the progressive wing of the Labour Party that was committed to the progressive extension of self-government to the colonies.[12]

The sum of all these developments was that by the end of 1945, American policy regarding the British Caribbean was shifting toward support for the reassertion of imperial authority in these colonies. There was a growing willingness to accept British efforts to maintain control over these colonies and to respect British sensitivities in the administration of these territories. The decision to ease pressures upon the British government to pursue economic reform in the West Indies was one indication of the American acceptance of its reduced role in the area's affairs. While American policies toward Puerto Rico and the Virgin Islands continued to focus upon economic and political reform, there was little active concern with the same issues displayed by the United States toward the British colonies. Rather, as the severity of Britain's economic straits manifested itself in the immediate postwar period and in the face of the mounting evidence that the immediate implementation of a postwar international monetary and trade order based on liberal economic principles was impossible, American policy shifted. American policymakers recognized and accepted that the European states needed to use discriminatory trade policies as a means of coping with the economic crisis of the immediate postwar period.[13] Consequently, the issue of the economic situation of the West Indian colonies became a function of metropolitan economic policy and its emphasis on the restoration of the British economy. With Britain's recovery assuming primacy, the importance of the colonies dwindled even further in the eyes of American policymakers.

These developments were evidenced in the establishment and operations of the Caribbean Commission. The expansion of the AACC to include France and the Netherlands encouraged the European powers from the outset to block any attempt by the United States to make the commission into a dynamic regional organization. At the Second West Indian Conference held in St. Thomas from February 21 to March 13, 1946, Taussig's speech to the conference specifically linked the work of the Caribbean Commission to Chapter XI of the UN Charter, especially the preparation of these territories for self-government. He further proposed to the conference the elaboration and acceptance of a charter for human rights in the colonial territories in the Caribbean. The European official delegates took vigorous exception to these proposals from Taussig. According to D. J. Morgan, this initial fracas effectively sealed the fate of the Caribbean Commission, rendering it useless at least from the British perspective. Sir John MacPherson, the new comptroller for development and welfare, criticized Taussig for the orientation of the conference.[14] Interestingly enough, support for the Taussig position came from West Indian delegates, Grantley Adams and Garnett Gordon. The French Antillean delegate, Remy Nainsouta, was also reportedly supportive of Taussig's views though he was not prepared to take a public stand.[15] According to a State Department representative at the meeting, the conflict over the Taussig proposal for a charter of human rights was rooted in the fear of the European representatives that discussion of such issues would open the way for political issues to be debated within the conference and the Caribbean Commission. This was a development the Europeans were not prepared to countenance.[16]

In July 1946, at a meeting of the four colonial powers in Washington called to discuss the Caribbean Commission, the French and Dutch showed their determination to restrict the scope and operations of the organization. Both powers objected to proposals to create formal linkages between the Caribbean Commission and the United Nations. The French also sought to deliberately limit the influence of the British and the Americans in the commission, by seeking to have a French secretary-general appointed, or failing that, by limiting the authority of the office.[17] The European powers gained their objective of preventing the establishment of any formal links between the UN and the commission. Through the appointment of French and Dutch deputies to the American Secretary-General, they also effectively placed constraints upon American initiatives within the day-to-day operation of the secretariat. The British role seemed to be one of quiet support for the French and the Dutch, while not openly challenging the United States. The decision to place the headquarters of the commission in Trinidad, with an American secretary-general, seemed to have been one strategy of reconciling the conflicting perspectives of the member countries.

From birth, the Caribbean Commission was afflicted with the problem that had plagued its predecessor, the AACC. There were fundamentally conflicting objectives among the member countries with regard to policy within their respective colonies. It was a symbol of collaboration, acting as a facade for the perennial suspicion of each other's motives. The situation was well described in early 1946 in an editorial of *The Times* of London, commenting on the Anglo-American Joint Statement which dismissed the recommendations for a Caribbean customs union and regional planning that had been advanced by the First West Indian Conference of 1944. According to The Times: "There is, in fact, still no sign that when it comes to positive action, as distinct from the enunciation of principles of policy, international cooperation, even between two colonial powers with such a common outlook as the United Kingdom and the United States, can achieve very much."[18] Notwithstanding this lack of agreement on positive action, the four partners in the Caribbean colonial enterprise continued to support the continued existence of the Caribbean Commission. However, several events in 1948 demonstrated both the moribund nature of the organization and the seething dissension underlying its operation. As early as 1946, Taussig had indicated a desire to leave the post of American co-chairman to the Caribbean Commission but congressional approval of his proposed successor, Ralph Bunche, was considered difficult and doubtful.[19] With his growing isolation within the Truman administration, it was not inconceivable that he continued to nourish thoughts of leaving. In early 1948, Taussig indicated to Dean Rusk that he had held discussions with the representatives from the other member countries about the Caribbean Commission. These conversations had arisen within a context in which Taussig was doubtful of the commitment of the European members to the work of the commission. The discussions had resulted in agreement that staff relations in the secretariat of the commission, particularly between the secretary-general and his assistants were difficult. It was agreed that the secretary-general would continue in his post but with new assistants. Taussig indicated that he was more optimistic about the Caribbean Commission after these discussions.[20]

But Taussig's confidence was either misplaced or represented a deliberate effort to paper over the deep-seated animus that bedeviled the organization. His special assistant, John Fuqua, resigned in early April. The reported reasons for his resignation painted a very different picture to the one presented by Taussig to Rusk. Fuqua listed continued opposition from the Dutch and French to the Caribbean Commission, with the Dutch privately suggesting that the organization be given a decent burial. The organization was unable to get anything done when confronted by assertions of sovereignty by the various governments. Finally, Taussig had lost interest in the Caribbean Commission as a result of his lack of influence in the Truman administration.[21] This reported evidence of crisis within the Caribbean Commission was further strengthened by reports that the British, French, and Dutch were seeking to remove the American secretary-general, Lawrence Cramer. Taussig was reportedly embarrassed by charges of malfeasance leveled against Cramer. Taussig was also reported to have met with President Truman to discuss his future role and/or resignation from the Caribbean Commission.[22]

In any event, Taussig died in early May 1948, before there was a resolution to the crisis and without any indication of what had been the outcome of his meeting with Truman. In this context of uncertainty and crisis, the Department of State moved to fill the gap created by Taussig's death. The British notified the State Department of their intention to continue the campaign to oust Cramer, even with the knowledge that the delegates from the Caribbean territories were likely to oppose their efforts and that Cramer was prepared to fight to keep his job.[23] Subsequently, the State Department swung its support behind the British and informed the latter that it had decided to seek Cramer's resignation.[24] An official of the department was sent to notify the other three American representatives of the decision. However, both the British and State Department were subjected to rebuffs by the delegates from the Caribbean territories. Governor Hastie of the Virgin Islands, and Dr. Rafael Pico of Puerto Rico, refused to accept the State Department's position and indicated their support for Cramer. The American representatives blamed the attitude of the other member countries for the problems of the commission.[25] Similarly, the British representative retreated from his demand for the removal of Cramer to one requesting his transfer to another post, and finally abandoned the entire scheme for fear of being opposed by Norman Manley and Garnet Gordon from the British West Indies. Cramer later argued that the source of British opposition to him lay in his proposals for research that would have demonstrated the problems confronting some of the British colonies.[26] The entire episode demonstrated the alacrity with which the State Department sought to take advantage of Taussig's demise to find common cause with the European powers and to assert a greater measure of control over the American section of the Caribbean Commission. In August 1948, the State Department recommended one of its officers Laurence Duggan, to Secretary of State, General George C. Marshall, as the replacement for Taussig. The bureaus for European, American Republics, and United Nations Affairs, all endorsed Duggan's nomination.[27]

The death of Taussig, the crisis over the secretary-general, and the continued opposition of the European member states to an activist role for the Caribbean Commission, continued to raise questions about the future of the organization. The death of Taussig amidst the crisis could presumably have served as an opportunity for the United States to reassess its position and role. However, no such review seems to have occurred. The choice of Taussig's successor reflected the lack of studied attention toward the organization. President Truman selected Ward Canaday, a businessman who had retired to the Virgin Islands and had hosted the president in his home during the latter's visit to the territory in 1948. It would seem that considerations of patronage played a more important role in the president's decision than a desire to reinvigorate the Caribbean Commission. Governor Hastie, while appreciative of Canaday's support in dealings with the Congress, questioned whether Canaday had the outlook or commitment necessary to deal with the problems of the people of the Caribbean.[28] In spite of these questions raised by Hastie, the appointment of Canaday as Taussig's replacement went ahead.

Notwithstanding the selection of a new American co-chairman, the sense of crisis in the Caribbean Commission continued. At the Third West Indian Conference in Guadeloupe in December 1948, the state of the organization was fully revealed. Repeated calls by delegates from the territories for metropolitan commitment and action to devise a coordinated approach to the solution of the problems of these colonies, did not elicit a tangible response. As a result, the Caribbean Commission had done little to justify its continued existence. The British were critical of the lack of realism among the colonial delegates, while the United States was concerned about whether the money spent for the organization was bringing an adequate return. Both the Dutch and French delegates were content with the progress of the commission. Despite these conflicting perspectives and the sense of frustration revealed, the final document expressed general satisfaction with the commission.[29] This paralysis of the organization was further exacerbated by the reported conflict between Canaday and the other American representatives on the commission. The latter held the view that Canaday was relying on the State Department for advice.

They viewed the department as more interested in supporting the policies of the European powers than in addressing the concerns of the people of the region. Even Canaday admitted that the European powers were less than ardent in pursuing the objectives of the organization.[30] This loss of commitment led to the evolution of the agency into a vehicle for providing technical assistance to the European colonies, a function that led to its marginalisation and subsequent demise.[31] Thus, the death of Taussig, combined with the hostility of the European members to the Caribbean Commission and the unwillingness of American policymakers to confront the Europeans, effectively transformed the organization into a forum for discussion among the colonial powers in the region. The commission ceased to serve as a source of independent influence on American policy toward the British Caribbean territories after the State Department assumed greater responsibility for policy in the region.

The decline in importance assigned to the British West Indies in American policy during the postwar period was further accelerated by the decision to deactivate the majority of Caribbean bases that had been established during the war. By 1949, the number of American troops stationed in the Caribbean had been reduced to 13,000--based largely in Puerto Rico, Panama, and Cuba. Of the bases in the British territories, only the naval base in Trinidad was not deactivated, though its status was reduced to standby in early 1950.[32] Negotiations begun in 1946 between Britain and the United States on the future of these deactivated bases resulted in 1948 in an agreement that provided for the use of the airfields by civilian aircraft without American military rights being rescinded. The responsibility for maintenance and operation of these bases was transferred to Britain under the terms of the agreement. Further negotiations also resulted in the return of land from the deactivated base areas for agricultural use, though with the United States reserving the right to requisition these areas on short notice.[33] The decision to deactivate these bases, and for their conversion to civilian purposes did much to lower the discontent that had begun to emerge at the end of the war. While American military rights to use of the areas continued to exist and responsibility for defense of the islands remained an American responsibility after 1945, the reduction in the American presence in the territories muted the undercurrent of discontent in American-West Indian relations. By early 1950, then, the principal reason for American involvement in the British Caribbean--the acquisition and operation of military bases--had declined in importance. Notwithstanding the continued American defense responsibility for the region, the absence of a credible external military threat to the area effectively facilitated the increasing American disengagement from the British territories.

The sterling crisis of mid-1947, following upon the British request to the United States to assume responsibility for British commitments in Greece and southern Europe, reflected the continuing problem of postwar recovery for the United Kingdom. Despite the efforts to accelerate the conversion to a peacetime economy, it became clear that British economic policy by mid-1947 had not resolved the problems of production and exports which affected its ability to earn dollars. In addition, the dollar deficit made Britain unable to meet the demands of its trading partners and colonies in the sterling area whose import requirements had contributed to the run on sterling in 1947.[34] In a context where the key European ally of the United States was unable to overcome its problems of postwar adjustment while the rest of Europe remained similarly afflicted, American policy underwent an urgent reassessment.[35] A key element in this American reassessment was a reversal of policy favoring the establishment of a liberal international trade order. Since the 1930s, the Americans had been ardent champions of such an international trade regime and that policy had been a constant source of friction in Anglo-American relations. By late 1947, the United States accepted that Britain needed, in the interest of its recovery as a financial and trading power, to pursue a mercantilist trade policy within the empire and commonwealth. In accepting British mercantilism, the United States recognized that British policy would actively discriminate against American exports to British markets. The fact that the United States was prepared to surrender its demand for a liberal international trade regime was an indication of the severity of the economic crisis facing the United Kingdom. This decision reflected American willingness to underwrite Britain's reassertion of its imperial authority and a mercantilist trading system. It was a significant step beyond the decision taken at San Francisco to abandon advocacy of an end to colonial rule.[36]

For the British colonies in the Caribbean, this shift in American policy toward the acceptance of a British mercantilist policy in empire trade, meant that the demands for a restructuring of the West Indian economy would largely be ignored. This had been foreseen by the communication from the Colonial Office to Stockdale in 1943. For Britain, from mid-1947 onward, the preeminent concern of policy was the integration of colonial economies into a British-run trading order that would help to restore Britain's economic and financial stability. British policy was directed toward stimulating colonial production and exports to the dollar area, increasing production within the colonies to displace imports from outside the sterling area, and increasing production as a strategy of import substitution for local consumption. Britain was at the center of this network, acting as coordinator of dollar receipts and disbursements and serving as a trading entrepot. This system of highly centralized management of dollar earnings and trade had two key objectives--depressing demand in the colonies for dollar denominated imports and providing Britain, and the other independent members of the sterling area dollar pool, access to dollars for their own development at the expense of the colonial territories. The support of British business for empire and a mercantile trading system was undoubtedly linked to its success in maintaining a British share of international trade. However, the sizable profits to be made under preferential trade arrangements including income from the provision of carrier services were major incentives for supporting a mercantilist trading order.

After 1947, colonial development, which had originally been conceived as a strategy for improving the welfare and conditions of colonial subjects, changed into a strategy for economic integration of colonial economies with the British economy. This strategy was aimed at facilitating British economic recovery and the management of sterling area trade and earnings imbalances with the rest of the world. This switch in focus assumed that the new strategy also worked in favor of the colonies themselves and criticism of the scheme could be overruled by references to empire solidarity, or even the refusal to acknowledge that Britain was benefiting enormously from the scheme.[37]

The workings of this system was revealed by the American consulate in Georgetown, British Guiana. As a result of investigations into the operation of the scheme, the consulate was able to report that dollar allocations to the colonies were determined in London on the basis of estimates made by colonial officials. The comptroller of supplies in each colony was advised of the amount of the allocation but was forbidden from divulging the information, even to his counterparts in other colonies, as the allocations were classified as top secret. Further, under the scheme for the regulation of imports, the United Kingdom was to be the first source of imports, and Canada was to be the alternative supplier only if Britain was unable to meet the demand. In addition, imports from Canada were to be reduced on an annual basis, while imports from the United States were to be kept to an absolute minimum without giving the impression of having done so.[38] These measures had been introduced by the imperial government despite the fact that American goods were often cheaper and because British re-exports of goods from dollar areas to the colonies and other members of the sterling bloc enjoyed high profit margins. Thus, British trade policy after 1945 consciously sought to limit the growth of American and Canadian trade in the West Indies, to their disadvantage and for its own benefit.

As the perceived disadvantages of this British attempt to reorient colonial trade began to be felt in the West Indies, criticism began to be leveled at the imperial government. On a visit to London in 1951, the Jamaican leader, Alexander Bustamante, whose views had shifted from being pro-imperial to nationalist by 1951, threatened to switch Jamaican allegiance to the United States away from the Britain. Bustamante was very critical of British commercial policies toward the region. He demanded increased dollar allocations, higher prices for West Indian coffee and citrus, a share in the profits of British re-exports of coffee to Canada, reduced tariffs on Jamaican cigars, and a reduction of British purchases of cigars from Cuba. Bustamante's comments were attributed to "discontent in the British West Indies with the continuation of original wartime controls exercised over currency and trade, as sanctioned by the Colonial Office, which serve to divert trade toward the United Kingdom, the Commonwealth and soft currency countries while limiting or prohibiting trade with the United States."[39]

This discontent was apparently influenced by the display of British insensitivity toward, and short shrift given to the West Indian delegation that went to London in mid-1950 seeking an increase in the sugar quota allocated to the West Indies. The British response was a memorandum that informed the West Indian delegation that colonial farmers were not entitled to the same help offered to British farmers and that the colonies were not part of the British fiscal system. The memorandum indicated that further help should be obtained from the respective governments in the territories, and that while willing to recognize the importance of the sugar industry to the West Indies, the territories had failed to take into account other exports and new industries. It also reminded West Indians that their purchases of British goods at high prices were part of the burden to be borne in shoring up the sterling area.[40]

Even the conservative *Daily Gleaner* in Jamaica responded to the British memorandum by criticizing British trade policy and called for a diversification of West Indian trading ties to escape the burdens of the British mercantile trading system.[41] While the imperial government changed its stance in late 1951, it was clear that conflict over the operation of the sterling area was pushing sentiment in the West Indies toward diversifying the area's economic and trading ties, especially by expanding commercial relations with North America. The problems affecting West Indian trade were exacerbated in 1951 when the Canadian National Steamship Company announced its decision to reduce its operations in the Caribbean at the end of 1952. The Canadian company, which was the sole operator of regular services northwards and southwards in the British Caribbean, made the decision as a result of the decrease in Canada's export trade to the area. According to the *Manchester Guardian*, the shipping situation in the British Caribbean was "worse off today in some respects than before the Boer War."[42] For the territories whose dependence on shipping links with the outside world was critical, the decision by the Canadian company could only be perceived as catastrophic.

The clash between the dictates of British economic policy and the economic future of the British West Indies was further highlighted in 1951. In May of that year, the United Kingdom and Canadian governments announced the decision to purchase Cuban sugar in return for tariff reductions on Cuban imports of British and Canadian goods.[43] The decision reflected the continued insensitivity of imperial commercial policy to the concerns and fears of the British sugar colonies in the Caribbean. These signs of the imperial government's willingness to abandon colonial interests in the pursuit of imperial well-being were not counterbalanced by any indication of a willingness to promote diversification of the economy of the colonies. Despite paying lip service to the idea of economic diversification, British officials remained hostile to proposals for industrial development in the territories. In 1945, a commission appointed to examine proposals for industrialization in Jamaica was pessimistic about its viability. The commission had been headed by the economic adviser to the comptroller for development and welfare, F. C.

Benham. Its conclusions were attacked as defeatist by T. S. Simey, who had also served on the staff of the Development and Welfare Organization, and who argued that the development of industry in the West Indies should be actively pursued.[44] The Benham Report was also subject to criticism by Arthur Lewis, a young West Indian economist at the Caribbean Commission.[45] In 1952, another commission was appointed by the imperial government to examine the issue. In an effort to refute Lewis's views, the commission sought to highlight the constraints against the establishment of industries in the region.[46]

This opposition to industrial development was rooted in British efforts to preserve its role as a supplier of finished goods to colonial producers of raw materials. It also reflected the continued inability, or unwillingness, of British officialdom to acknowledge that fiscal, economic, and trade policies enacted by the metropolitan government were significant constraints upon the ability of these colonial territories to pursue strategies of economic diversification. The 1947 comment by Sir Frank Stockdale to an American diplomat that "the trouble with the West Indies was that the people were not willing to work" captured the blame-the-victim approach that continued to operate in the Colonial Office.[47] Instead of addressing the weaknesses of the West Indian economy, and the contribution of imperial government policies to that situation, it was easier to fault the inhabitants of the territories.

A critical constraint upon the West Indian territories was the sentiment among British policymakers that the colonies were to be jealously guarded as an exclusive preserve for British enterprise. The Colonial Office remained wary of foreign investment (primarily American) in the British colonies. It was only as the evidence mounted in favor of the view that American assistance to Britain and its investment in the colonies were important to British postwar recovery that there was a weakening of this opposition. The British Treasury had supported American investment in the colonies as a means of stimulating exports to the dollar areas, and official policy on foreign investment in the empire reflected this Treasury preference.[48] In the case of the Jamaican government's decision to expedite approval of the Reynolds Metals Company's efforts to exploit Jamaican bauxite, British officials were critical of the haste to conclude an agreement. It was feared that the quick action would lead to a failure to safeguard the interests of future potential British investors.[49] Again, imperial government policy continued to reflect the priority accorded to British interests at the expense of the colonial territories. Inevitably, these policies gave rise to tensions in the relationship between the colonies and the metropolitan government.

The British failure to provide a new vision of economic organization in the West Indies was also demonstrated by its response to the problem of unemployment in the territories. During the war, the creation of a contractual labor scheme through which laborers from the colonies were sent to the United States to work in the agricultural sector had helped to alleviate unemployment in the region. With the end of hostilities, British policy was still directed toward maintaining the viability of the export-agriculture sector. London's opposition to industrial development blocked avenues for employment generation and British officials looked toward the expansion of the wartime scheme as an alternative. In November 1950, a delegation from the West Indian territories, led by officials from the Development and Welfare Organization, visited Washington. They sought to persuade American policymakers that an expansion of the program would help to reduce population pressures on the islands. According to the British official leading the team, Sir George Seel, 90,000 to 100,000 workers could be made available immediately, and a further 50,000 could be recruited in a serious emergency. A member of the delegation from the Jamaican Labour party also proposed the expansion of the program to recruit women in large numbers as nurses, hospital workers, domestic servants, and seamstresses.[50] The scale of the proposed expansion of the program suggested that the exportation of the region's unemployment was the preferred strategy. This option was obviously easier than the pursuit of economic diversification in the territories. In mid-1951, the House of Commons debated the situation in the West Indies, but beyond a reiteration of support for federation by both the Conservative and Labour parties, and a recognition of the importance of the sugar industry to these colonies, no specific remedies were proposed for dealing with the unemployment in the territories.[51]

The inability of the imperial government to devise a strategy for the economic reorganization of the territories was ultimately reflected in the problems and status of the Development and Welfare Organization in the post-1945 period. Its failure to make a significant impact upon the situation in the region by the end of the war had not led to its demise. As a symbol of the British commitment to a new colonial dispensation, it was hardly likely that it would suffer such a fate. The agency was suspect among colonial officials since it was a threat to their authority. It was also treated skeptically by West Indians. This wariness about its value extended to the Treasury, which questioned the size and return on expenditure of the organization. The organization, in turn, attacked the practice and consequences of Treasury control over the allocation of funds from the imperial exchequer for the pursuit of its own work.

Beyond these problems, the policy of extending self-government to the territories implied that greater control over budgeting decisions and allocations was exercised by these territories. This shift in control undercut the authority and relevance of an agency whose mandate derived from the Colonial Office rather than the territories themselves. Moreover, "local resources had emerged as an important and, in some cases, dominant factor in the financing of development plans."[52] Inevitably, with development expenditure being generated preponderantly from local resources--rather than through imperial largesse--the relevance of the organization was brought into question. Finally, the worsening financial plight of the smaller territories, despite the activities of the organization, raised the issue of whether imperial largesse could pave the way for their return to solvency. Their misfortune had led them to reliance upon the imperial exchequer and they had little to show for that policy. In effect, the concept of balanced development as a justification for the organization's existence had yet to be vindicated.

In this context of decreasing relevance, the shift in authority to local administrations, and the intractability of the economic problems of the target territories, the organization was in search of a role by 1949. It was decided that it should become a corps of advisers for the colonies and the eventual federal project, without any executive authority.[53] The fate of the Caribbean Commission as an advisory institution was apparently no deterrent to this decision.

By 1952, the imperial government's decision to shore up the main agricultural exports of the West Indian territories was the only sign that policy was not driven by incoherence and drift. The years between the submission of the findings of the Moyne Commission and the publication of the 1952 report on industrialization had failed to produce a viable strategy for economic transformation. Despite rhetoric to the contrary, neither London nor the individual administrations had been able to overcome the inertia afflicting the region. This failure of British policy, and the evidence of perfidy that it implied for many West Indian political leaders, fueled the postwar resentment toward the colonial order. The 1951 blast by Bustamante against British policy revealed the extent of discontent in the colonies. In 1950, Rita Hinden, a member of the Waddington Commission visiting British Guiana to examine demands for a new constitution, reported that sentiment in favor of the withdrawal of the British government from the colony was widespread. It was felt that the British withdrawal would open the way for investment needed to develop the colony in the interest of its inhabitants. In 1952, on a visit to British Guiana, Lord Munster held out the hope of remarkable development strides for the colony over the next decade. All three of the colony's daily newspapers revealed themselves critical of the lack of action by both the imperial and colonial governments to hasten the pace of development. The *Daily Chronicle* referred to Munster's remarks as empty propaganda.[54]

This disenchantment with and suspicion of British policy was not restricted solely to economic issues. They existed in perceptions of constitutional reform and the federal project. Despite Stanley's dispatch of March 1945 promising "to quicken the progress of all Colonial peoples towards the ultimate goal of self-government," considerable skepticism existed about the imperial government's decision to sponsor a West Indian Federation. For West Indian nationalist and labor leaders, the British decision to accept such a fundamental demand was not cause for rejoicing but rather one for concern and suspicion. The reaction of these leaders to the Colonial Office's embrace of their pet project revealed the extent to which British policy was held in suspicion. The Colonial Office's decision to soft-pedal the issue, and to seek to build a consensus in support of the federal project, was an acknowledgment that West Indian distrust of imperial policy could jeopardize the entire venture.[55] A conference on the proposed federation was held in September 1947 at Montego Bay in Jamaica, at which representatives from the territories met with the colonial secretary, Arthur Creech-Jones. The decision to hold the conference triggered the assessment by the individual territories of the costs and benefits of adherence to the federation.

In late 1945, British Honduras and Trinidad had announced support for the project while the Bahamas had elected to be excluded. In early 1946, the Jamaican legislature joined with Trinidad and British Honduras in endorsing the establishment of a federation. In so doing, the Jamaican legislators welcomed the project as a strategy for coordinating regional approaches on issues such as prices for agricultural exports, support for the University College of the West Indies, establishing a customs union, opening opportunities for migration to British Guiana and British Honduras, and providing a framework for action on a regional basis which the Caribbean Commission had not done. Albert Gomes, who represented Trinidad at the Montego Bay Conference, argued for federation as a mechanism of regional planning and coordination of policy for the various territories. He attacked the Caribbean Commission as a hindrance to development in the Caribbean, stating "It serves international cooperation to a much greater extent than it does the political progress of the Caribbean countries."[56] There was thus sentiment in favor of the federation project as part of a general process of reorganization of the political economy of the region. However, there were also very strong fears about the implications of federation for individual territories and groups within those territories. There seemed to be two major concerns: first, the federal project was viewed as a strategy for slowing the process of extension of self-government within the individual territories; and second, it appeared to be a means of shifting the burden of the weaker territories onto those whose budgetary situation was in better shape. Bustamante raised both issues at the conference. Delegates from British Guiana who shared Bustamante's skepticism also raised similar concerns. Grenadian sentiment was fearful of the burden that the financial difficulties of the territories of the Eastern Caribbean would place on the proposed federation, a concern shared by Barbados. Trinidad's delegates were seeking to get a commitment to the advancement of self-government, and the American consul to Trinidad reported that:

> The Colonial Government hopes to delay more active agitation for increased local participation in the government of this Colony by directing the thoughts and energies of the local population towards the eventual Federation. I understand this to be attitude adopted by the Colonial Office in London and that Colonial Officials in Trinidad do not share the optimism of the Colonial Office.[57]

If true, the West Indian concerns were not misplaced. In addition, considerations of race were also emerging as a problem. The East Indian communities in British Guiana and Trinidad were large enough to act as a brake on the policies of these colonies toward accepting federation. The white communities in Barbados and British Guiana were similarly wary of the federal project. In the case of Barbados, fear of the emergence of a black-dominated political order was especially strong and the proposed federation was seen as the embodiment of that new order.[58]

At the Montego Bay Conference, the colonial secretary was able to hold firm on federation. He garnered an acceptance of the principle and the project from the majority of the delegates, including Bustamante. Jamaica, as the largest of the islands, and with just over one-half of the population, was seen to be critical to the success of the venture. However, the price of West Indian acceptance was an explicit commitment by the Colonial Office that the extension of self-government in the individual territories would not be contingent upon progress toward a federation.[59] In effect, the West Indian delegates were making it clear that federation had to be made compatible with the extension of self-government in the individual territories. It was not to be conceived of as a substitute for, and an alternative to, constitutional progress in the various colonies. With this agreement in place (British Guiana's reservations notwithstanding), the conference agreed to refer the mechanics of federation to a Standing Closer Association Committee (SCAC), chaired by Sir Hubert Rance of the Development and Welfare Organization. This committee was charged with drafting recommendations for the elaboration of a federal constitution, the creation of a federal judiciary, customs and tariff policies, and currency standardization.

It issued its report in early 1950. The report proposed a federation of all the British colonies in the Caribbean, including British Guiana and British Honduras but without the Bahamas. Trinidad was selected as the capital site. It also proposed a weak federal government without the ability to raise taxes and financed by a contribution of 25 percent of the customs revenue from each constituent unit. The proposed federal structure would be headed by a governor-general who would have extensive reserve and veto powers over defense, finance, public order, and external affairs. In addition, the entire upper chamber of the bicameral legislature would be appointed by the governor-general. The Executive Council of State would also be chaired by the governor-general. The proposed federation seemed to be based more on the principles of Crown colony government than on an effort to implement constitutional devolution.[60] In effect, the proposals of the SCAC reflected the effort by both the territories and the Colonial Office to cripple the proposed federal government. The former by depriving it of independent taxing authority and an independent source of revenue; and, the latter by seeking to perpetuate the autocracy of the Crown Colony system of government that was already being abandoned in the individual territories. Notwithstanding the agreement reached at the Montego Bay Conference in 1947, the SCAC report provided unmistakable evidence of the the desire of British officials to secure their authority against the challenge from the new emerging political leaders.

The report also reflected the view, still held in the Colonial Office, that the only conceivable path to dominion status for the West Indian territories lay in federation. It was still inconceivable in the minds of British officials that the West Indian territories could seek dominion status on an individual basis. However, the response to the SCAC report when it was presented to the various legislatures revealed the extent to which there was a gap between British policy and nationalist views. In Jamaica, the leadership of both the PNP and the JLP criticized the proposed federal government and the considerable authority vested in the governor-general, on the grounds that the structure was designed to constrain the exercise of self government. The JLP also made it clear that Jamaica could achieve dominion status on its own, but was prepared to accept federation to obtain self-government for the poorer territories. However, the party expected the British to provide financial support to the federal government to ensure that Jamaica would not bear the burden of the poorer territories. The PNP criticized the weak structure of the federal government as providing too little power for the national government. As an indication of its lukewarm support for the proposals in the SCAC report, the Jamaican legislature accepted it only as a basis for discussion.[61]

In Trinidad, the legislature accepted the SCAC report but it was becoming increasingly evident that the Indian community feared being reduced to minority status within a federal state.[62] As in the case of Jamaica, there was considerable criticism of the authority vested in the governor-general and the failure of the proposed federal government to provide for independence. Objections were also raised to the financial arrangements for supporting the federal structure that was seen as a threat to the financial position of individual territories. In Barbados, Grantley Adams, the leader of the majority in the legislature, attacked the authority vested in the governor-general's office. He described such authority as making the federation little more than a Crown colony, and a step backward for Barbados. Questions were also raised about the location of the capital in Trinidad and fears expressed about Jamaican domination of the federation.[63]

British Honduras, under the influence of George Price and the People's United Party (PUP), rejected the proposed federation.[64] The nationalist campaign in the territory began to identify federation as a British project to subjugate British Honduras and the governor was obliged to issue a statement that federation was not being forced upon the colony. British Guiana also rejected the SCAC proposals and even a proposal from the People's Progressive Party (PPP) for a federation with dominion status was given short shrift in the colony's legislature. The Indian and white communities in the colony were fearful of being relegated to minority status in the federation and were instrumental in the rejection of the SCAC report. Support for Federation came from black labor leaders and the PPP which had a pronounced leftist orientation. There was also fear of migration from the island territories and the burden that the latter would impose on British Guiana as a price to be paid for participation in any federal system.[65] The Leeward and Windward Islands all endorsed the SCAC report. However, Albert Marryshow, the Grenadian political activist who had been an early proponent of federation before the war, gave a halfhearted endorsement of the proposals since they failed to address the issue of a date for accession to dominion status.[66]

By early 1952, it had become clear that the federal project was in trouble. Its proposed structure, with considerable authority vested in the governor-general and the Colonial Office, combined with the weakness of its financial base, did not make it an attractive proposition outside of London. The opposition of various ethnic groups within individual colonies, and the realization that federation would not constitute political advance in tandem with, or ahead of developments in individual territories, were powerful obstacles to the endorsement of federation as a project. The financial problems of the weaker territories were emerging as a major obstacle. The leaders of the larger territories saw federation as a British strategy for getting rid of a burden and compromising their progress toward the achievement of self-government. As late as June 1952, Bustamante, who was still perceived as a major stumbling block, reiterated his view that while prepared to support federation, "Jamaica will not be railroaded into a Federation without full and indisputable evidence that a BWI Federation will benefit this island and the region as a whole."[67] The decisions by British Honduras and British Guiana to reject the SCAC proposals had also delivered a serious blow to a major promise of the project. The movement of people from overpopulated islands to the underpopulated mainland territories was not going to be automatic. For both Jamaica and Barbados, which were looking to migration as a means for dealing with population pressure, the refusal of these colonies to participate represented a major setback.

Just as important, during the period 1945-52, the Colonial Office adopted a piecemeal approach to the process of constitutional and political reform in the region. Jamaica had its first election based on universal suffrage in 1944. It took eight more years before universal suffrage was approved for British Guiana, with elections scheduled in 1953. Trinidad obtained universal suffrage in 1946 but did not hold elections until 1950 under the new constitution. Similarly, universal suffrage was introduced in the individual Leeward and Windward islands between 1951 and 1953, while it was not introduced in British Honduras until 1954.[68] The uneven pace of political reform, at the level of the individual colonies, did little to inspire confidence that significant change was underway and probably contributed to the wariness with which the federal project was viewed by the nationalist leaders.

By 1952, it had also become clear that the political leadership in the various territories had serious political and personal differences among themselves that had a negative impact upon their ability to collaborate at the federal level. While Norman Manley and Grantley Adams were prepared to cooperate with each other, neither was prepared to assume responsibility for a federation in which either Albert Gomes or Alexander Bustamante played a leading role.[69] The latter pair had clashed on previous occasions, and their inability to win support from Adams in Barbados meant that there was little hope for the development of consensus among the three leading territories in the proposed federation. As a result, cooperation among West Indian leaders was visibly absent between 1945 and 1952. With Bustamante leading Jamaica and still wary about federation, the context for advancing the federal project was not highly propitious.

In retrospect, the period between 1945 and 1952 constituted a time of transition in the political life of the region. In all of the territories, as universal suffrage was introduced and competitive political systems were established, new leadership began to emerge. In British Honduras after 1950, George Price and the PUP were in the ascendant. By 1952, the left-wing PPP in British Guiana had become a major political force. In Trinidad, the elections in 1950 brought about the demise of Tubal Uriah Butler who had been catapulted into prominence by the unrest of the 1930s. However, the growing political weight of the Indian community had already begun to produce a leadership in competition with these early popular leaders. In Barbados, Grantley Adams and the Barbados Labour party was able to outmaneuver the white Electors' Association and effectively use his appeal to the black majority to consolidate his power. By late 1952, a challenge led by Errol Barrow, who subsequently established the Democratic Labour Party (DLP), was directed against the leadership of Adams. In Jamaica, Manley's PNP was riven by an ideological split over the variant of socialism, Fabian or Marxist-Leninist, that the party should espouse and it led to the expulsion of four leading members. In Grenada, unrest in 1951 brought Eric Gairy to the fore as he eclipsed T. Albert Marryshow as a political and labor leader. The emergence of a new generation of leaders, the competitive struggle for constituencies, and the emphasis on obtaining self-government, combined to shift the focus of political leaders. They began to expend greater energy upon consolidating their domestic base of support at the expense of the federal project. The period also reflected the process of political realignment underway in the individual territories, realignments that encompassed ideological shifts of individuals and parties, changes in style of political mobilization, and the growing impact of ethnic political mobilization among both whites and Indians.

These changes in the political context of the region were accompanied by the decline in American interest in the Caribbean and the inability of British policy to address the economic problems of the territories. The nationalist leaders began to articulate their dissatisfaction with this state of affairs and undertake initiatives to find alternatives to British policy. They began to explore the possibilities of greater economic links with North America and consciously sought to force changes in British trade and economic policies that would bring an improvement in the economic situation in the colonies. In early 1947, the American consul in Jamaica reported widespread media commentary in favor of the retention of imperial preferences for Jamaica. The media leveled criticism at American calls for free trade while the latter subsidized Puerto Rico through tariff preferences.[70] The commentary also revealed fears about having to compete on an open market with Cuban sugar. This demand for the continuation of imperial preferences for agricultural exports, especially sugar, reflected the continuing importance of the sugar industry as a leading source of exports and employment. Perceptions of mutual interest in the West Indian sugar industry led to the strengthening of the mercantile arrangements between Britain and the West Indian colonies. The British government initially agreed to purchase all of the West Indian output until the end of 1952. After refusing to increase the quota of West Indian sugar exports to Britain in mid-1950, the British government in December 1951 reversed its position and introduced an eight year agreement starting in 1953. Under the terms of this agreement, the West Indies were accorded a higher quota and prices for its sugar, and the colonies were free to trade directly with Canada, with an option to cut their quota in the British market and increase sales to Canada.[71] Thus, the imperial relationship was seen as a continued necessity for the stability of the sugar industry, though as the 1951 agreement made clear, the colonies were also seeking to widen their trading relationship with Canada. The value of the imperial relationship in securing export markets for West Indian products was also extended to West Indian citrus exports. In 1952 when American-subsidized citrus exports began to undercut their sales in Europe and Canada, the West Indian producers sought to get the British government to invoke General Agreement on Trade and Tariff (GATT) rules to force the removal of American subsidies on citrus exports.[72] The economic dimensions of the imperial relationship remained a critical factor in the political economy of these colonies.

The mercantile ties with Britain were not a constraint on West Indian governments in their pursuit of economic betterment. By 1950, both Jamaica and Trinidad were seeking to attract foreign investment for diversification of their respective economies. Jamaica opened its bauxite resources to investment from Canadian and American companies to promote diversification and to increase its dollar earnings. In addition, in January 1950, restrictions on repatriation of capital investment and earnings on such investment by foreigners were eased. According to the *Daily Gleaner*, the easing of the restrictions had been done with the aim of "stimulating dollar investment in Jamaican industry."[73] In Trinidad, the government also enacted provisions to attract foreign investment as a means of establishing new industries. Among these provisions were incentives offering tax breaks, relief from customs duties, and guarantees of repatriation of capital and profits. The economic adviser to the territory also proposed to visit the United States to promote

Trinidad as a site for investment in manufacturing industry.[74] The effort to attract manufacturing industry was aimed at offsetting the effects of trade controls with hard currency areas. These industries were also encouraged as a means for stimulating employment. While the British government sought to discourage this process of industrialization, the West Indian governments paid scant heed to British reservations. Wills Issacs, a leading member of the PNP in Jamaica, voiced criticism of continued restrictions on dollar purchases as a burden for the colony since it contributed to the high cost of textiles.[75] A delegation from the chambers of commerce of Kingston and Montego Bay visited the United States seeking to establish institutional arrangements through which American funds could help to promote Jamaican and West Indian development. According to a report of the visit, "the delegation made it plain that the position of these Islands places them fully within the sphere of North American influence. There was no question of less than complete allegiance to Britain, but Britain's `many problems' made that country unable to offer immediate major economic assistance."[76] Later in the year, the American consulate reported that Jamaican businessmen were critical of the operations of the sterling area dollar pool. They were especially negative about the officials of the colonial government who sanctioned the diversion of Jamaica's dollar earnings, in excess of expenditure on imports, to the pool. They also admonished the imperial government for its failure to appreciate the gravity of the situation.[77] Jamaican merchants had become convinced that the long-run commercial interests of the colony were best served by ties with the North American members of the dollar bloc.

This growing attraction with North America among Jamaicans was also mirrored by a shift in attitude at the level of the colonial administration. In 1950, the *Daily Gleaner*, commenting on the decision by Aluminium of Canada (ALCAN) to establish a plant for converting bauxite into alumina on the island, took the opportunity to level criticisms at the Jamaican government for its apathy in seeking capital investment from international financial organizations.[78] Government policies on attracting investment, providing protection for local industries, and increasing local production continued to be criticized. Unemployment was estimated at 80,000 to 100,000 in a total population of 1,388,000 people in 1950. By early 1952, the American consulate reported that the governor in Jamaica was open to getting assistance from the United States, the United Nations, and other sources. This approach was contrasted with those of previous governors who "tended to snub activities, ideas and organizations which were not of British origin."[79]

This search for American investment and the cultivation of American ties extended to even that most British of the West Indian colonies--Barbados. In 1948, in response to the unemployment situation in the colony, there was a march of the unemployed to the governor's residence demanding employment. The lack of jobs was attributed to the failure to promote economic diversification in the colony. The government's expectation was that migration to the United States would help to resolve the problem. By 1950, hopes were being pinned on the development of potential petroleum resources to stimulate economic diversification and reduce the dependence on sugar. It was also seen as a means of lowering unemployment levels. However, the issue of leases for petroleum exploration revealed the shift in thinking occurring in Barbados. Two firms applied for the leases: one was the British Union Oil Company-Trinidad Leaseholds, and the other, Gulf Oil, an American company. Opinion in the colony was divided on whether the British firm should be granted a monopoly, as it desired, or whether the American firm should be given a share of the leases. The Barbados Labour party, led by Grantley Adams, was reportedly in favor of granting some of the leases to the American company in the belief that the latter was likely to pay higher royalties. Such royalties would enable the party to influence government expenditure toward the expansion of the social security and welfare system. The decision was taken by the Executive committee chaired by the governor, and it was decided that Gulf Oil would be granted leases for exploration over 45 percent of the land surface and 50 percent of the territorial waters. The British company walked out of the meeting upon learning the decision of the Executive committee.[80] This dispute in Barbados reflected the growing divergences between West Indian needs and British desires. This cultivation of the relationship with the United States was further strengthened by the growth of the tourist industry in Barbados. By 1952, tourism had become the island's second most important industry after sugar. Americans and Canadians had increasingly found it an attractive destination, though racial tensions were reportedly being sharpened by the new industry.[81] The American connection had begun to assume a greater significance in the economic life of the territories.

North American ties were also useful in helping West Indian leaders to change the terms of their relationship with Britain. As Bustamante's remarks in London in 1951 revealed, West Indian leaders raised the specter of a closer relationship with Canada and the United States as a means of embarrassing Britain into providing concessions in negotiations with the colonies. British sensitivities to its image as a colonial power provided a lever that the West Indian leaders exploited to extract concessions from the imperial government. Fear of the American connection was a continuing factor in British policy toward the West Indies in the postwar period, especially as revealed in the attitudes of colonial officials.

This courtship of ties with North America was not limited to trade and economic issues. It also began a process of political interaction through which nationalist leaders sought to invoke support from American sources against their rivals, and resulted in efforts by the United States to set ideological limits on the nationalist movements. As early as 1947, Taussig and the State Department had been concerned about a visit to the United States by Norman Manley and Grantley Adams.[82] They were scheduled to appear on the same platform as Paul Robeson, the black American opera and film star who endured persecution by the American government for his political activism, at a rally in Madison Square Garden during their stay. Their visit had been arranged to raise funds for the Caribbean Labour Congress and to inform black groups in the United States about recent political developments in the British West Indies. It is not clear whether the two were informed of Taussig's concern, but the appearance was canceled. Both Manley and Adams maintained their Socialist label, but under the pressure of events in the West Indies and the wider world, they hastened to distance themselves from Marxists and other radicals in the West Indies and sought to purge radical left-wing activists from the regional and Jamaican political scene.

From 1945 onward, the *Daily Gleaner* in Jamaica, abetted by the Jamaican Labour Party, and one would suspect the colonial administration, had maintained a barrage of attacks and allegations about the PNP's ideological orientation. In 1948, the *Daily Gleaner* renewed the campaign following the unionization of the company's workers by a PNP-backed union and a strike to force its recognition by the company. This revival of the charges against the PNP prompted a member of the American consulate to meet with Manley to discuss the allegations of the PNP as a Communist organization.[83] Bowing to these multiple pressures, the PNP began to issue public denials of communism in the party ranks. Further action was taken in September 1949 when the Trades Union Congress, backed by the PNP, withdrew from the World Federation of Trade Unions (WFTU) in response to the split in that organization between Communist and anti-Communist unions.[84] The party's failure to win a parliamentary majority in the December 1949 election, despite having won a majority of the popular vote, led to its determination to neutralize perceptions of radicalism that had tainted the party. In 1952, four leading radical members were purged following a power struggle within the executive of the party. Hearings that led to the expulsion of the four were held in secret and these findings led to the dissolution of the party's executive.[85] This cleansing of the party's image was extended to a wider level when in late 1952, Manley and Adams were reported to be involved in an effort to expel Richard Hart from his post as secretary of the Caribbean Labour Congress.[86] Hart was one of the four members of the executive who had been expelled from the PNP earlier that year. The politics of anti-Communism had become an essential factor for success in West Indian politics.

Similarly, in British Guiana, Barbados, and Trinidad political leaders used allegations of communism to neutralize their opponents in intraparty and interparty conflicts. The American consular officials in the colonies conscientiously reported on these allegations, undoubtedly prompted in part by the hysteria and anti-Communist sentiment sweeping American politics at that time. In British Guiana, a leading anti-Jagan critic approached the American consul for information on Jagan's ties to the Communist states. He also distributed anti-communist propaganda that the consul supplied for dissemination in British Guiana.[87] Albert Gomes inveighed against Communist influence in the trade unions in Trinidad, and the refusal of the island's Trades Union Council to break with the WFTU was one piece of evidence for these charges.[88] In Barbados, allegations of communism were levelled against Errol Barrow, a leading challenger to Grantley Adams within the Barbados Labour party, and a fellow dissident Lorenzo Williams. The evidence adduced to demonstrate their ties to the British Communist party was the belief that they had served in an advisory capacity to the Colonial Office under the Labour government.[89] It was unclear whether the Colonial Office itself would have seen service on its behalf as evidence of Communist affiliation but the charges do suggest that there was some element of hyperbole in these campaigns.

The extent to which this effort to isolate and purge Communist elements in the West Indies was a joint campaign conducted by British and American agencies is not clear. As early as 1949, the head of counter espionage in the British War Office, Sir Percy Sillitoe, had identified Cheddi and Janet Jagan of British Guiana and John Kelshall of Trinidad as Communist activists. Sillitoe, in his discussions with American military officials in the West Indies offered the assessment that "his department expected active communism to take place somewhere in the British West Indies, but was not aware as to where it would break out, and in this appeared to be very much concerned."[90] The fact that these discussions were held and that they served as an opportunity to share information on Communist activities do suggest that some coordination was occurring. There were efforts by British officials to get British and American trade union leaders to persuade the leader of the Oilfield Workers Trade Union and president of the Trades Union Council in Trinidad to break with the WFTU.[91] Similarly, the decision to establish a Caribbean branch of the anti-communist Inter-American Workers' Organization in Barbados, with support from the International Confederation of Free Trade Unions (ICFTU), does suggest a measure of cooperation to influence the direction of the labor movement in the West Indies.[92] These developments demonstrated that the nationalist movements were themselves being influenced by ideological divisions in the wider world. While anticolonialism represented a broad consensus across the movements, ideological conflict was also increasing within them by 1952, thus spurring the growth of factionalist tensions.

The period 1945-52 was a transition period from all perspectives. Where the United States began a process of disengagement from the region and the United Kingdom an effort to reassert imperial control, developments in the region set in train by these parallel processes worked toward West Indians seeking closer economic and political ties with the United States. On the other hand, the demand for greater self-government by these colonies set in train not only a process of disengagement from Britain but also a renewed dependence on the trade and economic benefits accruing from the imperial relationship. In the colonies themselves, the introduction of universal suffrage began to present new leaders and new ideological tendencies in a framework of competitive politics. This fluidity was bequeathed to the Eisenhower Administration in 1953.

NOTES

1. For a discussion of the establishment of the Caribbean Commission see Bernard L. Poole, *The Caribbean Commission* (Columbia: University of South Carolina Press, 1951); and Herbert Corkran, *Patterns of International Co-operation in the Caribbean, 1942-1969* (Dallas, Texas: Southern Methodist University Press, 1970). Both are written from a perspective of the Caribbean Commission as the embodiment of trusteeship. As the preceding chapter has shown, policy toward the Caribbean by the colonial powers had not been driven by altruism. As the rest of this chapter shows, altruism had an even lesser role in the operations of the Caribbean Commission.

2. For a discussion of the shift in American policy see chapter 1.

3. *Foreign Relations of the United States* (Washington, D.C.: Department of State, 1945) 1: 792-97

4. 844.00/12-445. Memorandum of conversation, Participants: Charles Taussig, Abe Fortas, E. G. Arnold, E. T. Wailes, Ralph Bunche, Spruille Braden, James H. Wright, Ellis O. Briggs, George H. Butler, William P. Cochran, Willard F. Barber, and John H. Fuqua, December 4, 1945. R.G. 59, State Decimal File, Box 6047.

5. Ibid.

6. Ibid.

7. George Herring "The Truman Administration and the Restoration of French Sovereignty in Indo-China." *Diplomatic History* 1, no. 2 (1977), 98-100, reveals a similar process in the case of American policy to Southeast Asia.

8. 844.00/7-545. Dispatch, Ordway to DOS, March 14, 1945. R.G. 59, State Decimal File, Box 6042. The text of Stanley's dispatch was appended to this document.

9. Ibid.

10. Trevor Munroe, *The Politics of Constitutional Decolonization: Jamaica 1944-62* (Jamaica: ISER, 1972), 42.

11. 844D. 00/1-2345. Despatch, Blanshard to the Secretary of State, January 23, 1945. R.G. 59, State Decimal File, Box 6052.

12. This paradox was only the first of many occasions in the post-1945 period when developments in British politics were not in tandem with those in the West Indies, as the twin process of imperial disengagement and nationalist assertion began to unfold. For an analysis of the Jamaican election in 1944, see Munroe, *The Politics of Constitutional Decolonization*, 36-74

13. See R. T. Maddock, "The Politics of Trade--The American Experience since 1945," *International Relations*, 6, no. 12 (1978) 285-87; and Richard N. Gardner, *Sterling-Dollar Diplomacy in Current Perspective* (New York: Columbia University Press, 1980), 325-36.

14 . D. J. Morgan, *The Origins of British Aid Policy*, vol. 1 of *The Official History of Colonial Development* (London: Macmillan, 1980), 176-78

15. 844.00/3-1846. Memorandum, Stevenson to Briggs, March 18, 1946. R.G. 59, State Decimal File, Box 6060.

16. Ibid., and Morgan confirms this interpretation in, *The Origins of British Aid Policy*, 176-78.

17. 844.00/7-1546. Memorandum, Raynor to Hickerson, July 15, 1946. R.G. 59, State Decimal File, Box 6060.

18. Editorial, *The Times*, 28 January 1946.

19. 844.00/2-1146. Memorandum, Braden to Briggs, February 11, 1946. R.G. 59, State Decimal File, Box 6043.

20. 844.00/9-2349. Memorandum, Taussig to Rusk, March 8, 1948. R.G. 59, State Decimal File, Box 6046.

21. 844.00/4-548. Memorandum, Mackay to Woodward, April 5, 1948. R.G. 59, State Decimal File, Box 6045.

22. 844.00/4-3048. Memorandum, Mackay to Woodward, April 30, 1948. R.G. 59, State Decimal File, Box 6060.

23. 844.00/5-1848. Memorandum of Conversation, Participants: Balfour, Sabben-Clare, Armour, and Wailes, May 18, 1948. R.G. 59, State Decimal File, Box 6045.

24. 844.00/5-1848. Memorandum of Conversation, Participants: Green, Sabben-Clare, and Wailes, May 19, 1948. R.G. 59, State Decimal File, Box 6045.

25. 844.00/9-2349. Memorandum, Green to Sandifer, June 4, 1948. R.G. 59, State Decimal File, Box 6046.

26. 844.00/9-2349. Memorandum of Conversation, Participants: Cramer and Gerig, June 18, 1949. R.G. 59, State Decimal File, Box 6046.

27. 844.00/7-2148. Memorandum, Rusk to Marshall, August 6, 1948. R.G. 59, State Decimal File, Box 6046.

28. 844.00/9-2349. Memorandum of Conversation, Participants: Hastie and Green, September 10, 1948. R.G. 59, State Decimal File, Box 6046.

29. 844.00/12-2848. Memorandum, Mackay to Woodward, December 28, 1948. R.G. 59, State Decimal File, Box 6046.

30. 844.00/5-449. Memorandum of Conversation, Participants: Canaday, Hastie, Pico, Pinero, Acheson, Sandifer and Gerig, May 4, 1949. R.G. 59, State Decimal File, Box 6046.

31. For the evolution of the Commission see in its entirety, Herbert Corkran, *Patterns of International Co-operation.*

32. North Burn, "United States Base Rights in the British West Indies, 1940-1962," (Ph.D. diss., Tufts University, 1964), 59-66.

33. Ibid.

34. P. S. Gupta, *Imperialism and the British Labour Movement* (London: Macmillan, 1975), 303-48; Allister E. Hinds, "Sterling and Imperial Policy" *The Journal of Imperial and Commonwealth History* (JICH) 15, no. 2 (1987), 148-69; C. C. S. Newton, "The Sterling Crisis of 1947 and the British Response to the Marshall Plan", *Economic History Review* 37, no. 3 (1984), 391-408; B. R. Tomlinson, "Indo-

British Relations in the Post-Colonial Era: The Sterling Balances Negotiations, 1947-49" *JICH* 13, no. 3 (1985), 142-62.

35. Gardner, *Sterling-Dollar Diplomacy*, 325-36; and Maddock, "The Politics of Trade", 285-87.

36. Ibid.

37. This discussion of British post-1947 economic policy and the role of the colonies draws heavily from Morgan, *Developing British Colonial Resources*, passim.

38. 841 E. 131/5-2251. Dispatch, Burke to DOS, May 22, 1951. R.G. 59, State Decimal File, Box 4815.

39. 741 H. 00/7-2051. Dispatch, Brown to DOS, July 20, 1951. R.G. 59, State Decimal File, Box 3544.

40. 841 H. 2351/6-2050. Dispatch, Park to DOS, June 20, 1950. R.G. 59, State Decimal File, Box 4818.

41. Editorial, *Daily Gleaner*, June 9, 1950.

42. *Manchester Guardian*, January 23, 1951, cited in IR 4924, "Progress toward a British West Indian Federation," State Department, Office of Intelligence Research, March 20, 1953.

43. 841 H. 235/5-1451. Dispatch, Wilson to DOS, May 14, 1951. R.G. 59, State Decimal File, Box 4817.

44. 844.00/11-845. Dispatch, Hare to DOS, November 8, 1945. R.G. 59, State Decimal File.

45. W.A. Lewis from St. Lucia later won a Nobel Prize in Economics. His involvement in the economic problems of the B. W. I. dated from the 1930s as a student in London. He served as an adviser to the Labour party, taught at the University of London, and later worked for the Caribbean Commission. For his role in promoting industrial development in the B. W. I. see Terrence Farrell, "Arthur Lewis and the Case for Caribbean Industrialization," *Social and Economic Studies*, 29, no. 4 (1980), 52-75.

46. Ibid., 59

47. 844 C. 50/9-2547. Telegram, Douglas to DOS, September 25, 1947. R.G. 59, State Decimal File, Box 6050.

48. D.J. Morgan, *Developing British Colonial Resources*, pp. 97-111

49. Ibid., pp. 112-119.

50. 841 G. 00/12-450. Memorandum, "Meeting with the British West Indian Delegation on Migratory Labour," November 9-10, 1950. R.G. 59, State Decimal File, Box 4815.

51. 741 E. 00/7-1351. Dispatch, Tibbetts to DOS, July 13, 1951. R.G. 59, State Decimal File, Box 3544.

52. D.J. Morgan, *Developing British Colonial Resources, 1945-1951*, p. 138.

53. Ibid., p. 141.

54. 741 E. 13/5-252. Dispatch, Burke to DOS, May 2, 1952. R.G. 59, State Decimal File, Box 3544.

55. Morgan, *Developing British Colonial Resources*, 149-51.

56. 844 D. 00/10-2546. Dispatch, Kemp to DOS, October 25, 1946. R.G. 59, State Decimal File, Box 6052.

57. 844.00/9-447. Dispatch, Bonnet to DOS, September 4, 1947. R.G. 59, State Decimal File, Box 6045.

58. 844.00/8-647. Dispatch, Young to DOS, August 6, 1947; and 844.00/7-2147. Dispatch, Skora to DOS, July 21, 1947. R.G. 59, State Decimal File, Box 6045.

59. 844.00/9-1747. Dispatch, Hooper to DOS, September 17, 1947. R.G. 59, State Decimal File, Box 6045; and Morgan, *Developing British Colonial Resources*, 147.

60. Munroe, *The Politics of Constitutional Decolonization*, 122-24.

61. Ibid.

62. IR 4924. "Progress toward a British West Indian Federation," 34-36.

63. Ibid., 40-46.

64. Ibid., 63-65.

65. Ibid., 54-62.

66. Ibid., 50.

67. Cited in Morgan, *Developing British Colonial Resources*, 153.

68. For a brief overview of the introduction of universal suffrage see Elizabeth Wallace, *The British Caribbean* (Toronto: University of Toronto Press, 1977), 109-37.

69. 841 G. 062/8-752. Despatch, Ernest to DOS, August 7, 1952. R.G. 59, State Decimal File, Box 4817.

70. 844 D. 00/2-2447. Dispatch, Kelly to DOS, February 24, 1947. R.G. 59, State Decimal File, Box 6052.

71. See D.J. Morgan, *A Reassessment of British Aid Policy, 1951-1965*, vol. 5 of *The Official History of Colonial Development* (London: Macmillan, 1980), 117-28; and 841H. 2351/2-2152. Dispatch, Parker Wilson to DOS, February 21, 1952. R.G. 59, State Decimal File, Box 4817.

72. Ibid., 129-40; and 841M. 2371/1-1653. Dispatch, Miller to DOS, January 16, 1953. R.G. 59, State Decimal File, Box 4819.

73. 841 H. 131/1-3150. Dispatch, Park to DOS, January 31, 1950. R.G. 59, State Decimal File, Box 4817.

74. 841 M. 00A/5-1550. Dispatch, Hale to DOS, May 15, 1990. R.G. 59, State Decimal File, Box 4819.

75. 841 H. 00/5-2352. Dispatch, Brown to DOS, May 23, 1952. R.G. 59, State Decimal File, Box 4816.

76. Ibid.

77. 841 H. 00/6-1052. Dispatch, Brown to DOS, June 10, 1952. R.G. 59, State Decimal File, Box 4816.

78. Editorial, *Daily Gleaner*, August 24, 1950.

79. 841 H. 00/5-2352. Dispatch, Brown to DOS, May 23, 1952. R.G. 59, State Decimal File, Box 4816.

80. 841 G. 2553/3-1450. Dispatch, Nyren to DOS, March 14, 1950. R.G. 59, State Decimal File, Box 4815; and 841 G. 2553/5-1850. Dispatch, Nyren to DOS, May 18, 1950. R.G. 59, State Decimal File, Box 4817.

81. 741G.00/3-1852. Dispatch, Ernst to DOS, March 18, 1952. R.G. 59, State Decimal File, Box 3544.

82. 844 C. 5043/6-547. Memorandum, Mackay to McReynolds, June 5, 1947. R.G. 59, State Decimal File, Box 6060; and 844.00/8-647. Dispatch, Young to DOS, August 6, 1947. R.G. 59, State Decimal File, Box 6045.

83. 844 D. 00/1-2248. Dispatch, Hooper to DOS, January 22, 1948. R.G. 59, State Decimal File, Box 6052.

84. 844 D. 00/9-3049. Dispatch, Park to DOS, September 30, 1949. R.G. 59, State Decimal File, Box 6052. For an account sympathetic to those expelled see Trevor Munroe, "The Marxist `Left' in Jamaica 1940-1950," *Working Paper* No. 15 (Jamaica: ISER/UWI, 1977), passim.

85. 841 H. 06/6-2552. Dispatch, Wilson to DOS, June 25, 1952. R.G. 59, State Decimal File, Box 4817.

86. 741 D. 001/5-553. Dispatch, Hamlin to DOS, May 5, 1953. R.G. 59, State Decimal File, Box 3543.

87. 741 D. 00/3-851. Dispatch, Burke to DOS, March 8, 1951. R.G. 59, State Decimal File, Box 3542.

88. 841 M. 062/6-452. Dispatch, Hale to DOS, June 4, 1952. R.G. 59, State Decimal File, Box 4819.

89. 841 G. 06/2-253. Dispatch, Clark to DOS, February 2, 1953. R.G. 59, State Decimal File, Box 4817.

90. 844 G. 00/2-1449. Intelligence Report, "British West Indies-Threat of Communist Activity", February 14, 1949. Office of Naval Intelligence. R.G. 59, State Decimal File, Box 6060.

91. 841 M. 062/9-2151. Despatch, Hale to DOS, September 21, 1951. R.G. 59, State Decimal File, Box 4819.

92. 841B. 062/2-1953. Despatch, Clark to DOS, February 19,1953. R.G. 59, State Decimal File, Box 4815.

5

From British Guiana to Chaguarmas: The American Response to West Indian Nationalism and British Disengagement, 1953-61

The year 1953 was of critical importance to the challenge to the colonial order in the British Caribbean. The ascendancy of radical nationalist leadership in British Guiana and British Honduras occurred in a context where there had been a political shift to the right in the United States confirmed by the accession to office of the Eisenhower administration. This shift in American politics followed upon the return to office in Britain of the conservatives led by Winston Churchill. The Conservative government was seeking to slow the process of imperial disengagement that had been set in train by the postwar Labour administrations. This shift to the right in both the United States and the United Kingdom set the context for conflict over the pace of decolonization in the British Caribbean, as the demand for decolonization began to assume a momentum that escaped the preparedness of the two powers to deal with the issue.

The Eisenhower administration had entered office on a platform that implied a more vigorous anti-Communist strategy--rollback--in foreign policy. The Eisenhower campaign had skillfully utilized the anti-Communist hysteria generated by McCarthyism and wooed southern Democrats alienated by Truman's civil rights policies to build a coalition of conservatives across American society. This conservative triumph in American politics, embracing both domestic and foreign policies, implied little tolerance for radicalism.[1] As the administration's policies evolved between 1953 and 1961, this intolerance, particularly in foreign policy, increasingly manifested itself in the American response to the process of decolonization.

Similarly, in Britain, the Conservatives led by Winston Churchill were returned to office in 1951. The new government sought to hedge the promise of imperial disengagement around which the post-1945 Labour governments had constructed their colonial policy. Despite a consensus on postwar colonial policy within the British political establishment--that decolonization would occur after a period of training of colonial leadership in the art of self-government--the Churchill government had reservations about the policies of its predecessors.[2] One element of Churchill's strategy was to attempt to woo the Eisenhower administration into slowing the process of decolonization.[3] The British strategy of using its dependence on its alliance with the America to maintain its role as a major international power was now directed at persuading the Eisenhower administration to underwrite a leisurely pace of disengagement.

It was against this background of the resurgence of American conservatism and the return to power of the Conservative party in Britain that the issues of the pace and direction of decolonization in the British Caribbean gained saliency. As the decade progressed, the three parties, the British West Indies, the United Kingdom, and the United States found themselves engaged in a process of redefining the parameters of their relationship. This process engendered both conflict and collaboration among the various parties. It also set the stage for the collapse of federation as a strategy of decolonization for the British Caribbean and consequent decolonization on a unit basis. This was a result that no single protagonist would have dared to forecast in 1953. However, several events of that year served as catalysts for the transformation of West Indian politics and Anglo-American relations in the region.

In April 1953, the People's Progressive Party, against which charges of communism were leveled by its opponents, defied all expectations and won eighteen of the twenty-four elected seats in the colony's legislature under the new constitution. On the basis of these results, it was expected that the PPP would select six of the ten members of the Executive Council and enjoy a majority in both the lower house and the combined lower and upper houses of the legislature.[4] In effect, by winning the elections in such a handsome fashion, the PPP translated popular discontent with colonial administration into a mandate for a vigorous challenge to colonial rule. At that point in the colony's history, the PPP's nationalist platform helped to forge an ideologically diverse collection of groups and individuals into an effective political party. Given the colony's ethnic diversity and its inherent potential for political fragmentation, the election results were a stunning vindication of the PPP's strategy. The significance of the PPP's victory transcended the politics of the colony itself and transformed the context within which decolonization in the British Caribbean proceeded after 1953. It also precipitated a hasty search by both the United States and Britain for mechanisms to coordinate their responses to the growing influence of nationalism in the region. The PPP victory reversed the process of disengagement that had characterized American policy over the period of the Truman administration. Despite its communist reputation, the PPP had been elected to office at the peak of the cold war in the American backyard and in a region where Britain had exerted considerable influence over several centuries.[5] For policymakers in both countries, it was an extraordinary event and immediately provoked alarm. To both governments, the turn of events in British Guiana challenged their expectations of a gradual and noncontroversial winding down of the British imperial role in the area. The State Department, which had closed its consular office in British Guiana as an economy measure, was confounded by the PPP's election victory. It was a chastening experience that a party, among whose leadership were numbered individuals with ties and ideological affinities to the Communist world, could be elected to office in a freely contested election in a British colony in the Western Hemisphere. In view of the administration's effort to portray itself as more vigorously anti-Communist than its predecessor, the PPP's election challenged the Eisenhower administration's fundamental views of the world.

To the British government on the other hand, which had assumed that complacency was an effective substitute for policy, events in British Guiana were a telling reminder that refurbished empire was not a sufficient condition for the continuation of colonialism. In effect, the results of the elections in British Guiana raised serious questions about British hopes for slowing the pace of imperial disengagement. Most troubling of all was the scale of the PPP victory and its ability to maintain its unity across the political and ethnic divisions of the society. The PPP had forced the colonial administration on the defensive. The governor, who had only assumed his post in early 1953 just prior to the elections, found his very authority in question.[6] For his superiors in London, the PPP's victory demanded an adequate response.

Similarly, the emergence of the PPP as the dominant political force in British Guiana posed a major problem for the other West Indian nationalist movements. Even prior to the PPP election victory, strains had already emerged in the relations between its leaders and those in the other territories. The PPP leadership's support for Richard Hart, one of the four Jamaican labor activists expelled from the PNP, against efforts led by Manley and Adams to oust him from the Caribbean Labour Congress was a major factor in this strained relationship.[7] This conflict reflected the growing impact of the cold war upon nationalism in the British Caribbean. For the majority of leaders outside of British Guiana in 1953, nationalism and anticommunism were part and parcel of their campaign for decolonization. For the more influential leaders in British Guiana in 1953, there was little willingness to pursue an anti-Communist strategy or to sever ties with institutions linked to the Communist world. Another difference distinguishing the PPP leadership from its counterparts in the other British Caribbean territories was the strength of anti-British sentiment upon which the PPP was able to build its political support. Where the nationalist leadership in the other territories conceived of decolonization as a gradual process through which they would earn the benediction of the imperial government, the PPP made it clear that it was not prepared to accept the ritual of tutelage in the art of self-government.[8] The party's electoral success signaled the emergence of leadership in the British

Caribbean which was impatient with the pace of imperial disengagement. It also ran counter to the consensus on the process of gradual devolution of responsibility that had been forged by the West Indian nationalist leadership in other territories and the Colonial Office over the preceding decade. As a consequence, the PPP victory had transformed the context of the Caribbean and the debate over the pace and strategy of constitutional devolution. Thus, the emergence of the PPP as a radical nationalist force, influenced by Marxist ideology and intent on forcing the pace of decolonization, confronted the United Kingdom, the United States, and other West Indian nationalist movements with a dilemma. Given the party's electoral triumph and its legitimacy, the PPP had seized the initiative and was catapulted to the center of the West Indian nationalist arena.

Even before the elections in British Guiana in 1953, there had been concern about the ideological orientation of the leadership of the PPP, especially that of Cheddi and Janet Jagan.[9] Cheddi Jagan was a dentist whose parents had worked as field laborers in the sugar industry. As a result of his intellectual gifts, he was able to attend the elitist Queen's College for his secondary education and later went to Northwestern University in Illinois for his professional training. Jagan managed to leap social and intellectual barriers in British Guiana upon his return in 1943. By the late 1940s, Jagan and his wife Janet, née Rosenburg who had been active in student politics in Chicago, had propelled themselves to prominence in the burgeoning nationalist movement. They engaged in building political alliances in both urban and rural areas and establishing the Political Affairs Committee that evolved into the PPP.[10] In the decade between his return to British Guiana and the election victory in 1953, Jagan was able to spearhead the formation of a political front across ethnic communities, solidly anchored in both rural and urban areas. The enormous legitimacy accorded to the PPP by the electorate in the colony reflected the gulf between the colonial administration and its subjects. Interpreting their victory as a mandate for the vigorous pursuit of a nationalist agenda, the PPP embarked on a campaign directed at forcing devolution of constitutional authority to the elected representatives of the government. This set the PPP on a collision course with the colonial administration, the imperial government, and the United States that led to military intervention by the imperial government and the suspension of the constitution within six months of the elections.

The platform upon which the PPP had conducted its electoral campaign called for self-government for British Guiana. It also endorsed participation in a West Indian federation in which all units had self-government and which would achieve dominion status. This platform objective was similar to that espoused by all the other nationalist movements at this period in the British Caribbean. The significant difference was that where the other nationalists were prepared to accept a tutelary relationship with the imperial government, in the wake of the elections the PPP sought to accelerate the process of constitutional devolution. From the moment that the extent of support for the PPP became evident, the leadership of the party began a campaign for the removal of the authority vested in the governor and other nonelected officials.[11] Further, a staple theme of its campaign was that the imperial relationship was an impediment to political and economic progress in the colony, and that the party's energies would be focused on changing the terms of that relationship. Just as important, the election victory encouraged the PPP to attempt to consolidate its support in the sugar industry where the large majority of the labour force was Indian. Ownership of the industry was concentrated in the hands of the British Booker Group with a minor stake in the industry held by local white interests.[12] It was a two-pronged strategy aimed at ensuring the party's ability to control the pace of events and define the political agenda for the colony.

In its challenge to the colonial administration, the PPP denigrated imperialism and the British connection as well as heatedly criticized administration officials. Its most obvious affront to the imperial connection was the decision not to send representatives to meet with the queen while she was passing through Jamaica on the way to an official visit to Australia. The official explanation was that the colony's finances could not support the expenditure required.[13] In the emotionally charged context of mid-1953, the PPP's decision could not but be perceived as evidence of its view of the empire. For colonial and imperial officialdom, the PPP's behaviour smacked of irresponsibility. It was a clear signal that for the PPP the relationship between Britain and the colony was of diminishing importance.

The party's perspective of the relationship was made evident in a meeting between PPP leaders and the American consul-general during the latter's visit to British Guiana in June 1953. At that meeting, the PPP leaders emphasized that they were anxious to secure capital investment from the United States and diversify the colony's trade away from the sterling bloc through increased trade with the United States. The American consul general reminded them that American investors would be sensitive to the investment climate in the colony, and that the ability to attract such investment would have to take that factor into account. The Guianese stressed that nationalization did not feature in their immediate objectives since they had not campaigned for office on those grounds. They also revealed their concerns about the negative image of the PPP portrayed in the American media. Notwithstanding the consul general's reticence, the nationalist leaders sought to obtain from him a sense of American receptivity to British Guiana's search for independence. The nationalists specifically sought to discover the extent to which economic ties could be strengthened with the United States by obtaining political independence for the colony. They were particularly interested in discovering the extent to which the United States would include British Guiana in its plans to strengthen economic ties in the hemisphere. The consul general did not respond to a question along these lines when it was put to him during the course of his meeting with the PPP leadership. In his report on the meeting, the consul general indicated that the PPP were committed to forcing the pace of constitutional change in the colony. He thought that the British government, after an initial trial period, would probably offer further constitutional devolution. From the tone of the report, the consul general did not appear to anticipate the crisis that exploded within the next three months.[14]

In subsequent reports, however, he became increasingly critical of the PPP as the struggle for control over the colony's political future intensified. Just as important, his reports reflected the sense of panic that beset the colonial administration and the business community at their loss of control over events in British Guiana. In late July he reported that the governor was seeking to boost his popularity in the colony in the event of a crisis.[15] Further, despite public statements by Jagan that capitalists would be offered every protection, the general manager of the Esso Standard Oil Company in Trinidad, the American firm doing the largest volume in business in British Guiana, depicted the PPP as the most serious threat to Western interests in the Americas. As a consequence, the firm sought to have the Department of State reopen a consulate in the colony.[16] The PPP's decision to reject the invitation of the Jamaican government to send a delegation to greet the queen was also announced during this period.[17] Political tension was further intensified by the PPP's continuing campaign to revoke the reserve powers of the governor and other nonelected officials. This included a signature campaign to petition the colonial secretary for the removal of these powers. At their public meetings, the PPP's speakers continued to berate the colonial administration and the imperial connection. By mid-September, when the PPP announced that it was contemplating state control over education, the American consul general reported that "Although the development of state-operated schools is not in itself objectionable, the apparent intention to give them a monopoly in the field of education savors of totalitarian policy."[18]

The event that triggered the British decision to send in troops was a struggle for control over the labor force in the sugar industry. The bargaining rights of workers in the industry had been accorded to the Man Power Citizens' Association (MPCA) and the Sugar Producers' Association (SPA) negotiated with the MPCA. However, in September 1953, the Guiana Industrial Workers' Union (GIWU) led by PPP activists called a strike in the sugar industry that rapidly spread and closed down the entire industry. For the first time in the history of the sugar cultivation in British Guiana, the entire industry was brought to a halt by industrial action. The refusal of the GIWU to accept a proposal by the SPA for the GIWU to be accorded bargaining rights for field-workers and the MPCA to remain as agent for factory workers, paved the way for the crisis that erupted.[19] The minister of labor introduced a bill in the legislature providing for a poll in any industry with recognition being granted to the union gaining the majority of votes. The governor sought to delay passage of the bill. As it became clear that the PPP would be able to override the governor's attempts to forestall the legislation, the British government resorted to military intervention. This latter course of action had been under consideration since early September.[20] The crisis provoked by the Labour Relations Act was more than just a conflict over bargaining rights in the sugar industry. The total rout of the MPCA from the industry would have meant that the company union would no longer offer the SPA a mechanism of influence among the workers. It would have meant that the new union, whose strength had been demonstrated by the strike, would have been buttressed by a sympathetic government. For the colonial administration, the unfolding crisis demonstrated that the governor's reserve powers could be thwarted by the parliamentary strength and discipline of the PPP. Left unchallenged, the authority of the governor would have been eroded by the parliamentary power of the majority party. The passage of the legislation would have also implied that the PPP's dominance in the colony had destroyed any pretensions to British control over the pace and agenda of constitutional devolution. To the American government, the image of a communist takeover began to generate an intense anxiety. According to the consul general on October 1: "With PPP leaders pressing hard to establish complete control colony, consolidated Communist bridgehead this area distinctly possible unless menace firmly met."[21] By early October, the American Embassy in London was keeping Washington abreast of British thinking and preparations for military intervention and suspension of the constitution in the colony.[22]

It is not clear from the records the extent to which the American government influenced British policy, but Dulles in a message to American envoys in Latin America and the Caribbean indicated that

> Although we (sic) not officially consulted re. situation in British Guiana or action contemplated, we have been generally informed of developments. Our view is that establishment Commie bridgehead there would be matter deep concern all republics hemisphere which value their sovereign independence. . . . FYI only, we have expressed deep concern to British re. developments and opinion situation should be met with great firmness.[23]

The British government publicly denied that any American pressure played a role in the decision to resort to military intervention. However, it did extend thanks to the American government for its offer of assistance in dealing with the crisis, indicating that a statement of support for British action would suffice.[24] The State Department complied. In the face of criticism of the British action from Latin American countries, the American government went even further to convince skeptical Latin American countries. American missions in Latin America were instructed to stress the Communist threat posed by developments in British Guiana "which forthright British action has apparently thwarted."[25] Beyond anti-PPP sentiment and a desire to support the United Kingdom, American policy was influenced by the perception that

British Guiana was a major source of the world's bauxite production.[26] The colony's proximity to the other American republics and the fear of PPP activity having a demonstration effect on other nationalist movements further encouraged American support for the British action.[27] One element that may have contributed to the American stance was the fact that the MPCA had been identified as a nucleus of anti-Communist and anti-Jagan leadership. Its threatened demise as a result of the Labour Relations Act, may have generated anxiety among American policymakers.[28] Thus, American policy toward Britain's action reflected a complex series of concerns, but fear of the communism of the PPP, a reaction to the latter's militancy and rhetoric rather than its ideological program, proved dominant.

The propaganda developed to justify the British resort to military intervention systematically emphasized the threat that the PPP represented. In a white paper issued to justify its action, the Colonial Office depicted the PPP as both Communist and committed to violence to advance its political agenda. In its background briefing to the press on the British decision, the Colonial Office also provided extensive details on PPP ties to European groups considered Communist.[29] Despite the propaganda, the British resort to intervention and suspension of the constitution in British Guiana raised concerns about the credibility of British policy. Officials in the Foreign Office expressed reservations about the number of charges leveled against the PPP in the white paper.[30] In a masterpiece of understatement, *The Spectator* reported:

> What Mr. Lyttleton has failed, or declined, to establish is the precise nature of the threat and the precise reason for the remedy employed. Though Dr. Jagan emerges as beyond all doubt a potential Guy Fawkes, his gun powder and his plot are still missing. It is one thing to encourage a strike and incite a riot; but it may be still another to plan a Communist coup. . . . The removal of democratic rights is not a matter which can, or should, be left to the imagination and the Colonial Office should be the last to overrate this particular faculty.[31]

Notwithstanding the patent weakness of the British government's case of a coup, labeling the PPP as a Communist party was enough to convince the Labour party's leadership and other nationalist leaders in the Caribbean that British action to deal with the PPP had been necessary.[32] On the American side, there was a preference for unconditional support for the British action. This was evidenced by the efforts to convince skeptical Latin American countries that the PPP constituted a serious threat to the American hemisphere.

The entire episode was a watershed in the process of imperial disengagement in the British Caribbean. Through military intervention, the British were seeking to demonstrate to nationalist movements throughout the Empire that it was determined to control the pace of constitutional devolution. Its efforts to discredit the PPP leadership and its collaboration with the United States toward that end was significant. In British Guiana, Britain was prepared to use American support to manage the process of imperial disengagement. The concurrence of other nationalist movements with the British campaign to portray the PPP as Communist reflected both the consensus among the nationalists that Fabian socialism should represent the leftward limits of ideology in the Caribbean, and a tactical unwillingness to pursue the path followed by the PPP in forcing the pace of constitutional devolution.[33] The alacrity with which both the People's National Party in Jamaica and the Barbados Labour party condemned the PPP and endorsed the policy of the British government pointed to their antipathy toward the PPP. Just as important, the crisis portended the deep rift that would be created over the question of British Guiana's participation in a West Indian Federation, as the anti-Communist issue was now no longer a matter of internal party politics in any single territory. The anti-PPP stance of the other West Indian leaders in 1953 impaired the willingness of the PPP to lead British Guiana into the federation after its return to office in 1957. Finally, the crisis revealed British deference to American sensitivities in the Caribbean, and the need for the United States to develop a policy to deal with the changing context within the Caribbean. Imperial disengagement and a communist threat were at the center of the political agenda. The crisis in British Guiana was a catalyst in moving American policy toward assuming a more activist stance in the West Indies. The American government believed that it had to participate in the creation of a new political dispensation in the region as the British prepared their departure. For the remainder of the Eisenhower administration, the issues of the West Indian Federation, the future of British Guiana, and the American role in an independent West Indies were the foci of American concern.

The need for a more activist American response to the unfolding situation in the British Caribbean was reinforced by the simultaneous emergence of a stridently anti-British nationalist leadership in British Honduras. The British sought to portray the movement as Communist-inspired and under the influence of the neighbouring Guatemalan government which had been branded as communist by the Eisenhower administration.[34] Unlike the PPP in British Guiana, which had refused to engage in anti-Communist politics, the People's United Party in British Honduras was openly and enthusiastically pro-American. Further, its leadership was prepared to pursue anti-Communist policies and maintained very close links with the American consulate in the colony.[35] Despite British efforts to paint the PUP as a Communist and pro-Guatemalan movement, the American consulate in British Honduras consistently played down these charges and provided a more sympathetic explanation of the attitudes of the PUP leadership.[36] The fact that the governor of the colony did not feel threatened by the rise of the PUP, and sought to co-opt the party's leadership in the process of constitutional devolution was a significant factor in calming the political climate in the colony.[37] Consequently, the American response to developments in British Honduras was qualitatively different to its response to the situation in British Guiana.

The distinction was due to the differing images of the PUP and PPP held by American policymakers. While both parties represented militantly anti-British nationalist forces, the latter represented a serious threat because of the ideological leanings of its leadership. Given the developments in British Guiana and the relative lack of overt American hostility to the PUP in British Honduras, it was obvious that the West Indian nationalist movements would have to ensure that their agendas did not provoke American anti-Communist sentiment. Such sentiment had already shown its impact upon the evolution of the decolonization process in the area. For various factions of the West Indian nationalist movements and for the British imperial government charges of communism became a useful device for attempting to slow the progress of political leadership whose objectives or strategies were perceived as inimical to their interests.

The institutionalization of anti-Communism as an element of the political culture of the West Indies was attested to by developments in the various colonies. In his speech at the opening of the legislature in Trinidad in October 1953, the governor lauded the actions of the British government in British Guiana and continued "It will show once and for all that we will not tolerate in the Commonwealth a communist government disavowing loyalty to Her Majesty the Queen and working for the elimination of every safeguard and for the subversion of the Constitution itself."[38] A subsequent report by a British trade unionist, F. W. Dalley, was highly critical of Communist activity in Trinidad. The Dalley mission resulted from an effort Chief Minister Albert Gomes in collaboration with the colony's administration, the British government, and the British TUC to force the WFTU-linked unions in the colony to sever their ties to both the WFTU and the West Indies Independence Party (WIIP).[39] In 1954, challenges to Grantley Adams' leadership of the Barbados Labour party led to allegations that some of these dissidents were Communist. Adams also lent his standing in the labor movement to the efforts to purge Communists from the movement in the region. These efforts were supported by both the ICFTU and North American unions.[40]

The issue of anti-Communist nationalism was of particular salience to American policy in the region. Even before the PPP victory, the Department of State's Office of Intelligence Research had emphasized the strategic importance of the region in light of the political and economic changes underway. Its report pointed out that the process could promote growth of Communist influence in the area. It urged that the United States needed to to define a policy response to these developments. According to the report,

> Whether the region progresses or stagnates will significantly affect American prestige and security. The British government is trying to increase and diversify West Indian production while giving the inhabitants substantial control of their government at both territorial and regional levels. The success or failure of this program will be widely regarded as a test of the capacity of Western democracy to build a stable society in its

own backyard. . . . A federated West Indies may provide a dynamic symbol for democratic progress and regional unity which would bar Communism more effectively that the most enlightened colonial paternalism.[41]

This sense that the end of colonialism was nigh and that a new dispensation was in the offing was confirmed by the American co-chairman of the Caribbean Commission in early 1954. There had been a demand by delegates to the West Indian Conference in 1952 for the commission's charter to be revised. The American chairman had been empowered by the Department of State to review the effectiveness of the commission. In April 1954, he indicated that an effort should be made to revitalize the organization by removing the stigma of colonialism that it bore. Failing this, he advised "it should be allowed to die and other means sought to advance the stability of the area."[42]

In the wake of the British Guiana episode and the accelerating pace of constitutional devolution in the other British colonies, it was incumbent upon the Americans to participate in elaborating a new dispensation to safeguard its interests in the area. The 1953 crisis in British Guiana had revealed the tenuous nature of Anglo-American collaboration in the region. After that episode, the two powers, with fitful cooperation from Canada, began to construct a condominium to manage the process of West Indian decolonization. It was a process in which the leadership of the nationalist movements actively participated. The accelerating pace of constituional devolution had produced a shift among the various parties and set the stage for conflict over their respective attitudes and agendas. The fact that Britain was both incapable of, and unwilling to, shoulder the burden of restructuring the economies of these territories began to influence the attitude of the West Indian leadership. The severity of Britian's postwar economic problems had demonstrated the manifest weakening of Britian's economy. However, the West Indians were not inclined to let the imperial government off the hook of providing economic assistance to their territories. Instead, their attention began to focus upon developing strategies of economic diversification through economic ties to North America. This was complemented by an effort to maintain preferential access to the British market and to obtain higher levels of imperial assistance. By the mid-1950s, the British search for disengagement, the West Indian attempts to create diversified economies, and the American desire for stability were the central themes in the debate over the future of these colonies. The efforts to reconcile these objectives among the protagonists led to conflict and crisis as the increasing assertiveness of the West Indian leaders began to weigh upon the tripartite relationship.

The first signs of the changes underway in the 1950s were manifested in attitudes toward the federal project. By increasing the scope of self-government through the introduction of universal suffrage, Britain found itself confronted by a triumph of insular concerns over the plans for a federation.

The introduction of ministerial government, with executive responsibilities progressively transferred from appointed officials to elected members in the legislature, helped to bring about the prominence given to parochial concerns. Legitimacy and performance, as indices of responsibility in the art of self-government, were almost entirely linked to territorial concerns. Inevitably, perceptions of the utility of federation were modified. Up until the Montego Bay Conference in 1947, federation had been a strategy for achieving a greater degree of self-government. However, by the early 1950s, attention began to focus upon the cost and benefits of a federal structure for both self-government and economic diversification.

In addition, the fitful interest in federation that had followed upon the submission of the 1950 SCAC report was only worsened by developments in British Guiana and British Honduras. In the former case, the suspension of the constitution had effectively disrupted the process of constitutional devolution which would have facilitated the integration of the colony into the constitutional framework of the federation. Even if British Guiana had been able to participate, it was not evident that the other territories would have accepted such collaboration with the PPP. The size of the Indian population in the territory and the strength of support enjoyed by the Jagans in that community also constituted an inhibiting factor in the colony's participation in the federation. In the case of British Honduras, the PUP's militancy was directed against the colonial administration and the proposed federation since the party saw the colony's future within Central America rather than with the other British colonies.[43] The active unwillingness of both major underpopulated mainland colonies to support the federal project raised fundamental questions about its viability. For the islands where population export emerged as a strategy for dealing with unemployment and lack of economic diversification, particularly Jamaica and Barbados, it was doubtful that a federation without the mainland territories would be appealing. In the absence of these two territories, attention shifted to Trinidad that had a relatively low population density and an economy more prosperous and stable than its partners in the embryonic federal project. The nonparticipation of the mainland colonies created greater expectations of Trinidad's role and burden within the federal project.[44] As a consequence, by 1954, both the expectations and roles of the various territories within the federal project had undergone significant modification.

In early 1953, the Colonial Office had convened a meeting of representatives from the British West Indies to discuss the SCAC proposals. British Guiana had announced its reluctance to participate in the proposed federation as did British Honduras. However, both colonies sent observers to the meeting. At this meeting the Trinidad delegation split on the issue of freedom of movement within the federation. One of the two Trinidad delegates explicitly rejected the decision of the conference to restrict Trinidad's control over immigration into the islands, except on grounds of health or security.[45]

The fear of the disruptive consequences of migration upon Trinidad's relative prosperity had emerged as a significant stumbling block to the federal project. In 1955, a conference on migration was held in Port of Spain and the earlier decision was reversed to allow Trinidad to maintain control over immigration. It was agreed that Trinidad would retain that authority for five years after the establishment of the federation.[46] The 1953 conference also resulted in an explicit commitment from Britain to provide budgetary support to the federal government, while £500,000 would be donated toward the establishment of the federal capital.

As planning for the federation moved ahead, the continuing financial predicament of the Eastern Caribbean, the lack of economic diversification in the colonies, the unabated population pressures in Barbados and Jamaica, and the inadequacy of an imperial policy that perceived disengagement as more important than diversification were all burdens imposed upon the project. Initially, the federal project had been seen as a framework for achieving greater self-government and political reform. From 1950 onward, as the project and planning became more detailed, it began to appear as an unwieldy enterprise whose primary purpose was to facilitate imperial disengagement without delivering the economic diversification imperative for the region's viability. Britain's plight after 1945 certainly contributed to its failure to marshal resources for the economic diversification of the West Indies. It was the nationalist leadership that inherited the problem of finding a strategy to overcome the problems confronting these territories. In this context, the utility of the federal project began to be evaluated in terms of its potential to contribute to economic diversification, to facilitate migration, and to reduce chronic unemployment in these territories. The fear that Britain's support for the proposed federation was little more than an effort to divest itself of the burden of the financially weaker colonies in the Caribbean constituted a powerful source of distrust among West Indian nationalists.[47] British policy after 1945 had not calmed those fears and Britain's inability to provide capital investment for the territories only exacerbated the situation. The governments in Barbados, Jamaica, and Trinidad had embarked upon policies designed to increase investment in these territories, often in the face of opposition from the imperial government. The failure of the other territories to pursue similar strategies did little to promote their financial independence from the Imperial Exchequer. Their dependence on London later proved to be a major source of conflict within the federation. As late as 1955 there continued to be serious doubts about the viability of the federal project. The 1953 conference in London had not dispelled West Indian unease and British hopes for its establishment were held hostage to sentiment in the colonies.

Even as the federal project marked time, however, the pace of constitutional devolution was accelerating and, in hindsight, further undermined the appeal of the federation. The victory of the People's National Party at the general elections in Jamaica in 1955 reflected the shifts taking place in the Caribbean. From the outset, the PNP made it clear that its priorities were the problems confronting Jamaica and that attention to the issue of federation would be deferred.[48] This shift in focus reflected the strength of sentiment already evident in Jamaica that federation was a constraint upon Jamaica's own development. Norman Manley had been one of the early nationalist leaders who had championed the idea of a West Indian federation. However, in late 1955 the Colonial Office reported that both Manley and Adams were lukewarm about the project. Manley's reservations were based upon the drop in support for the project among Jamaicans and in the ranks of the PNP itself.[49] The fact that Adams was also identifiably cool to the federation was significant since he had also been an early proponent of the project. The PNP's assumption of the reins of government did not provide impetus for federation, as had been anticipated by the Colonial Office.[50] Rather, it confirmed the strength of anti-federation sentiment among the Jamaican political leadership and the strong emphasis on Jamaica dealing with its own political problems as a priority. Given their long-standing political ties, it would have been inconceivable that Adams and Manley had not shared their reservations about the project.

The Jamaica-first orientation of the PNP government was emphasized from the outset. After his accession to office, Manley made it clear that he was prepared to cultivate closer ties with the United States even in the face of opposition from the Colonial Office.[51] The PNP moved rapidly to obtain technical assistance from the United States and actively solicited American investment to finance the economic diversification of the island's economy. Beyond the promotion of ties to the United States for Jamaica's benefit, the PNP leadership sought to accelerate the pace of Jamaica's constitutional devolution through the introduction of cabinet government which would allow elected ministers to exercise greater authority over departments and reduce the power of nonelected officials.[52]

This focus on Jamaica's problems was vividly demonstrated in the negotiations leading up to the establishment of the federation. In February 1956, a conference of delegates from the British Caribbean was convened by the Colonial Office in London. At this conference the decision to proceed with the establishment of the federation was taken. The Jamaican delegates made it clear that Jamaica's support for federation was contingent upon Jamaica maintaining control over its own economic development strategy. This strategy included the maintenance of high tariffs for revenue and to encourage industrial development.[53] The Jamaican position was directly related to the diversification of the economy and the territory's unwillingness to underwrite the administrative costs of the federal government. The inflexibility of the Jamaican position demonstrated the consensus within the territory about the value of federation. For the Jamaicans, Britain's stake in the federal project required it to provide substantial financial support to underwrite the establishment and formative phase of the federal government's life.

This strategy of forcing economic aid out of the British government was also manifested in the refusal of the Jamaican government to exercise any controls over the flow of Jamaican migrants into Britain.[54] The arrival of West Indians into the United Kingdom began to generate tensions and conflict over housing and employment conditions. In response to these tensions, the British political establishment became concerned about the fruits of empire being dropped into the lap of the mother country. The migrants were largely Jamaican and Barbadian, and the growth in the numbers of those migrating to the United Kingdom was one consequence of the small quota of migrants accorded by the U.S. to the West Indies. The PNP government in Jamaica made it clear that, despite a loss of skilled labor, it saw the migration as a mechanism for reducing the population pressure in the colony.[55] The export of seasonal workers to the United States, as well as nurses and domestic servants to Canada, continued to serve as a mechanism for reducing unemployment. The Barbadian government also actively supported migration through financial support for the migrants.[56] The lack of other outlets, particularly in British Honduras, British Guiana, and the United States, effectively left the United Kingdom as the only destination for the surplus population of these territories. In response to queries about the disruptive effects of the migration to Britain, the Jamaican government argued that the refusal of the imperial government to increase aid to the West Indian colonies made the migration inevitable. Further, it was not prepared to act unilaterally in either slowing or interrupting the flow.[57] This use of migration to force increased aid out of the British government was accompanied by requests for aid to the federation that exceeded the levels proposed by the imperial government. While the latter proved willing to establish a fund for the building of a capital site for the federation and to continue aid at existing levels, West Indian leaders considered this aid insufficient to support the federal project.[58] The fear of a Federation of paupers continued to inform West Indian thinking about the objectives of British policy. The British government's unwillingness to increase its aid to the West Indies constituted a powerful constraint upon acceptance of the Federal project by West Indian leaders.

The growing divergence between Jamaica's views and those of the British government reflected an emerging trend in the political economy of the British Caribbean. The colonies of Jamaica, Trinidad and Barbados were pursuing strategies of economic diversification that provided a measure of financial stability. This relative financial stability created a context in which these colonies were able to pursue strategies of economic diversification that were largely independent of the British government. The other colonies remained dependent upon the British Treasury and consequently, subject to British control. This difference in the degree of autonomy enjoyed by the various colonies implied considerable difficulty in reaching consensus on the Federal project--both in terms of its objectives and its *modus operandi*. The degree of autonomy enjoyed by Jamaica was also a reflection of the improved position in which Jamaica found itself after its decision to revise taxation agreements with the bauxite producing companies in Jamaica.[59] The rapid increase in government revenues accruing to the Jamaican government enhanced its financial position and its autonomy vis-à-vis the other West Indian colonies and the British government. The PNP government also sought to take advantage of America's status as a creditor nation by seeking to establish a tax agreement with the United States that would provide incentives for American investment in Jamaica.[60] With the rising cost of loans on the London market to finance development in the colonies, Jamaica also began to explore possibilities of securing loans in the United States.[61] When the British government conceded that Britain could not provide adequate capital to meet colonial needs, Jamaica was set to solicit American investment in the island's economy. In addition, Norman Manley also set out to obtain the services of an economic advisor, independent of the British government, who could provide advice on Jamaica's strategy of economic diversification.[62]

By asserting its growing autonomy from the British government and courting the United States, the Jamaican government was demonstrating that it would not be bound by British visions of the future of these territories. It was making it clear that Jamaica's economic transformation would not be held hostage to the economic problems of the smaller territories. Its promotion of a protected industrial sector was also setting it on a path to competition with Trinidad as a producer of manufactured goods for the other colonies.[63] Thus, on the eve of federation in 1958, Jamaica had become the centerpiece around which the federation would be built. Norman Manley had emerged as the dominant political figure in the region and the key to the establishment of a successful federation. This status had been achieved despite the opposition to the project within Jamaica and the PNP itself.[64] He also represented, with Grantley Adams, the embodiment of the West Indian nationalism that preceded World War II and championed the idea of federation. It was to be the paradox of the federal project that would ultimately lead to its failure. Manley, who vigorously pursued a Jamaica-first strategy that unleashed centrifugal tendencies in the West Indies was at the same time perceived as the bulwark of federation.

However, the centrifugal tendencies at work in the British Caribbean were not restricted solely to Jamaica. Due to the latter's prominence and economic growth, it best exemplified these developments. Among the smaller territories, there was a fear that the federation would be dominated by Jamaica and Trinidad, and early efforts were devoted to ensuring the location of the capital in another territory.[65] There was also an effort by the smaller territories to exploit the differences between the two leading colonies. Much of the Barbadian interest in the federal project revolved around the possible choice of the island as the federal capital, even though there was considerable skepticism among the other territories about race relations in the island.[66] In Trinidad, the rapid rise of Eric Williams and the People's National Movement

(PNM) in the colony's political life resulted in the eclipse of the older generation of political figures at the 1956 elections. Williams' prominence within Trinidad had followed upon his public denunciation of the Caribbean Commission, with which he had been associated for over a decade, and his adoption of a strident anticolonial and anticorruption platform in the election campaign.[67] He had identified himself with Norman Manley after his break with the Caribbean Commission in 1955 and had patterned the PNM on the People's National Party in Jamaica.[68] However, following the election victory in Trinidad, he demonstrated an increasing independence of Manley, best exemplified by his refusal to have the sobriquet socialist, favored by Manley and Adams, designate either himself or the PNM.[69]

The strident anticolonialism that marked Williams and the PNM demonstrated strong similarities to the militancy displayed by the PPP in British Guiana and the PUP in British Honduras. This militancy and the popular support it enjoyed in the various colonies reflected the changing climate in the West Indies. It also was not coincidental that this militancy was most obviously associated with leaders and parties that had emerged after 1945. The changed climate had produced a new generation of nationalist leaders whose tone and style differed significantly from that of Norman Manley and Grantley Adams. The election of Williams to leadership in Trinidad, a rival to Jamaica as a leading force within the proposed federation, promised both possibilities of increased cooperation as well as potential conflict. Given the differences in style, and a generation gap among the leaders of the nationalist movements in the various territories, problems were bound to arise. These differences of style and militancy affected perceptions of the pace of decolonization in the region. Manley was committed to pursuing a gradualist approach, whereas Williams sought to push the pace, envisaging a date for independence prior to that of the Gold Coast, which became independent in 1957.[70] Williams's sense of independence from Britain and his fellow West Indian nationalists also prompted him to pursue the development of Trinidad's ties with the United States. Even before assuming office as leader of the majority in the legislature, Williams approached the American consulate in Trinidad about obtaining American technical assistance for the colony.[71] He also solicited advice from Puerto Rican officials about strategies for promoting industrial development in Trinidad. The consulate reported that Williams and the PNM, despite their anticolonial militancy, demonstrated respect for the United States. He was also insistent that negotiations for technical assistance with the United States be conducted directly with the American government rather than through the Caribbean Commission.[72] His attitude on this issue was undoubtedly related to his animosity to the commission, but it may also have been shaped by his desire to establish a relationship with the Americans independent of British involvement.

Trinidad's pursuit of industrialization had been a cause for concern in Jamaica prior to Williams's victory. The latter's determination to continue with that strategy of economic diversification set the stage for heightened competition between the two major poles in the federation. Even before the formal inauguration of the federation, the competitive dimension of regional politics had begun to undermine the efforts at collaboration. The strategies of economic diversification pursued by the individual colonies were proving to be less than complementary and the survival of the Federation demanded large doses of compromise. It was not obvious that many of the nationalist leaders could display that facility. This transformation of the context in the West Indies and the changes in expectations of what the federation should achieve, as well as the reduction in the number of participating colonies, did not lead to a reassessment of the project itself by the imperial government. British policymakers conceived of federation as the only viable strategy for political independence for the West Indian colonies, given their size and economic difficulties.[73] Despite the evidence of dwindling commitment to the project among West Indian leaders and the difficulties of achieving agreement among them, the British government was bereft of an alternative strategy for the West Indian colonies. The lack of an alternative seemed to make the imperial government even more desperate to hold on to the federal project. In addition, by 1956 the British government publicly admitted that Britain was not capable of providing the levels of capital needed for colonial development and that American capital would inevitably fill the breach.[74] In the wake of the Suez episode, when the benefits of empire appeared increasingly dubious, the imperial government began to hasten the process of decolonization. By early 1957, it was the considered view within the imperial government that the British West Indian colonies would be eligible for independence by 1963, with British Guiana and British Honduras following by 1967.[75] In this context, the proposed federation had begun to assume, for British policymakers, an aura of inevitability and represented the only viable mechanism for colonial divestiture in the British West Indies.

For West Indian nationalists, the perception that the burden was being shifted unto the federation and unto the financially secure territories was hardly an exaggerated view of British policy. In effect, federation was beginning to represent an imperial bailout in the minds of both British policymakers and West Indian nationalists. The leader of the anti-federation faction of the PNP in Jamaica claimed that federation was a process forced upon Jamaica by the imperial government. He also described it as an effort to forestall the development of closer ties between Jamaica and the United States.[76] Further evidence of West Indian skepticism about British objectives was provided by the American consulate in Trinidad. A confidante of Albert Gomes (the leader of the majority in the legislature before the 1956 elections that brought Williams to office), James Bain, had offered the view that British support for the federation had two objectives: "(1) to impress the United Nations with its eagerness to grant self-government and independence to its colonial dependencies; and more important, (2) to rid itself of the continuing financial drain of supporting an area which is dependent upon grants and development aid."[77]

The February 1956 conference in London, where the structure of the federal government was agreed upon, did not provide any indication that West Indian skepticism had been overcome. The American embassy in London reported that "Both as regards the work of the Conference and the nature of the Federation the attitude of the Colonial Office is far from enthusiastic or optimistic. The general feeling is that the constitutional arrangements envisaged will provide at best for a flimsy structure."[78] In effect, West Indian skepticism was beginning to infect the British government itself about the viability of the proposed federation. Without a willingness, or express policy, to provide increased British financial support to the federation, British officials had little leverage to induce changes in the structure of the proposed federal government. The federal government had no independent capacity to raise revenues for the first five years of its existence. Even before its inauguration, there was an obvious lack of commitment to the enterprise from both the colonies and the imperial government.

In its subsequent decision to appoint a governor-general for the West Indies Federation, the Macmillan government in London selected Lord Hailes, who had previously served as the chief whip for the conservatives in the House of Commons. Hailes's appointment did not evoke enthusiasm in either Britain or in the West Indies as he had had no prior experience in the area. In an assessment of reaction to the appointment in London, the American embassy reported that opinion had been generally unfavorable across the political spectrum, even within the Conservative party itself. According to the embassy, critics said that

> His lack of distinction meant that this appointment was not particularly complimentary to the new Federation, nor was he likely to be a first-rate Governor General. Furthermore, his appointment gave the appearance of a political deal whereby Macmillan fobbed off on the West Indies a man to whom he was politically indebted but whom he considered too incompetent to become a member of his Cabinet. They added that the appointment showed the Prime Minister really was not interested in the far-flung parts of the Commonwealth, but instead concentrated his attention on the United States and on Western Europe.[79]

By choosing Hailes as governor-general, the Macmillan government had managed to convey the message that the West Indies and the federation were of little import to Britain. It was a message that did little to shore up the crumbling commitment to the federation.

While developments in the West Indies and Britain's haste to divest itself of its empire were helping to undermine the federal project, American policy toward the region showed an interest in increasing American influence. However, the Americans sought to remove any suspicion that the United States was either competing with Britain, or seeking to displace the latter's influence. Despite its rhetorical posturing about supporting the right to self-determination, American policy toward the British Caribbean reflected a willingness to allow Britain to set the lead in the area. There was an early American acceptance of the idea of political independence for the West Indies and for the federal project. It was also recognized that the economic viability of the federation would be problematic and that American aid and technical assistance would be sought by an independent West Indies Federation. There was little likelihood of increased trade between the West Indies and the United States as the latter was unlikely to open its market to West Indian sugar. In addition, the West Indies had actively engaged in trying to keep the British market closed to American citrus exports to have preferences continued for their own exports.[80] Notwithstanding these potential problems, it was felt that "it would appear that Federation would be consistent with our foreign policy objectives and not detrimental--perhaps even beneficial--to our relations with Latin America." It was also conceived that the Federation would be eligible for membership in the Organization of American States and become a signatory to the Rio Pact.[81]

This relatively low-keyed approach was fortified by the extension of technical assistance to Jamaica and British Guiana by 1955 and by opening discussions with the other territories toward that end in subsequent years. In the case of British Guiana, American assistance had been extended with the explicit objective of undermining the influence of the PPP and the Jagans in the colony. An example of this assistance was the funding of a seminar in workers' education in British Guiana, the organization of which was handled by the University of Maryland. In approving the funding for the seminar, the State Department instructed the consulate in Trinidad that

> Prior to taking any action with local authorities or British trade union representatives in British Guiana, however, the Department desires to be certain that the British TUC approves of the project and that the TUC does not regard this as an intrusion on its functions by the U.S. Government. Naturally the entire project could fail in its purpose should there be any such feeling.[82]

Even in British Guiana, where American policy was most interventionist in trying to shape political developments, priority was given to the American desire for coordination with the British on shaping the political evolution of the British Caribbean. The motives shaping American policy toward the British Caribbean were detailed by the American consul in British Honduras in early 1958. According to the consul:

> the United States, despite the obvious delicacy of projecting itself into countries where a colonial power--in this case Great Britain--has primary responsibility and authority, has undertaken ICA programs in the colonial dependencies of the Caribbean because

they are located in a geographical area of primary concern to the United States. It is further understood that we must avoid: (1) any impression that we wish to supersede the British in their primary responsibility; (2) any special encouragement to British Honduras aspirations for self-government or independence that would seem to be dangling before them an alternative to British assistance, financial or otherwise; (3) any temptation prematurely to capitalize on the strong underlying pro-US sentiment among the British Honduras population; (4) any impression of support, direct or indirect, for the colonial aspect of the regime, which might interfere with a posture most likely to reap eventual value from this pro-US sentiment.[83]

Obviously, American policy toward British Honduras was informed by a wider view of the Anglo-American relationship.

The extent to which the United States was prepared to go to evade confrontation with the British over decolonization was revealed in a subsequent exchange of correspondence between the American consulate in British Honduras and the Department of State. After playing a mediating role in the hostile and bitter relationship between George Price, the leader of the People's United Party, and the governor of British Honduras, the American consul suggested in October 1958 that the United States should issue a public declaration that the future of British Honduras should be determined by the inhabitants of the colony. He suggested that the statement should be made in Washington or at the United Nations and indicated that George Price had often voiced a desire for American intervention on this issue.[84] In a response to this recommendation by the Consulate, the Department of State stated that while agreeing with the consul on much of his analysis of the situation in British Honduras, the department was reluctant to pursue an activist policy. In elaborating on the reasons for the position adopted by the department, Dulles took the position that

In general Department does not wish intervene in British Honduras affairs and in particular does not wish give British impression U.S. meddling or pressuring. Close relations with British on broad front are of paramount importance to U.S. particularly at present. . . . Under circumstances Department does not contemplate high level public statement that U.S. believes future B.H. should be determined by people thereof and reluctant as well authorize any such statement by you. Department would not object, however, your making statement before Rotary Club as casual and platitudinous part unofficial local talk other subjects. You should attempt avoid appear propose change in status B.H. which would upset Guatemala. In order avoid British suspicion of meddling, you show text informally to Governor or Colonial Secretary beforehand. *If objection encountered, do not deliver. Do not repeat not indicate statement cleared Department or that talk anything more than your idea* (emphasis added).[85]

The instructions to the American consulate in British Honduras reflected the fundamental unwillingness of the American government to champion decolonization in the Caribbean. Even with a pro-American nationalist leadership importuning American support against Britain, American policy reflected its preference for collaboration with the colonial power.

However, this preference for a collaborative relationship with the colonial power, the United Kingdom, was sorely tested as the proposed Federation of the British West Indies began to take shape after 1956. As constitutional devolution progressed, the West Indian nationalist leadership had been assertively demonstrating their independent stance vis-à-vis the British government. And as Britain began to accelerate its pace of disengagement from the Caribbean, the issue of the American role and influence in these territories began to loom larger. West Indian assertiveness generated tensions with both Britain and the United States; it forced both powers to confront West Indian nationalism and recognize the limits to their influence in the changing context of the British Caribbean.

The 1956 conference in London of West Indian delegates had fashioned a federal constitutional structure that reflected the unwillingness of both the British government and West Indian leaders to confer significant authority on the new entity. The West Indian delegates had agreed to finance the federal government through a mandatory levy on revenues from each territory, with the federal government shorn of any revenue-raising authority. Jamaica's contribution constituted 43.1 percent of the levy, Trinidad provided 38.6 percent, Barbados 8.5 percent and the seven other territories provided the remainder.[86] The size of the contributions from the individual colonies made it evident that the two major territories, Jamaica and Trinidad, were indeed being asked to shoulder the lion's share of the federal structure, however inadequate that structure. It also reflected the disproportionate influence that the two colonies would have over the federation. It was inconceivable that the federation could proceed without one, or the other, and demonstrated the necessity for a consensus between the two for the federation to achieve a measure of credibility. Without such a consensus, it was already obvious that the centrifugal tendencies at work could cripple, if not destroy, the federation.

The British government's inability to persuade the West Indian leaders to adopt a constitutional structure that would provide greater authority to the federal government demonstrated its lessening influence over developments in the Caribbean. The British government was unwilling to provide significant increases in aid to the federation, and without the leverage that such aid could provide, resorted to investing significant authority in the governor-general's powers under the federal constitution. However, at the 1956 London Conference, West Indian criticism of these reserve powers led to a revision of the specific clauses.[87] The lack of confidence in federation and in each other, shared by West Indian leaders and British officials, was thus embodied in the constitutional framework of the proposed federation. From its conception, through its establishment, the federal project was developed in a climate of distrust among the most influential West Indian leaders and the British government. This ambiance of distrust was not propitious for the future of federation, and the further the project advanced the less inclined did the participants seem to desire a confrontation over the issue. It was in this context that controversy over the West Indian decision to establish the federal capital in an area leased to the United States erupted, sowed increased distrust among the participants in the federal project, and effectively crippled the federation itself.

The roots of the controversy lay in the shifting parameters of the federal project during the decade of its development. In 1953, the conference of West Indian delegates had agreed upon Grenada as the site of the proposed federal capital. However, in 1956, that decision was reversed by the delegates and the task of selecting an alternative site was entrusted to a commission of British officials empowered to recommend a list of suitable sites in the various colonies.[88] Even before the 1956 conference had agreed to reverse the decision to locate the capital in Grenada, influential voices in Trinidad were already raising arguments in favor of establishing the capital in an area leased by the Americans. *The Guardian*, the leading newspaper in the island, had pronounced itself in favor of locating the capital in Tucker Valley, an area leased to the United States.[89] The American consul-general in Trinidad indicated that the Colonial Secretary had previously expressed similar views and may have been behind the position taken by *The Guardian*.[90] Leading members of the government prior to 1956 had also endorsed the site chosen by the newspaper. Albert Gomes, the majority leader in the government, even broached the possibility that siting the capital in Tucker Valley would be raised at the conference in London. He was also of the view that Trinidad would ultimately be selected as the capital site.[91] A Trinidadian lobby was already building support for the siting of the federal capital in an area leased by the Americans, even before the decision in favor of Grenada had been reversed. The People's National Movement led by Eric Williams later campaigned in the 1956 elections on a platform endorsing both the federation and the siting of its capital in Trinidad. Thus, a strong consensus had emerged in Trinidad for the island to serve as the host to the federal government.

This consensus, and the positive sentiments that underlay it, received a rude shock when the report of the commission charged with recommending a site was issued in January 1957. The commission had opted to identify a site that had an infrastructure capable of supporting both a territorial and federal capital. On these grounds, only Jamaica, Trinidad, and Barbados could reasonably claim to offer the twin capital option. The commission's report expressed a clear preference for Barbados. Jamaica, despite its distance from the other territories, was placed second, and Trinidad an undignified third. The lack of dignity accorded to Trinidad was reflected in the language used to relegate its candidacy. The report referred disparagingly to the politics of the territory as unstable, with low standards, widespread corruption, and cited the presence of the community of East Indian origin as a disturbing element.[92] If the commission had sought to ensure that Trinidad would not be selected as the site of the federal capital, its recommendations were a serious miscalculation. On the second round of balloting in the meeting to decide on the site of the federal capital, the West Indian delegates overwhelmingly voted in favor of Trinidad.[93] The commission's report had an inflammatory impact upon West Indian opinion and did little to shore up the credibility of colonial officials in the eyes of West Indians.

The commission's report may have been influenced by the unwillingness of the Defense Department to consider the surrender any of the leased areas. In a letter from the Department of State to the Department of Defense, the former indicated that the commission had solicited American opinion on the capital site. The State Department itself was of the view that

> if it is consistent with other national interests, we should make every effort to meet a request for the release of a site if it is required for the new capital. . . . As you know there is always a certain degree of resentment among the British West Indies peoples over the United States bases as representing land over which they have lost sovereignty for a period of 99 years. If we are to afford the whole population of the British West Indies a site for the capital of their country, the rewards in goodwill toward the United States would not be limited to the island in which the site was located, but would extend throughout the area.[94]

However sympathetically the State Department may have considered the request, the commission's report itself reflected little sympathy for the request to locate the federal capital in a leased area. The language of the report may have been an accurate reflection of the thinking of the American Department of Defense. In rejecting the proposal to use the buildings on the naval base at Chaguaramas as a temporary site for the federal capital, the report stated:

> This base has not been "deactivated." Rather, the probability appears to be that its strength will be increased. We see therefore no prospect of the Government of the United States abandoning any part of it permanently and we consider that it would be highly damaging to the prestige of the new Federation to have its capital, even temporarily, situated in an area which is under the control of a foreign power, however friendly that power may be.[95]

With such a categorical rejection of the proposal to use the leased areas as a site for the federal capital already in the report, the commentaries on the quality of political life in Trinidad were gratuitous. In the final analysis, it produced a result that probably was not intended--the West Indian leaders opted to locate the federal capital in Trinidad in February 1957.

As a consequence of this decision by the Standing Federation Committee (SFC) composed of West Indian delegates and British officials charged with laying the groundwork for the establishment of the federal government, the Trinidad government appointed a site committee of local business leaders and civil servants to recommend a range of possible sites in Trinidad. This committee listed seven possible sites but indicated that the north west peninsula of Trinidad, which included the American Naval Base at Chaguaramas, was far and above the most suitable site. It was a decision that placed the newly elected PNM government on the horns of a dilemma. The PNM had explicitly pledged to respect existing international agreements and was reluctant to ask the American government to release the base.[96]

In May 1957, at a meeting of the SFC, the Trinidadian delegates including Eric Williams sought to avoid a confrontation with the United States by intimating their unwillingness to request the release of Chaguaramas. However, with leadership from Manley and Adams, the SFC pressed the case for seeking the release of the naval base. The Trinidad delegates abstained from voting on the issue at the meeting. Notwithstanding the reluctance of the Trinidad delegation, the SFC decided that the British government would be asked to arrange a meeting with the American government to discuss the release of the naval base and a defense agreement among the three parties--the West Indies, the United Kingdom, and the United States of America. However, it was also decided to include Eric Williams as an observer in the West Indian delegation sent to the meeting.[97] The May 1957 meeting of the SFC, and its decisions on the federal capital site, set the stage for the nascent West Indian nation to define its relationship with the United States. In seeking to secure the release of the American naval base, the West Indian political leadership was obviously attempting to solicit from the United States an expression of its policy toward the federation. By tabling the proposal for tripartite discussions on a defense agreement, the West Indian leaders were probably attempting to reassure both domestic and international audiences that the request for the release of the Chaguaramas base was not an expression of hostility toward the United States. It was also a signal that the West Indians would not simply accept the Bases-for-Destroyers Agreement that had come to symbolize the arbitrariness of the colonial order. The issue of the capital site and the release of Chaguaramas had begun to assume a critical psychological importance to West Indian leaders. The response of the American and British governments to West Indian decisions about the location of the federal capital would obviously serve as an index, at least in West Indian eyes, of their sensitivity to West Indian national sentiment.

If the Mudie Commission's report reflected British dismissivenes of nationalist sentiment in the West Indies, the American response to the British request for the release of Chaguaramas, on behalf of the SFC, opened the way for a full-blown confrontation between the United States and West Indian leaders. In the process, the imperial government again found itself the object of West Indian opprobrium. A meeting of the three parties was arranged for London on July 16-24, 1957. Prior to the meeting, the Department of State had circulated a memorandum in which it was made clear that the base was of such importance to American global strategy that its release would be a disservice to both the United States and the West Indies. It was a categorical rejection of the West Indian request.[98] The West Indian delegation arrived in London to find that the Colonial Office was reluctant to provide them with advice and information that would be helpful in their preparations for the meeting with American officials. In addition, the American delegation consisted of high-ranking officers from the military whose views did not diverge from the position adopted in the memorandum circulated prior to the meeting. The leader of the American delegation, John Hay Whitney, the ambassador to the United Kingdom, deferred to the military officials in the meeting. It was not obvious that the Americans had arrived prepared to negotiate with the West Indians.

The British foreign secretary opened the meeting, departed, and left the chair to John Profumo, the parliamentary under secretary in the Colonial Office. The latter was not considered impartial in the exercise of his functions by the West Indian delegates. In effect, the meeting proceeded in a manner that offered scant consideration for their concerns. Moreover, West Indian efforts to elicit information about the operations and facilities at Chaguaramas were countered with the invocation of security concerns against the release of information by the American delegation.[99] It was in this context that Eric Williams shed his status as an observer and intervened in the meeting. Basing his comments upon records of the Trinidad government from the negotiations of 1940-41, Williams launched an attack on the American position at the meeting. He described the American attitude as seeking to perpetuate, in 1957, the sin of disregarding Trinidadian views that had occurred in 1940. He called for a renegotiation of the agreement in accordance with Article 28; indicated that the government of Trinidad and Tobago wished to have Chaguaramas evacuated; and suggested that the United Kingdom, the United States, and Trinidad and Tobago should negotiate on an equal footing for the American base to be relocated elsewhere in Trinidad. In his attack on the American position, Williams indicated that in 1940 the governor of Trinidad had raised several issues about the suitability of Chaguaramas for the American base, and the need for a joint commission to select the site for the base. The Governor had been overruled by the imperial government, but Williams was determined that he should not be perceived as less willing in 1957 than the colonial governor in 1941 to defend Trinidad's interests.[100] Williams's stance at the conference shifted the entire negotiations. In abandoning his previous reservations about siting the federal capital in the leased area, Williams effectively redefined the issue as one central to West Indian and Trinidadian nationalism. His shift also raised the issues of moral value of the agreement, and whether it agreement could continue to be justified in light of changed circumstances in the West Indies.

The final communiqué of the meeting revealed the gap that had been opened. Both sides agreed on the need for an American Naval Base in the Eastern Caribbean but the United States continued to insist that Chaguaramas was essential. The West Indian view was that the base at Chaguaramas should be released and an alternative site be located. There was agreement to establish a joint commission whose task was to investigate the feasibility of the releasing Chaguaramas after consideration of the military and economic dimensions of the issue.[101] The divergence between the West Indian leaders on one side, and the American and British governments on the other, was only one consequence of events in 1957. The issue of locating the federal capital in Chaguaramas also created strains among leaders in the West Indies. In both Jamaica and Trinidad, the opposition parties had criticized the decision to request the release of the American base.[102] Some of the critics of the decision were fearful that American assistance to the federation would be jeopardized. Of greater import, the issue had begun to create strains among Manley, Adams, and Williams who had emerged as the troika of regional leaders entrusted with the task of constructing a federation. In reversing the position he had adopted prior to the July 1957 conference, Williams opted for confrontation with both the American and British governments. His confrontational stance and his insistence upon the release of Chaguaramas by the United States perturbed Manley and Adams. They sought to moderate Williams's vigorous espousal of Trinidadian and West Indian claims. Williams, in turn, resented their attitude. It was one example of the clash of generations among West Indian nationalist leaders.[103] This schism among the leaders was further widened by subsequent developments. Inadvertently, American policy had begun to exert centrifugal pressures upon the politics of the British Caribbean even as the federal system was being set in place. If, at the London Conference in 1957, these pressures had not consciously sought to exploit the differences among the West Indian leadership, from 1958 American policy increasingly followed this path. The United States sought to undercut the militant nationalism of Eric Williams over the issue of Chaguaramas. It was a policy to which the British government lent its support and, in the process, helped to undermine the federation which it had labored to bring into existence over the previous decade.

The federal government was officially inaugurated on January 3, 1958, with the swearing-in of Governor-General Lord Hailes. Elections for the federal legislature however did not occur until March 25. In the interim, both Eric Williams and Norman Manley indicated that they would not seek federal Office.[104] After the election resulted in a victory for the West Indian Federal Labour party (WIFLP) with which they were affiliated, Grantley Adams was elected as prime minister of the federal government. Both Williams and Manley preferred to remain in their respective territories to consolidate their authority in territorial politics. Manley's decision not to seek the office of prime minister of the federation was perceived as a serious setback and latent doubts about the durability of the federation began to surface.[105] In any event, the election results in both Trinidad and Jamaica had resulted in an electoral defeat for the ruling parties in each territory--the PNP in Jamaica and the PNM in Trinidad. As a result, the WIFLP government and the prime minister's authority rested upon the parliamentary representatives of the smaller territories. It was a reflection of the fragility of the federal project that the ruling parties in the two major territories, Jamaica and Trinidad, were not in a position of strength in the federal legislature. Further, it created a context in which Prime Minister Adams was independent of Manley and Williams, both by his status as federal prime minister and the source of his support in the legislature. Having lived in the shadow of Norman Manley for most of his political career and having been eclipsed by the rise of Eric Williams, the office of prime minister of the Federation offered Grantley Adams his moment in the sun.[106] The election results confirmed the tenuous nature of the federation. The lack of either unambiguous commitment or electoral support for the federal government from the two major territories resulted in the overwhelming dependence of the federal government upon the smaller territories. The weakness of federation was never more obvious than at the very moment that it was being set in place. It was a fragility that would not be able to withstand the consequences of the confrontation over the federal capital.

The first major test of the stability and durability of the federal government arose out of the publication of the report prepared by the joint commission established by the 1957 conference. Despite indications from Manley that the federation would be prepared to consider the partition of the leased areas on Trinidad's north west peninsula as one way of resolving the dispute, there was little indication that the United States was prepared to move beyond the position adopted in July 1957.[107] In addition, statements by American military and naval officials publicly stressed the importance of the base to American security and global strategy.[108] Even before the joint commission submitted its report, the American government had announced that a missile-tracking station would be established at Chaguaramas.[109] In mid-January 1958, newspapers in the West Indies were carrying stories out of London indicating that the United States was not prepared to surrender Chaguaramas and that Britain was not inclined to support the West Indian demand. It was also reported that the United States would offer an inducement to the West Indies to establish the federal capital elsewhere.[110] The accuracy of these press reports based on British sources was revealed in a message from Secretary of State Dulles to the American consul general in Trinidad. Emphasizing that the United States government would not comment on the press reports, Dulles indicated that the United States had been prepared to offer $2.5 million to the West Indies Federation at the London Conference in July 1957 to help establish its capital. A new offer of $5 million was being considered although the British government, which had been apprised of the previous offer, was not aware of the new proposal.[111] The proposed inducement to the West Indies to select another site for the federal capital was accompanied by an effort to solicit British help in persuading the West Indies to accept the American position. The Department of State instructed the American embassy in London that it should stress to the British government "that it would be an error to argue that U.S. should make concessions on Naval Base issue for purpose of bolstering Federation, since over long run, Federation would lose more from ill-will created in U.S. through insistence on repossession of base area than through changing its preference for capital site."[112]

The inflexibility of the American position was undoubtedly rooted in a calculation that, despite opposition criticism in Britain, the imperial government was not prepared to champion the West Indian position. Opinion in the West Indies was also divided. In Trinidad, the opposition Democratic Labour party had campaigned in the elections for the federal legislature on a platform rejecting the demand for the release of Chaguaramas. The assumption that standing firm would force Williams and the other leaders to retreat may have played a considerable role in shaping American policy. The report of the joint commission was completed in March 1958 but its release was delayed until after the inauguration of the federal government. On April 30, the United States announced that the headquarters of the South Atlantic Force Command was being established at Chaguaramas.[113] This announcement was followed by the release in May of the Joint Commission's Report which reiterated that Chaguaramas could not be released either on military or financial grounds. The simultaneous release of the report by the British and American governments was accompanied by unilateral statements issued by each party. The American statement described the report as comprehensive and obviating the need for further discussion by its conclusion that there was no viable strategic alternative to the Chaguaramas base.[114] The statement by the British government indicated that it was not prepared to ask the American government to move the base, nor would it consider providing financial support for such a move. Both governments obviously sought to force a closure of the Chaguaramas issue.[115]

An earlier warning by the Department of State that a refusal to release Chaguaramas without an offer of negotiations would generate a West Indian backlash proved true.[116] Neither the British government nor the United States seemed to be aware of the consequences that would follow from their stand, nor did it seem that they appreciated the stigma attached to the Bases-for-Destroyers Agreement in the psyche of West Indian nationalists. It was a critical failure of foresight. After consultations, Manley, Adams, and Williams decided to reject the report and advocate a resumption of discussions in London to discuss the next step.[117] However, the desire of Britain and the United States to close the entire affair, combined with plans of the opposition in the federal legislature to bring down the government, derailed the collaboration among these leaders. The opposition tabled a motion in the federal legislature calling for an acceptance of the joint commission's report, and the ruling WIFLP became aware that it would not be able to marshall enough votes in the legislature to defeat the motion.[118] Trapped between a threat to the survival of his government and the firm rejection of the joint commission's report by Manley and Williams, Adams decided to abandon his colleagues.

The American consul in Port-of-Spain, in an obvious attempt to increase pressure on the West Indians to abandon their demands for the release of the base, issued a statement rejecting any further meeting to discuss Chaguaramas. To add insult to injury, he declared that since Britain had not requested the release of Chaguaramas, the issue was closed. Released for maximum effect on the debate in the federal legislature, the consul's statement displayed a singular dismissiveness of West Indian sensibilities.[119] This statement by the American consul was followed by a British-American proposal that the release of Chaguaramas would be subject to review in ten years' time. In the interim, the agreement governing the base would be modified to accommodate mutually acceptable amendments.[120] Adams, forsaking consultation with Williams and Manley, issued a statement accepting the proposal from the British and American governments.[121] His acceptance saved his government from defeat in the federal legislature, and undoubtedly, won him approval in both London and Washington. However, his decision undermined his relationship with Williams and Manley and raised the question of whether the federal government could adequately represent the interests of the major territories.

The outcome of this first round of the Chaguaramas issue reflected American intransigence, British willingness to collaborate with the United States, the fragmented state of West Indian political opinion, and the uncertain grip on power exercised by the federal government. The most durable consequence of this confrontation was the rift it opened among Manley, Adams, and Williams that subsequent developments in the Chaguaramas controversy widened. The immediate consequence of the agreement struck among the British, American, and West Indian governments was Eric Williams's adoption of the Chaguaramas issue as a responsibility of the Trinidad government.[122] Upon assuming this responsibility, Williams began to question the validity and legal status of the agreement under which the base had been leased and operated in Trinidad. The thrust of his campaign was to embarrass the United States and the United Kingdom through the portrayal of their stance as an attempt to maintain the colonial order in the West Indies.[123] Given the alacrity with which his domestic opponents had seized upon the issue, Williams also sought to exploit the Chaguaramas issue to consolidate nationalist sentiment in Trinidad behind the PNM and to target the opposition as traitors.[124] The federal government was similarly labeled and for the rest of its life was accorded quasi-pariah status by Williams and the ruling party in

Trinidad. Williams also exploited the issue to discredit the ability of the federal government and Britain to represent Trinidad's interest in foreign affairs. Williams' strategy was multifaceted and designed to project the Chaguaramas issue as symbolic of the inequities of the colonial order.

Even before the announcement of the agreement reached between Adams and the British and American governments, Williams, in remarks to the Trinidad legislature on the joint commission's report, had reported that the Chaguaramas base was underutilized. Further, based upon his own research on American negotiations for base rights with various countries, Williams pointed out that the leases in these other countries were shorter, most of twenty-year duration. In addition, he argued that these agreements had resulted from negotiations between the host government and the United States. He emphasized Trinidad's desire to have a resumption of the talks in London as a forum to discuss, among other issues, the revision of the agreement requested by Trinidad under the terms of Article 28.[125] Williams returned to the attack within a week of Adams' acceptance of the Anglo-American offer to freeze the Chaguaramas issue for ten years. On June 20, he raised the issue of whether the leases were valid since they had not been registered under Trinidad law. In addition, existing legislation did not allow for the lease of land beyond thirty years, and no provision had been made for special treatment to the United States. In any event, it was not evident that the British government had the authority to impose an agreement with a foreign power upon a colony in violation of the colony's laws. Finally, Williams raised the issue of whether rent was due for the lands leased in light of the fact that existing legislation explicitly forbade rent-free lease of lands belonging to the Crown.[126]

The case that Williams laid out challenged the legal validity of the 1940 agreement. He had also effectively raised the issue of whether the accession to independence by Trinidad, or the federation, would render the agreement invalid. As the United States and the United Kingdom attempted to ignore Williams's demands for a resumption of the London Conference, he launched a wide-ranging assault on the operations of the Chaguaramas base. The rhetoric surrounding the Chaguaramas became increasingly heated as Williams insistently painted the issue as emblematic of the desire of the two powers to perpetuate the colonial order in the Caribbean.[127] During this phase of Williams's campaign, he raised questions about the use of leased territory for the commercial cultivation of citrus in Trinidad, an activity that was in explicit violation of the terms of the agreement. He queried the relationship between activities on the base and the wider society, including allegations of smuggling of duty-free goods from the base for sale in Trinidad. He indicated that the practice of opening membership in the base club on a selective basis to Trinidadians was a violation of existing legislation. Even more damaging, he questioned the nature of ties between the base authorities and the political opposition in Trinidad. The campaign was later expanded to allegations that the construction of radar tracking facilities at Chaguaramas posed radiation risks for the island's population. Williams's campaign was two-pronged: first, the legality of the agreement and the lease arrangements was in question; and, second, the operations of the base itself were of dubious significance for Trinidad. This campaign thrust the Trinidadian leader into direct and sustained confrontation with the United States until early 1960.

As a consequence, the United States was forced to define its policy and relationship to the federation and to articulate a general response to West Indian nationalism. The American response to Williams's strategy of heightened rhetorical confrontation was to adopt a dual strategy; first, find a way to quiet Williams; and, second, try to improve its image in the West Indies and strengthen its relationship with federal leaders (apparently in an effort to isolate Williams).[128] It was obvious that Chaguaramas had become the central issue in American-West Indian relations and the American response revealed the imperiousness with which its policymakers viewed the Caribbean. After Adams's decision to accept the Anglo-American proposal for a freeze of the Chaguaramas issue, the United States continued to ignore Williams's demand for the reconvening of the London Conference. However, Williams's campaign against both the Agreement and the operations of the base, did not provide any respite. The PNM's official organ, *The Nation*, also began to raise allegations of racial discrimination against Trinidadians by the base authorities.[129] The campaign by the PNM had already provoked concerns about American attitudes toward West Indians when an American team of officials visited Trinidad to meet with the federal authorities for discussions on American aid. The visit was proposed as an exploratory one but the lack of announcement of any aid program at the end of the visit led to criticism of the United States in the West Indian press.[130] The West Indian perception of American parsimony had done little to improve the American image in the eyes of West Indians. The provision of $450,000 aid under a technical cooperation agreement in June 1959 did not improve the climate either. American assistance to the West Indies was also to be extended through the Economic Cooperation Administration Agreement of 1948, under which American aid had been extended to Britain during its economic crisis. Again, the low level of American assistance was the object of criticism in the West Indian press. This effort to create a positive image later led to a gift of $2.5 million to the West Indian Federation for lending at low rates of interest to the private sector. The Department of State also intervened to block efforts by the Congress and the Department of Labor to bring an end to the West Indian farm labor program. This intervention was motivated by the desire to improve the American image in the West Indies at a time when the American position was problematic because of the Chaguaramas controversy.[131]

In 1960, the PNP government in Jamaica also requested a continuation of American government purchases of Jamaican bauxite for the stockpile maintained by the General Services Administration. A downturn in other markets for Jamaican bauxite had motivated the Jamaican request. The United

States responded favorably at the urging of the Department of State that stressed the political importance of the issue.[132] Notwithstanding this mixed record in trying to cultivate West Indian public opinion and leadership, West Indian political leaders were not prepared to adopt a public stance that contradicted the campaign led by Williams. Both Manley and Adams--the latter obviously retreating from his position on the Chaguaramas issue--endorsed the legitimacy of Williams' demands to American consular officials.[133]

The campaign to isolate Williams became even more troubling when the British government--in this case the Colonial Office--indicated to the United States that the West Indies was in a strong legal position when arguing that upon accession to independence the existing agreement could be repudiated. This expression of Colonial Office views was followed by advice that the United States should opt to negotiate with the federal government of the West Indies, namely Grantley Adams, in an effort to undermine Williams and strengthen the authority of the federal government. Adams himself was reported to have a preference for concessions to be made to the federal government. It was felt that an outright rejection of the proposal for negotiations should be delivered to Williams directly.[134] The Colonial Office itself was involved in the effort to undercut Williams. In July 1958, when it had become evident that Williams was prepared to reject American efforts to close the Chaguaramas issue, the American consul general in Trinidad had requested the Department of State to ask the Colonial Office to exert pressure on the governor of Trinidad, Sir Edward Beetham. The latter, it was felt, was encouraging Williams' intransigence. According to the consul general, "we do believe that the sooner the U.K. reaches the same opinion of Dr. Williams as held by this office, the better. It would be desirable, to say the least, if they were to recognize that over the long-run the political presence and ambitions of Williams are damaging to U.K. as well as U.S. interests."[135] It is not clear to what extent the American efforts to isolate Williams directly influenced British policy. However, early British support for the American position and subsequent actions certainly reflected a willingness to facilitate American efforts to discredit Williams. In mid-1959, the Colonial Office reportedly attempted to exact concessions from Williams on Chaguaramas in return for approval of constitutional revisions allowing for greater self-government.[136] Williams correctly perceived that he was ranged against both the United States and the United Kingdom, and that the federation was being used as a mechanism to contain his militantly nationalist platform on Chaguaramas.

However, American efforts to quiet Williams were not restricted to seeking to isolate him from the United Kingdom and his colleagues within the federation. It would seem that during 1959 an effort was initiated at the level of the American consulate in Trinidad to provoke a split in the PNM. It appeared to be a strategy designed to secure the installation of a DLP government to replace the PNM. In early 1959 fears about communist infiltration of the PNM began to be raised as a result of the growing importance of C. L. R James within the PNM, and his appointment to the post of secretary of the West Indies Federal Labour Party. James had made no effort to disavow his Trotskyite leanings and the political opposition and press in Trinidad targeted James as a means of discrediting Williams. According to the American Consul General in Trinidad: "James is a particularly vulnerable target... Although the Consulate General has no evidence, there is always the possibility that James is under international communist discipline, and continues to use his Trotskyite identification as a cloak. It is rumored locally that James has access to communist money."[137] Despite the lack of evidence, the consul general saw James as a threatening figure within the PNM. The fact that Williams was close to James, whose party-building activities and views increased his influence, was also a source of concern. James's presence within the PNM meant, for the consul general, that communism was on the loose.[138] The red-baiting began to surface as a means of discrediting Williams and the PNM. James's rise within the PNM was also the subject of discussion with a leading member of the PNM, Kamaluddin Mohammed, who indicated that there was concern within the ranks of the PNM leadership about his influence.[139] Three members of the cabinet, including Mohammed, had become suspect within the PNM, either out of fear that their ethnic origins would lead them to identify with the opposition DLP which had its base in the Indian community, or their unwillingness to pursue the strategy of confrontation with the Americans. The political climate in Trinidad had become increasingly tense as both the PNM and DLP had pursued strategies of ethnic mobilization to consolidate their respective political positions. The ethnic cleavages in the society were further widened as Williams sought to define opposition to his campaign for the release of Chaguaramas as treachery.

It was in this context of ethnic polarization within Trinidad that the conversation occurred among Mohammed and the American consular officials. During the course of this discussion, the issue of the possible collaboration between dissidents within the PNM and the opposition DLP was raised by the American consular officials. Mohammed rejected this option and indicated that the dissidents were developing contingency plans should they be ousted. He further ruled out any possibility that the DLP could win any election because of its lack of effectiveness and the narrowness of its ethnic and political support.[140] This discussion with Mohammed followed upon a conversation among a leading member of the opposition DLP, Simboonath Capildeo, and the same American consular officials. During the course of that meeting, the American officials raised the issue of whether dissident members of the PNM had been consulted about DLP plans to force a new general election by resigning en masse from the legislature. Capildeo responded that no such contacts had occurred, but it was an option to be considered.[141] In a subsequent meeting at the State Department in Washington, Capildeo was asked about the political situation in Trinidad. On the issue of Chaguaramas, Capildeo indicated to his American audience that Williams had successfully transformed the issue into a symbol of the evils of colonialism and oppression. In response to a direct question:

> If Williams were removed from the scene, therefore, would the issue die with him? Capildeo said the issue would not die. If another PNM leader took over the government the issue would definitely be kept alive. . . . The DLP, if it came to power in Trinidad, would know how to handle the issue. He [Capildeo], probably with a government delegation, would come to the U.S. and talk it over with us quietly. He would probably ask us to give up a strip of Chaguaramas and he was sure we would agree. If we didn't agree at first, he was quite certain that he could convince us that we didn't need the whole base.[142]

Capildeo's views demonstrated the fact that whether Williams remained in office or not, the United States was expected to make concessions on Chaguaramas.

The indications that there was little likelihood of Williams' removal from office by electoral means, and that, in any event, his removal would not end demands for American concessions on the Chaguaramas issue, was accompanied by signals that Williams was prepared to be flexible on the American release of Chaguaramas. The chairman of the Petroleum Association of Trinidad, Patrick Hobson, in a meeting with the American consul general, said that Williams was prepared to negotiate with the Americans on their remaining at Chaguaramas within the context of a fixed date for their departure. Beyond conveying Williams's views to the American consul general, Hobson also argued that in his assessment Williams would win the next general election in Trinidad, and that the oil companies were prepared to work with Williams.[143] After more than a year, American policy had not found a way to keep Williams quiet. It was obvious that there was little hope for a resolution without American concessions. In September 1959, the United States expressed its willingness to open negotiations with the United Kingdom on the issue of Chaguaramas, with West Indian representatives being part of the British delegation.[144] Prime Minister Adams refused, demanding independent representation for the federation. In November 1959, the United States agreed to independent West Indian representation and Adams announced his acceptance of tripartite talks the following month.[145] Williams quickly rejected the proposed tripartite discussions emphasizing his demand for separate representation for Trinidad at any conference. In his rejection of the proposed tripartite talks, Williams declared that he had no faith in the ability of the federal government to represent Trinidad's interests. He also indicated that the Chaguaramas Agreement was invalid, and that Trinidad would reject any settlement of the dispute achieved by the tripartite conference. To emphasize Trinidad's objections to the proposed tripartite conference, the Trinidadian government instituted a ban on the use of Trinidad's airport by

American military aircraft. This ban was followed by a PNM-organized demonstration and march on the American consulate in the capital.[146]

To break the deadlock, the secretary of state for the Colonial Office flew to Trinidad where he negotiated a compromise solution under which the main conference would be tripartite, with representatives from the United States, the United Kingdom, and the federal government. However, each territory in which American military facilities were located would negotiate directly with the United States over the leased areas.[147] As a result of this compromise, and in the subsequent negotiations, the United States agreed to release all of the leased areas outside of Chaguaramas (some 21,000 acres) and committed itself to surrendering Chaguaramas by the end of 1977 at the latest. It also agreed to review the agreement at the end of 1967, and again in 1973. However, the United States closed its operations in mid-1967.[148] While the final negotiations could be construed as a major political victory for Williams, it had been achieved at the price of the breakdown of personal relationships among the nationalist leaders over the Chaguaramas issue. The entire affair had raised questions about the extent of the authority of the federal government over one of its constituent units, a sensitive issue in all federal systems. Ultimately, Adams's effort to exercise his authority over the Chaguaramas issue was construed as continued obeisance to the colonial order in the Caribbean, of which the original lease was a product.

While the Chaguaramas issue was a catalyst for the emergence of the federal-unit conflict within the federation, it was not the only one. As the Chaguaramas issue poisoned the atmosphere among West Indian leaders, British policy vacillated between accommodating the United States in its effort to discredit Williams and attempting to support a federal government whose foundations had been weak from the outset. Williams' campaign against the lease further discredited the British government in the West Indies. The crisis over Chaguaramas was followed by the strains caused by Jamaica's desire to limit federal authority over taxation and customs issues. Jamaica sought to acquire an effective veto on federal legislation and British policymakers were unable to intervene to halt this process. In 1960, the British government accepted Manley's position that Jamaica had the right to secede from the federation. It was a decision that arose from the increasing sentiment within Jamaica that federation was an encumbrance on Jamaica's own development.[149]

The inability of Britain to indicate the level of aid it anticipated providing to the federation after independence, did little to fortify West Indian enthusiasm for the federation. The major territories continued to be concerned that federation represented a shift of Britain's burden unto their shoulders. For the smaller territories, British aid was necessary to reduce their dependence upon the major territories and to enhance their ability to set their own agenda within the federation. The larger territories had already demonstrated the ability to attract foreign investment to finance their plans for economic diversification. For the smaller territories, the imperial connection represented the only viable channel for concessionary terms of finance for the diversification of their economies. The conflict over the scope of federal authority and the imperatives of economic diversification also set Trinidad and Jamaica at loggerheads. The Jamaican government's decision to solicit the construction of a petroleum refinery in Jamaica provoked critical comment from the Trinidadian and federal governments.[150] Trinidad's concern was that an oil refinery in Jamaica would compete with Trinidad's petroleum exports. This conflict over the refinery between Jamaica and Trinidad later escalated into a major confrontation over the kind of federal government that should be established and the scope of its authority. Williams sought a federal government vested with considerable power while Jamaica championed a weak center.[151] It was a debate that revealed the deep fissures within the West Indies. The eventual decision of the Jamaican electorate to reject federation in a national referendum resolved the debate and brought the federation to an effective end. The federation had begun on a note of desperation with little commitment or consensus among the participants. It was a climate that had not been improved over the three ensuing years. The controversy over Chaguaramas, and the centrifugal tendencies inherent in the absence of consensus among the West Indian leaders, exacerbated the weakness of the project.

However, notwithstanding the conflict generated by the Chaguaramas issue, and its role in undermining the federation, the relationship between the United States and the West Indian territories did not degenerate into hostility. With the collapse of the Federation, Trinidad and Jamaica decided to honor the Defense agreement signed by the federal government that had replaced the wartime agreement. Both Williams and Manley provided assurances about being part of the West. In addition, C. L. R. James was purged from the PNM as part of the general settlement of the Chaguaramas issue. Again, the American hostility to non-Western ideology had emerged and once more, even a militant nationalist like Eric Williams, bowed to the pressures from the United States.[152] The rigidity of American policy on the ideological limits of West Indian nationalism had become a major factor determining American policy. C. L. R. James represented only the most recent casualty of American fixations on the authenticity of West Indian nationalism, in which non-Western influences would not be tolerated. It was a harbinger of American policy toward British Guiana under the Kennedy administration.

NOTES

1. For a general discussion of the Eisenhower administration see Stephen Ambrose, *Eisenhower: The President* (London: George Allen and Unwin, 1984); for a discussion of Eisenhower courtship of white southerners during his 1952 election

campaign see Robert F. Burk, *The Eisenhower Administration and Black Civil Rights*, (Knoxville: University of Tennessee Press, 1984), 3-20; and for foreign policy issues, see John L. Gaddis, *Strategies of Containment* (New York: Oxford University Press, 1982).

2. For the development of the consensus on colonial policy see D.J. Morgan, *Guidance towards Self-Government in British Colonies, 1941-1971*, vol. 5 of *The Official History of Colonial Development* (London: Macmillan, 1980), 20-22; for the attitudes of the Conservative Party, see David Goldsworthy, *Colonial Issues in British Politics 1945-1961: From "Colonial Development" to "Wind of Change"* (Oxford: Clarendon Press, 1971), 168-74; and, "Keeping Change within Bounds: Aspects of Colonial Policy during the Churchill and Eden Governments, 1951-1957," *Journal of Imperial and Commonwealth History* 18, no.1 (1990), 81-108.

3. See Notes, Dwight D. Eisenhower, Pres., December 10, 1953. *Declassified Documents Quarterly Catalogue* 6, no. 1, 1980, WH 117A.

4. 741D. 00/4-3053. Memorandum, Campbell to Johnstone, April 30, 1953. R.G. 59, State Decimal File, Box 3542.

5. In an analysis of the election results, the American consul general to Trinidad, who was also accredited to British Guiana, demonstrated the bewilderment that the PPP occasioned. According to him, "it may be doubtful whether more than one or two of the central group of PPP leaders (some of whom may, for all practicable purposes, be called Communists) are solidly steeped in traditional doctrine. But they parrot Moscow phrases, they receive Moscow (or Vienna) guidance and funds, they maintain Vienna (and perhaps Moscow) contacts, and they profess support for some stated Communist objectives. Thus, whether ideologically they are Communists or not, some of these PPP leaders act and behave like Communists, and this is a hard political fact to be reckoned with." 741D. 00/5-453. Dispatch, Maddox to DOS, May 4, 1953. R.G. 59, State Decimal File, Box 3542.

6. Thomas Spinner, *A Political and Social History of Guyana 1945-1980* (Boulder, Colo.: Westview Press, 1984), 35-36.

7. 741D. 001/5-553. Dispatch, Hamlin to DOS, May 5, 1953. R.G. 59, State Decimal File, Box 3543.

8. In 1954, the British government admitted that this had been the root of the 1953 crisis. "It is agreed on both sides of the House of Commons that at every stage of constitutional development in the Colonial Territories short of the ultimate grant of self-government some powers must be reserved to Her Majesty's Government and some restrictions placed upon the elected representatives of the people. If the leaders of a colonial territory are not prepared to accept in principle some such limitations the whole basis for progress along the lines of this policy is lacking." The report continued: "It is, therefore, our conclusion that Her Majesty's Government's Colonial Policy failed in British Guiana not because of any defects in the Waddington Constitution but because the party which received the support of the majority of the electorate was unwilling to accept and work anything short of full self-government." *Report of the British Guiana Constitutional Commission 1954*, Cmd. 9274 (London: HMSO, 1954).

9. See chapter 4.

10. Spinner, *Guyana*, 17-31.

11. Ibid., 38; and 741D. 00/7-1653. Dispatch, Maddox to DOS, July 16, 1953. R.G. 59, State Decimal File, Box 3542.

12. Spinner, *Guyana*, 9.

13. 741D. 00/8-2053. Dispatch, Maddox to DOS, August 20, 1953. R.G. 59, State Decimal File, Box 3542.

14. 741D. 00/7-1653. Dispatch, Maddox to DOS, July 16, 1953. R.G. 59, State Decimal File, Box 3542.

15. 741D. 00/7-3153. Dispatch, Maddox to DOS, July 31, 1953. R.G. 59, State Decimal File, Box 3542.

16. 741D. 00/8-2053. Dispatch, Maddox to DOS, August 20, 1953. R.G. 59, State Decimal File, Box 3542.

17. Ibid.

18. 741D. 00/9-1753. Dispatch, Maddox to DOS, September 7, 1953. R.G. 59, State Decimal File, Box 3542.

19. Spinner, *Guyana*, pp. 39-46; and 741D. 00/9-1053. Dispatch, Maddox to DOS, September 10, 1953. R.G. 59, State Decimal File, Box 3542.

20. 741D. 00/9-1153. Telegram, Maddox to Secretary of State, September 11, 1953. R.G. 59, State Decimal File, Box 3542.

21. 741D. 00/10-153. Telegram, Maddox to DOS, October 1, 1953. R.G. 59, State Decimal File, Box 3542.

22. 741D. 00/10-553. Telegram, Aldrich to Secretary of State, October 5, 1953; and 741D. 00/10-653. Telegram, Aldrich to Secretary of State, October 6, 1953. R.G. 59, State Decimal File, Box 3542.

23. 741D. 00/10-653. Telegram, Dulles to All American Diplomatic Posts in the other American Republics, October 6, 1953. R.G. 59, State Decimal File, Box 3542.

24. 741D. 00/10-653. Telegram, Aldrich to Secretary of State, October 6, 1953. R.G. 59, State Decimal File, Box 3542.

25. 741D. 00/10-1653. Telegram, Dulles to American Embassy, Rio de Janeiro, October 20, 1953. R.G. 59, State Decimal File, Box 3543.

26. Memorandum, October 8, 1953, "Discussion at the 165th Meeting of the National Security Council, October 7, 1953," Dwight D. Eisenhower, Papers as President of the United States 1953-61 (Ann Whitman File) NSC Series Box 4.

27. 741D. 00/10-1653. Telegram, Dulles to American Embassy, Rio de Janeiro, October 20, 1953. R.G. 59, State Decimal File, Box 3543.

28. 511.41M/5-1253. Dispatch, Maddox to DOS, May 12, 1953. R.G. 59, State Decimal File, Box 2357; Serafino Romualdi had also prepared an article for publication which argued that the GIWU effort to displace the MPCA was a "Communist takeover," see 741D. 00/10-2753, Memorandum, Horowitz to Christensen, October 27, 1953. R.G. 59, State Decimal File, Box 3543.

29. 741D. 00/10-753. Telegram, Aldrich to Secretary of State, October 7, 1953. R.G. 59, State Decimal File, Box 3542.

30. 741D. 00/10-2653. Dispatch, Tibbetts to DOS, October 26, 1953. R.G. 59, State Decimal File, Box 3543.

31. Ibid., cited from *The Spectator*, October 23, 1953.

32. Ibid.

33. Ibid. Statements by Manley and Adams, critical of the PPP, were used by the colonial secretary in the Parliamentary debate over the suspension of the constitution in British Guiana.

34. 741C. 00/7-3053. Dispatch, Mazzeo to DOS, July 30, 1953. R.G. 59, State Decimal File, Box 3542. Consideration had also been given to suspending the elections scheduled for 1954 because of the militant anti-British position of the People's United Party and its perceived similarities to the PPP. See D.J. Morgan, *Guidance towards Self-Government*, pp. 86-87.

35. 741C.00/9-1153. Dispatch, Mazzeo to DOS, September 11, 1953; 741C. 00/10-553. Dispatch, Mazzeo to DOS, October 5, 1953. R.G. 59, State Decimal File, Box 3542. The PUP's pro-American stance was displayed by carrying the American flag and singing "God Bless America" during National Day celebrations in 1953. The official ceremonies sponsored by the colonial administration were boycotted by the PUP.

36. 741C. 00/9-1153. Dispatch, Mazzeo to DOS, September 11, 1953; 741C. 00/3-2454. Dispatch, Mazzeo to DOS, March 24, 1954. R.G. 59, State Decimal File, Box 3542.

37. 741C. 00/5-654. Dispatch, Bywater to DOS, May 6, 1954; 741C. 00/6-354. Dispatch, Bywater to DOS, June 3, 1954. R.G. 59, State Decimal File, Box 3542.

38. 741D. 00/10-2653. Dispatch, Maddox to DOS, October 26, 1953. R.G. 59, State Decimal File, Box 3543.

39. 841M. 06/7-3054. Dispatch, Maddox to DOS, July 30, 1954. R.G. 59, State Decimal File, Box 4819.

40. Editorial, *Barbados Advocate*, March 23, 1954.

41. IR4924 "Progress towards a British West Indian Federation," Office of Intelligence Research, State Department, March 20, 1953.

42. Memorandum, McIlvaine to Dulles, April 7, 1954. DDE 1953-61, WH Central Files, Confidential Files, Subject Series, Box 13.

43. In November 1953, the PUP leadership met with the minister of state for the colonies and the governor. During that meeting, the PUP leaders indicated that their country should not remain within the commonwealth as it had "suffered greatly through the connection to Britain." See 741c. 00/11-953. Dispatch, Mazzeo to DOS, November 9, 1953. R.G. 59, State Decimal Files, Box 3542.

44. In late 1953, Trinidad enacted legislation banning 147 categories of immigrants. Editorial *Barbados Advocate* November 25, 1953.

45. 741E. 00/5-1454. Dispatch, Maddox to DOS, May 14, 1954. R.G. 59, State Decimal File, Box 3544.

46. Elizabeth Wallace, *The British Caribbean* (Toronto: University of Toronto Press, 1977), 110.

47. Editorial, *Daily Gleaner*, April 16, 1953, and D. J. Morgan, *Changes in British Aid Policy*, vol. 4 of *The Official History of Colonial Development* (London: Macmillan, 1980), 42.

48. Ibid., 37

49. Ibid.

50. Morgan, *Changes in British Aid Policy*, 36-40.

51. 841H. 00/1-2155. Dispatch, Hamlin to DOS, January 21, 1955; and 841H. 00/4-755, Dispatch, Lee to DOS, April 7, 1955. R.G. 59, State Decimal File, Box 4453.

52. Rex Nettleford, "Manley and the Politics of Jamaica," *Social and Economic Studies*. 20, no. 3 (1971), 52-63.

53. Morgan, *Changes in British Aid Policy*, 39-40; and John Mordecai, *The West Indies: Federal Negotiations* (London: Allen & Unwin, 1968), 53-60.

54. 841H. 00/6-1055. Dispatch, Maynard to DOS, June 10, 1955. R.G. 59, State Decimal File, Box 4453.

55. 741H. 00/6-1755. Dispatch, Maynard to DOS, June 17, 1955. R.G. 59, State Decimal File, Box 3206.

56. 841G. 00/4-1056. Dispatch, Noziglia to DOS, April 10, 1956. R.G. 59, State Decimal File, Box 4452.

57. 841H. 00/4-1555. Dispatch, Lee to DOS, April 15, 1955. R.G. 59, State Decimal File, Box 4453.

58. Wallace, *The British Caribbean*, 110-14.

59. The increase in revenues accruing to the Jamaican government as a result of these revisions were estimated to be nearly twentyfold. In 1957, revenue was estimated to amount to £352,000; by 1961 it was expected to bring in £7,000,000. 841H. 00/4-1057. Dispatch, Maynard to DOS, April 10, 1957. R.G. 59, State Decimal File, Box 4453. See also Wallace, *The British Caribbean*, 130.

60. 841H. 00/3-1155. Dispatch, Hamlin to DOS, March 4, 1955. R.G. 59, State Decimal File, Box 4453.

61. 841H. 10/4-1356. Dispatch, Maynard to DOS, April 13, 1956. R.G. 59, State Decimal File, Box 4455.

62. 841H. 00/1-2155. Dispatch, Hamlin to DOS, January 21, 1955. R.G. 59, State Decimal File, Box 4453.

63. 841H. 10/8-657. Dispatch, Ringwalt to DOS, August 6, 1957. R.G. 59, State Decimal File, Box 4454; and Mordecai, *The West Indies*, 55-56.

64. Wallace, *The British Caribbean*, 142-45.

65. Ibid., 136.

66. 741G. 00/9-2853. Dispatch, Jester to DOS, September 28, 1953. R.G. 59, State Decimal File, Box 3544.

67. For Williams's relationship with the Caribbean Commission, see Eric Williams, "My Relations with the Caribbean Commission 1943-1955" in Paul Sutton (ed.), *Forged from the Love of Liberty* (Trinidad: Longman, 1981), 269-80.

68. 741H. 00/1-656. Dispatch, Maynard to DOS, January 6, 1956. R.G. 59, State Decimal File, Box 3207.

69. Selwyn Ryan, *Race and Nationalism in Trinidad and Tobago* (Toronto: University of Toronto Press, 1972), 184.

70. 741H. 00/12-1655. Dispatch, Lee to DOS, December 16, 1955. R.G. 59, State Decimal File, Box 3206.

71. 841M. 00/10-2456. Dispatch, Jenkins to DOS, October 24, 1956. R.G. 59, State Decimal File, Box 4457.

72. Ibid.

73. For the evolution of British thinking about the West Indies and other colonies which were being considered for independence, see in its entirety Morgan, *Guidance towards Self-Government.*

74. Ibid., 88-91. Harold Macmillan, the chancellor of the Exchequer, admitted that the U.K. government was unable to stop the purchase of a British oil company in Trinidad by Texaco. However, as early as May 1955, the Colonial Office had advised Colonial governments to seek external sources for development finance for the colonies. 841H. 00/5-2055. Dispatch, Maynard to DOS, May 20, 1955. R.G. 59, State Decimal File, Box 4453.

75. Ibid., 100-101.

76. 741H. 00/9-2557. Despatch, Ringwalt to DOS, September 25, 1957. R.G. 59, State Decimal File, Box 3207.

77. 741B. 00/2-2156. Despatch, Jenkins to DOS, February 21, 1956. R.G. 59, State Decimal File, Box 3202.

78. 741B. 00/2-2956. Dispatch, Rutter to DOS, February 29, 1956. R.G. 59, State Decimal File, Box 3202.

79. 741E. 111/7-257. Dispatch, Knox to DOS, July 2, 1957. R.G. 59, State Decimal File, Box 3206.

80. D. J. Morgan, *A Reassessment of British Aid Policy, 1951-1965*, vol. 3 of *The Official History of Colonial Development*, 128-40.

81. 741E. 022/5-2555. Memorandum, Holland to Murphy, May 25, 1955. R.G. 59, State Decimal File, Box 3206.

82. 841D. 06/5-2755. Telegram, Dulles to American Consulate, Port-of-Spain, May 27, 1955. R.G. 59, State Decimal File, Box 4451.

83. 741C. 5MSP/3-3158. Dispatch, Oakley to DOS, March 31, 1958. R.G. 59, State Decimal File, Box 3204.

84. 741C. 00/10-2858. Dispatch, Oakley to DOS, October 28, 1958. R.G. 59, State Decimal file, Box 3204.

85. 741C. 00/10-2858. Telegram, Dulles to American Consul, Belize, November 25, 1958. R.G. 59, State Decimal File, Box 3204.

86. Wallace, *The British Caribbean*, 121.

87. Mordecai, *The West Indies*, pp. 51-74.

88. Ibid., 67-71.

89. 741B. 00/1-956. Dispatch, Jenkins to DOS, January 9, 1956. R.G. 59, State Decimal File, Box 3202.

90. Ibid.

91. Ibid.

92. Mordecai, *The West Indies*, 67; Wallace, The British Caribbean, 116-17; and *Report of the British Caribbean Federal Capital Commission*, Colonial no. 328 (London: HMSO, 1956).

93. Mordecai, *The West Indies*, 70-71.

94. 741E. 022/5-2256. Memorandum, Murphy to Gray, May 22, 1956. R.G. 59, State Decimal File, Box 3206.

95. *Report of the British Caribbean Federal Capital Commission*.

96. Mordecai, *The West Indies*, 109-10; Wallace, The British Caribbean, 116-18; and C.A.P. St. Hill, *The Chaguaramas Question*, (M.Sc. thesis, U.W.I., Mona, Jamaica, 1967), 131-32.

97. Ibid., Mordecai.

98. Mordecai, *The West Indies*, 114.

99. Ibid.

100. Ibid., 100; and St. Hill, *The Chaguaramas Question*, 138-39.

101. North Burn, *United Stated Base Rights in the British West Indies, 1940-1962* (Ph.D. diss., Tufts University, 1964) 105; Mordecai, *The West Indies*, 115; and, St. Hill, *The Chaguaramas Question*, 138-44.

102. St. Hill, *The Chaguaramas Question*, 144; and 741B. 00/8-1557. Dispatch, Ringwalt to DOS, August 15, 1957. R.G. 59, State Decimal File, Box 3202.

103. Mordecai, *The West Indies*, p. 115.

104. Ryan, *Race and Nationalism*, 188; and Wallace, *The British Caribbean*, 144. In late 1957, W. Adolphe Roberts, a Jamaican historian and commentator, told the American consulate that Manley's relucance to join the federal government was shaped by the perception that a power struggle within the PNP would be unleashed. It was feared that Wills Isaacs, the leader of the anti-Federation rump of the party would win that struggle. Roberts also indicated that there was little faith in Jamaican political circles about the success of the federation, and that Jamaican secession from the federation was a distinct possibility. See 741B. 00/11-2557. Dispatch, Duke to DOS, November 25, 1957. R.G. 59, State Decimal File, Box 3202.

105. Wallace, *The British Caribbean*, 144-45.

106. For an account of Adams's sensitivities and eventually his paranoia about Williams and Manley plotting his removal, see Mordecai, *The West Indies*, 124-54, 236-44.

107. 741B. 00/7-3157. Dispatch, Ringwalt to DOS, July 31, 1957. R.G. 59, State Decimal File, Box 3202.

108. Ibid., and St. Hill, *The Chaguaramas Question*, 144.

109. St. Hill, *The Chaguaramas Question*, 144-45; Burn, *U.S. Base Rights*, 70-73. The Americans provided assurances that the construction of the tracking station would not prejudice the findings of the Joint Commission. However, the American Consul General in Jamaica indicated that the American military "had no intention whatever to surrender any part of the base." 741H. 111/10-2457. Dispatch, Ringwalt to DOS, October 24, 1957. R.G. 59, State Decimal File, Box 3207.

110. 741B. 00/1-1558. Despatch, Ringwalt to DOS, January 15, 1958, R.G. 59, State Decimal File, Box 3203; and 741B. 02/1-1558, Despatch, Orebaugh to DOS, January 15, 1958. R.G. 59, State Decimal File, Box 3204.

111. 741B. 00/1-1558. Telegram, Dulles to American Consul, Port-of-Spain, January 17, 1958. R.G. 59, State Decimal File, Box 3204.

112. 741J. 00/2-758. Telegram, Heiter to American Embassy, London, January 27, 1958. R.G. 59, State Decimal File, Box 3207.

113. 841J. 00/5-158. Dispatch, Orebaugh to DOS, May 1, 1958. R.G. 59, State Decimal File, Box 4455.

114. Burn, *U.S. Base Rights*, 106-08; St. Hill, *The Chaguaramas Question*, 151-52.

115. Ibid., Burn and St. Hill.

116. 741B. 00/8-2357. Memorandum, Parsons to Jones, August 23, 1957. R.G. 59, State Decimal File, Box 3202.

117. Mordecai, *The West Indies*, 115-19; St. Hill, *The Chaguaramas Question*, 156-162; Burn, *U.S. Base Rights*, 108-10.

118. 741J. 00/6-2058. Dispatch, Orebaugh to DOS, June 20, 1958. R.G. 59, State Decimal File, Box 3207; Mordecai, *The West Indies*, 119-23.

119. St. Hill, *The Chaguaramas Question*, 162-64; and Mordecai, *The West Indies*, 120-124.

120. Ibid., St. Hill and Mordecai.

121. Ibid., and Burn, *U.S. Base Rights*, 110-11.

122. St. Hill, *The Chaguaramas Issue*, 164-67.

123. Ibid., 169-72; Wallace, *The British Caribbean*, 118; and Ryan, *Race and Nationalism*, 209-15.

124. Ryan, *Race and Nationalism*, 186-87.

125. St. Hill, *The Chaguaramas Question*, 157-62.

126. Ibid., 169-72.

127. Ibid., 175-16; Ryan, *Race and Nationalism*, 209-19.

128. Burn, *U.S. Base Rights*, 121.

129. Ibid., 113.

130. Ibid., 123.

131. Ibid., 123-26.

132. Ibid., 126.

133. 741J. 00/3-2059. Memorandum of Conversation, Participants: Norman Manley and Robert G. McGregor, US consul general, March 20, 1959. R.G. 59, State Decimal File, Box 3207; and 741J. 13/5-1359. Dispatch, McGregor to DOS, May 13, 1959. R.G. 59, State Decimal File, Box 3208.

134. 741J. 13/4-3059. Telegram, Barbour to Secretary of State, April 30, 1959. R.G. 59, State Decimal File, Box 3208.

135. 741J. 03/7-358. Dispatch, Orebaugh to DOS, July 3, 1958. R.G. 59, State Decimal File, Box 3208.

136. Ryan, *Race and Nationalism*, 203.

137. 741J. 00/2-359. Dispatch, Orebaugh to DOS, February 3, 1959. R.G. 59, State Decimal File, Box 3207.

138. Ibid.

139. 741J. 13/8-759. Memorandum of Conversation, Participants: Mr. Kamaluddin Mohammed, Edwin G. Moline, and Philip C. Habib, July 29, 1959. R.G. 59, State Decimal File, Box 3208.

140. Ibid.

141. 741J. 00/7-3159. Memorandum of Conversation, Participants: Simboonath Capildeo, Edwin G. Moline, and Philip C. Habib, July 25, 1959. R.G. 59, State Decimal File, Box 3207.

142. 741J. 00/8-2859. Memorandum of Conversation, Participants: Simboonath Capildeo, Milton C. Rewinkel, James W. Swihart, and North Burn, August 28, 1959. R.G. 59, State Decimal File, Box 3207.

143. 741J. 2/8-559. Dispatch, Moline to DOS, August 5, 1959. R.G. 59, State Decimal File, Box 3207.

144. Burn, *U.S. Base Rights*, 136.

145. Ibid.

146. St. Hill, *The Chaguaramas Question*, 229-30.

147. Burn, *U.S. Base Rights*, 137-138; St. Hill, *The Chaguaramas Question*, 230-31; Mordecai, *The West Indies*, 237-38.

148. St. Hill, *The Chaguaramas Question*, 232-43; Burn, *U.S. Base Rights*, 135-58.

149. Wallace, *The British Caribbean*, 164.

150. Mordecai, *The West Indies*, 123-27.

151. Ryan, *Race and Nationalism*, 229-32.

152. Ibid.

6

American Policy Towards British Guiana, 1957-64: Setting the Limits on West Indian Nationalism

The decision of the British government to suspend the constitution of British Guiana in 1953 had effectively slowed the process of imperial disengagement from the colony. However, the removal of the PPP did not resolve the problem of its continued popularity and legitimacy as a nationalist movement within the colony. The suspension of the constitution and the accompanying military intervention had been followed by the detention, jailing, and other confinement of the PPP leadership.[1] An interim government of trusted influentials from the colony, of whom only one had demonstrated the capacity to win electoral support, was installed.[2] A hastily concocted development plan, with support from the United States was set in place in an effort to demonstrate British commitment to British Guiana's development. These efforts to undermine the popularity of the PPP were followed by the appointment of a royal commission to investigate events in the colony in 1953. This commission, chaired by Sir James Robertson, released its report in September 1954. The report identified two factions within the PPP, one Communist, the other Socialist. Fortuitously, Cheddi and Janet Jagan were described as the leaders of the Communist faction, while Forbes Burnham was depicted as the leader of the moderate socialists within the party. Whether by design or not, the Robertson Commission's report, in seeking to isolate the Jagans and their supporters within the PPP, opened the way for the nationalist movement to fragment into racial blocs. By identifying the two most important leaders of the PPP, Cheddi Jagan an Indo-Guianese, and Forbes Burnham an Afro-Guianese, as following ideologically divergent paths, the report exacerbated tensions in the multiracial alliance that had emerged under the PPP.[3]

The Robertson Commission's report was a watershed in the evolution of British Guiana's politics. Confronted by a nationalist movement, the militancy and ideological orientation of which was unprecedented in the British Caribbean, British policy was directed at reversing the process of imperial disengagement as a strategy for undermining the support for the PPP in the colony. When the PPP had emerged as a highly organized, multiracial alliance in the 1953 elections, the colonial government had felt threatened. The Robertson Commission's report endeavored to split the nationalist movement, on both ideological and racial grounds. This attempt by the authorities to promote divisions within the nationalist movement proved successful. After the release of the report, Forbes Burnham and his supporters led an effort to seize control of the party. With the tacit support of the colony's government which maintained restrictions upon the movement of key supporters of Jagan, Burnham attempted to convene a meeting of the party's leadership in early 1955.[4] He was rebuffed and the party split into two factions, both claiming to be the real PPP. This split in the leadership was the opening act in a tragedy that led to racial and ideological fragmentation, and eventually violence. The rift shattered the political consensus and cooperation that had been established before 1953.

However, the effort to undermine the PPP was not restricted solely to dividing the nationalist movement. In early 1955, the British Trades Union Congress provided a grant of £3,000 to the Man Power Citizens Association in British Guiana and designated the union as the instrument for the development of responsible trade unionism in the colony.[5] It was an obvious counter to the PPP's efforts to strengthen its hold in the sugar industry. This grant by the British TUC represented a further step in the effort to build an anti-PPP trade union center in British Guiana which could prevent the PPP from dominating the labor unions. It was also the beginning of a process of collaboration among American and Guyanese trade unions, with support from the British TUC, to build an anti-Jagan coalition within the colony.[6] The efforts to discredit and undermine the PPP reached another plane when prominent West Indian nationalist leaders, including Adams, Gomes, and Manley, visited British Guiana in mid-1955 and publicly castigated the PPP.[7] The fact that these nationalist leaders lent themselves to such a campaign was testimony to the power of anti-Communist sentiment within West Indian nationalist circles. It also reflected the growing divergences among the nationalist leadership in the Caribbean that made collaboration so difficult in subsequent years.

Despite these efforts to undermine the PPP, it had become evident by late 1955 that the interim government installed by the British had little credibility.[8] A replacement for Governor Alfred Savage, who had overseen the suspension of the constitution in 1953, had already been announced. Sir Patrick Renison who had successfully pursued a strategy of co-opting the People's United Party (PUP) in British Honduras was named as Savage's successor. Governor Savage had resigned on grounds of ill-health, though his ineffectiveness during his tenure may have contributed to the timing of his departure.[9] The American consulate reported that Renison's arrival in British Guiana implied that he had been mandated to develop a new policy toward the colony.[10] From the perspective of the American and British governments, the central problem remained the continuing legitimacy of the PPP in British Guiana which was reflected in the widespread view that elections would result in its return to office. The ineffectiveness of the interim government was worsened by the continued insensitivity of the Colonial Office to opinion in British Guiana. On a visit to British Guiana in late 1955, Norman Mayle, head of the West Indies Division of the Colonial Office, announced that the 1956-60 Development plan for the colony had not yet been approved by the Imperial government. This announcement opened the way for further criticism of the Colonial Office and for that institution to be reminded that the colony's problems predated the 1953 crisis.[11] The removal of the PPP had created a vacuum that neither the Interim government nor the Colonial Office could effectively fill. The PPP was able to maintain its legitimacy while the Colonial Office's policies continued to inspire criticism in the colony.

The new governor sought to reverse this situation. His early efforts were directed at building an anti-Jagan coalition that would displace the PPP in any future elections. Toward this end, he encouraged efforts to build an alternative Indo-Guianese leadership around Lionel Luckhoo, an Anglophile lawyer whose family had converted to Christianity.[12] This was followed by the removal of restrictions on members of the Burnham faction of the PPP leadership, while those on the Jagans and their supporters in the PPP leadership were maintained.[13] This policy was directed at widening the schism within the nationalist movement and further weakening the Jagans. The governor also sought to encourage Burnham to become part of the anti-PPP coalition, but for tactical reasons Burnham rejected a role in this grouping.[14] Renison also hoped that Burnham's contacts with Norman Manley and Grantley Adams would be helpful to the strategy of isolating the Jagans and their supporters.[15] As part of this strategy, the governor announced that new elections would be held under a new constitution. The key provisions of the new constitution vested considerable authority in the office of the governor by authorizing him to nominate majorities in the two chambers of the legislature and through the subordination of the elected ministers to his authority in the executive.[16] The new constitution represented an insurance policy for the colonial authorities.

The decision to return to electoral politics, and the effort to create an anti-Jagan coalition, set in train a dual process of political fragmentation and realignment in British Guiana's political system. The Jagan-led faction of the PPP was affected by these developments. In late 1956, three leading members of the Jagan faction resigned as a result of ideological differences with Jagan.[17] The de-Stalinization campaign in the Soviet Union, the Hungarian uprising, as well as Jagan's inability to tolerate challenges to his role as the

PPP's theoretician were all contributory factors to the departure of Sydney King, Rory Westmaas, and Martin Carter. These were the most prominent non-Indian members of the PPP, and the rupture within the party was evidence of the diminishing ability of the PPP to maintain its cohesion as a multiethnic movement. This fragmentation of the PPP's leadership was paralleled by the failure of the Governor Renison's strategy aimed at creating a viable anti-Jagan front. Race, class, and ideological differences all contributed to this dissension among the anti-Jagan forces. The parties that drew their support from the middle classes, the United Democratic Party (UDP), a lineal descendant of the League of Coloured People, and the National Labour Front (NLF) which drew support from the Portuguese and Christianized Indian middle class, found themselves unable to stand on common ground. Discussions about a merger of the UDP and Burnham's faction of the PPP failed to reach fruition prior to the 1957 elections. Burnham's political base lay largely in the Afro-Guianese working-class population of the capital, Georgetown, and he courted the support of Sydney King who ran on an independent platform designed to entice rural Afro-Guianese support away from the Jagan forces.[18] Both the Jagan and Burnham factions of the PPP campaigned using the PPP label, and a major issue in the campaign was the possibility of the reunification of the party.

Upon his return from the independence celebrations of Ghana, Jagan had publicly proposed reunification of the party. Burnham rejected this call from Jagan and the platform of his faction was overtly anti-Communist.[19] Burnham and Jagan had attended the Ghana independence celebrations at the invitation of the Nkrumah government. Though Jagan had apparently sought to effect a reconciliation with Burnham, the other West Indian leaders who had been invited--Norman Manley, Grantley Adams, and Patrick Solomon of the PNM in Trinidad--apparently advised Burnham that he would enjoy their support if he came out on an anti-Communist platform. Significantly, these leaders organized a meeting with Burnham but apparently never arranged to do likewise with Jagan.[20] They were apparently hopeful that a Burnham victory would bring British Guiana into the projected federation and thus treated Jagan with scant regard.

The 1957 election campaign mirrored the process of racial and political fragmentation that had beset the colony in the wake of the publication of the Robertson Commission's report in 1954. It also reflected the collapse of the PPP as a multiethnic alliance and the increasing importance of anti-Communist politics among the opposition forces. Effectively, events since 1953 had transformed the political context and climate in the colony in ways which boded ill for the future. Faced with this reversal of their fortunes, the Jagans had begun to shift ground. As early as mid-1956 Janet Jagan had publicly admitted that the PPP had made mistakes in 1953.[21] Earlier, the Jagan faction of the PPP had attended a meeting of all the political groups in British Guiana and had proposed the establishment of a coalition government that could negotiate for further constitutional devolution from the British.[22] While the colonial authorities sought to portray the Jagans as Communist, the Jagans emphasized the nationalist dimension of their political platform in negotiating with other Guyanese political forces and the colonial authorities. The Jagans stressed the ideological diversity of the party, admitting that Communists were members of the party. This willingness to tolerate ideological diversity within the party coexisted with an intolerance of any challenge to the leadership role of the Jagans. It was this unwillingness of the Jagans to tolerate challengers that precipitated the exodus of leading members from the PPP after 1953.

In spite of Renison's support for the anti-Jagan forces and the demarcation of election boundaries that increased the disadvantages under which the PPP were working, the Jagan faction remained the best-organized political grouping in British Guiana.[23] The factionalism of the anti-Jagan forces, and Burnham's unwillingness, or inability, to make common cause with the other anti-Jagan elements were major reasons for the failure of the governor's strategy. The American Consulate in British Guiana, reestablished in 1957, predicted that the Jagan faction was likely to win the elections.[24] Even the governor himself was sanguine about a Jagan victory and was prepared to work with Jagan after the elections. Renison, during a visit to Washington, informed his audience at the Department of State that the Jagans were politically astute, while the anti-Jagan forces needed further guidance to become effective. In his view, Jagan would either be tamed or hung by the responsibility of elected office. He went on to discount the legitimacy of communism in British Guiana.[25]

Communists or not, the Jagans enjoyed significant legitimacy in the eyes of the Guyanese population and the colonial authorities had reconciled themselves to fashioning a working relationship with these leaders. The election results confirmed the accuracy of the views of the American consul and the governor. Of the fourteen seats at stake, the Jagan PPP won nine with 47 percent of the vote. The PPP's victory was based on the overwhelming support of the rural, largely Indo-Guyanese vote. Sydney King, running as an independent in the rural constituency he won in 1953, lost to the PPP candidate. The Burnham faction won only three seats, all in the capital, two of which were close victories against the NLF. The latter had won only one seat in the hinterland areas where the Amerindian populations were in the majority, and the Anglican and Catholic churches were major influences. The UDP won a single seat in the urban center of New Amsterdam.[26] The results of the election were an endorsement of the Jagans' leadership and provided them with a secure advantage over their opponents. The distribution of seats and votes won by the opposition parties testified to the fragmentation of the anti-Jagan forces. The election also signaled that the Jagan-faction of the PPP could be expected to win any future elections with a plurality of the vote under the existing electoral system. It did not need an absolute majority to win an election under the first-past-the-post system and the anti-Jagan forces would later make that a major plank of their campaign to force the PPP from office.

The 1957 election also attested to the growing racial polarization in the colony which had become an inevitable consequence of the splintering of the nationalist movement.

Buoyed by the election results, the Jagans entered into negotiations with the governor about the formation of a new government. Despite the considerable authority vested in the governor under the constitution, Jagan's approach was to accept office with constrained powers and to seek further constitutional devolution.[27] Unlike 1953, the PPP leadership was prepared to work for change within the existing constitutional dispensation. It also decided to accept the tutelage of colonial officialdom in the process of constitutional devolution. Whatever the ideological preferences of the PPP leadership, they had embarked upon an effort to persuade the imperial government that the PPP would pursue a moderate path in the search for independence. Public opinion within the colony itself was favorable to the results of the election. The business community, which had anticipated the victory of the Jagan faction, was willing to give Jagan a second chance in light of his political moderation.[28] Given the disenchantment with the interim government and Colonial Office policy, and the fragmentation of the anti-Jagan forces, the PPP had emerged as an attractive, if not the sole, alternative.

But if the PPP had shifted ground and had moved toward establishing a working relationship with the colonial authorities, the United States remained perturbed by the evidence of the PPP's legitimacy. The State Department was bewildered by the fact that the United States had spent $1 million in technical assistance to British Guiana over the three preceding years, and that this expenditure had not served to counteract Communist influence. The British ambassador to Washington was informed about the deep American concern over the PPP's victory, since it was perceived as a precursor of Communist penetration of other countries in the hemisphere.[29] This reaction reflected the ideologically driven perceptions of American policymakers. It highlighted the uninformed appreciation of the nuances of politics in British Guiana that continued to characterize American policy. However, there was little alternative to the policies adopted by Britain. Since the elections had been organized by the latter, there was no viable basis for rejecting the outcome.

From the moment of its election victory, the PPP began to strike a moderate pose that sought to reassure its various critics. With the help of a liberal member of the management of the Booker Group of Companies, Jagan began the search for American and other economic consultants to do a study of British Guiana's problems and prospects.[30] The effort to secure economic advisers followed upon Jagan's attempt to persuade the American consul in the colony to continue the U.S. technical assistance program. He also stressed the importance the PPP accorded to attracting foreign investment to promote the colony's economic development, and its willingness to provide guarantees for investors.[31] Notwithstanding Jagan's efforts to reassure the United States of his moderation and his sensitivity to the concerns of potential foreign investors, the Department of State refused to abandon its hostility to the Jagans and the PPP. By December 1957, American policy toward British Guiana reflected continuing resistance to any accommodation with the PPP. A decision had been taken to establish an office of the United States Information Service in the colony and to undertake a serious effort to identify possible alternative leadership to the Jagans.[32] It was also decided that the United States would not support the idea of an American consultant doing a study of British Guiana's problems, as it did not wish to find itself in the embarrassing position of having to veto the recommendations of the adviser.[33]

Nonetheless, the PPP and the Jagans continued on their path of moderation. By mid-1958, British Guiana's chief secretary confided to the American consul that Jagan had developed a more reasoned approach to governing the colony and had established a rapport with officials of the colonial government.[34] The PPP had also begun to express an interest in following Puerto Rico's strategy of attracting foreign investment to finance industrial development. The inability of the United Kingdom to provide adequate levels of capital flows to the colonies had already begun to affect British Guiana's ability to finance its development program. In May 1958, a consultant of the International Labor Organization presented a report to the British Guiana government in which unemployment was tabulated at 18 percent of the labor force.[35] These developments followed upon the publication in February 1958 of the views of the American senator, George Aiken, who had criticized British neglect of British Guiana.[36] Thus, by mid-1958 the issues of foreign investment, economic development, and unemployment had emerged at the center of the political agenda in British Guiana. In a revealing conversation with the American Consul, Forbes Burnham indicated that

> Dr. Jagan's future political life depended chiefly on his ability to procure loans from abroad for the continuation and expansion of the colony's development program. He added that he was glad that this particular problem was Jagan's and not his at the moment. He declared that he and his party now realized that the failure of the PNC (then campaigning as the Burnhamite-PPP) to win the August 1957 elections was really a blessing in disguise.[37]

Jagan's ability to obtain development capital to promote economic diversification and employment had become an index of political credibility within British Guiana.

A mid-1958 visit by Jagan and Governor Renison to London to solicit funds from the imperial government brought little reward. The Exchequer was only able to offer a £5.5 million loan to help finance British Guiana's development, despite Jagan's efforts to use the urgent unemployment situation to induce greater assistance from Britain.[38] Britain's increasing inability to provide adequate capital flows to British Guiana mirrored developments elsewhere in the Caribbean and in the empire. The Colonial Office had taken the unusual step of providing Jagan with introductions to the German and Japanese embassies in London to help him solicit development financing from these countries.[39] While there was widespread public disappointment with the meagerness of British assistance, the American consul in British Guiana reported that the anti-Jagan leaders were privately relieved that Jagan had not enjoyed greater success. The PPP and British Guiana had become victims of the relative decline of Britain as a capital exporter and the desire of Jagan's domestic opponents to see his political credibility undermined.

The imperial government's recognition of its inability to provide the necessary capital to British Guiana had also led it to advise the United States that it should not withdraw its aid from British Guiana. The United Kingdom expressed its concern that such a step might force Jagan to approach the Soviet Union or India.[40] Despite this effort by the British government to persuade the Americans of the necessity to provide aid to British Guiana, Secretary of State Dulles, responding to information that Jagan planned to visit the United States, was very cool to the idea. He indicated that the administration would not oppose the visit, but was neither desirous of it nor wished to have it portrayed as resulting from an American invitation. He also saw it as an opportunity for Jagan to familiarize himself with procedures for American assistance.[41] The ambivalence of the Eisenhower administration about providing support for Jagan and the PPP was revealed in a memorandum in October 1958. In reviewing American policy to British Guiana, the memorandum outlined the reasons underlying the declining interest in providing aid to British Guiana: "Our TC program in British Guiana has been diminishing during the past year, partly because of `our wait and see' attitude toward the Government for political reasons, and partly because our technicians have not been getting the co-operation they need from local British colonial officials."[42] The issue of American assistance to British Guiana was becoming a central element in the increasingly complex relationship among the American and British governments and the PPP leadership in British Guiana.

By the second half of 1958, colonial officials were sufficiently impressed by Jagan's moderation to suggest that further constitutional devolution could be set in motion.[43] In November 1958, the governor announced the creation of a committee to recommend revisions of the existing constitution that would provide greater autonomy to elected officials. This process of accelerated constitutional devolution in British Guiana was also influenced by the inauguration of the West Indian Federation in 1958. The PPP had been holding discussions with the opposition in the federal legislature, the Democratic Labour party about participation in the federation.[44] The fact that the PPP was willing to engage in such discussions with the more conservative DLP than with the socialist Federal Labour Party was testimony to its moderation and the gulf separating the Jagans from Manley and Adams. The PPP had made a major shift in its political stance and the reward for this shift was the support of the imperial government for the resumption of the process of constitutional devolution in British Guiana with the PPP at the helm.

The evidence of PPP moderation convinced even the American consul in British Guiana. In February 1959, he penned a lengthy dispatch in which he argued for American assistance to the colony. The perceived benefit from such assistance was that it would encourage the growth of pro-Western sentiment in British Guiana. The consul argued that a loan from the United States to British Guiana would send a signal of American interest in the colony's development and serve as an insurance against the radicalization of British Guiana's politics. In essence, he was arguing that the United States could provide a signal of its willingness to work with the PPP as the future political leadership in British Guiana. In arguing the case for American assistance, the consul provided a thoughtful and nuanced analysis of political developments in British Guiana. He indicated that despite the ideological affinities of the PPP leadership, the rank and file supporters of the party and the majority of the population were not Communists. Rather popular sentiment tended to be either pro-Commonwealth or pro-Western. In addition, he portrayed Cheddi Jagan as idealistic while Janet Jagan tended to be much more pragmatic. Further, the Hungarian uprising of 1956 had created serious fissures within the PPP leadership leading to the departure of several leading figures. Given these developments, the consul dismissed the notion that the PPP's shift was only tactical, and argued that there were serious constraints upon the PPP's ability to pursue a Communist agenda. Among these constraints was the Indian business community that was a major source of financial support for the PPP. If the PPP were to adopt a Communist platform, it would lose the support of these influential members of the Indian community. It was also likely that open espousal of communism would undermine the PPP's effort to remain the leading political force in the colony, especially since the Indo-Guianese were not an absolute majority within the population, and further racial polarization could undermine the PPP. The geographic isolation of British Guiana from the Communist world also represented a barrier to the extension of Communist influence. Finally, the largely black militia was supportive of the People's National Congress and thus constituted a major obstacle for the PPP. In addition, there was little evidence of strong PPP ties to Moscow. Jagan had announced a desire for a loan from the Soviet Union, but there had been no serious effort to raise such a loan. The PPP's library had approached the USIS for material and its existing stock of literature on communism was unimpressive. The local press was also continuing its anti-Communist campaign against the PPP, thus reducing the latter's ability to propagate Communist views. Beyond these constraints, there were concrete benefits accruing to the PPP from its political shift. The first was that the colonial officials had established a collaborative relationship with the PPP, and they were little inclined to support the opposition PNC. Despite the party's pro-federation stance, its moderate image, and its anti-Communist platform, it did not enjoy the confidence of the colonial officials. Further, the non-Indian business community, including the Booker Group, were supportive of the PPP and uneasy about the PNC.[45] The consul's analysis of politics in British Guiana was remarkably insightful and appreciative of the dynamics of the society. It was measured and thoughtful in its assessments of the options open to the PPP.

Thus, by early 1959, the PPP had achieved a measure of respectability and the active support of the colonial administration. It remained the leading political force in the colony, and with the population growth rate significantly higher in the Indian community than in other communities, seemed set to enjoy a prolonged period in office. Its ideological shift and greater receptivity to the United States, as well as its acceptance of a gradual process of negotiated constitutional devolution, testified to its moderation of political positions and tactics. Notwithstanding this shift in the PPP's stance, the Jagans continued to define themselves as leftist in ideological orientation.[46] Their unwillingness to tolerate challenges to their leadership led to the departure of two leading members of the PPP, Fred Bowman and Edward Beharry in May 1959. The two left the party levelling charges against Cheddi Jagan that he was a Stalinist communist.[47] The personal ideological leanings of the Jagans, their effective control of the party, and the popular support they enjoyed, continued as barriers to challenges within and outside of the PPP. Whatever their ideological affinities, their leadership was not in doubt nor easily contested.

This undisputed preeminence enjoyed by the PPP did not diminish its determination to achieve control over the labor force in the sugar industry. In a change of strategy, the PPP mounted an effort in 1958 to have PPP supporters elected to the posts of president and general secretary of the Man Power Citizens Association (MPCA), the bargaining agent recognized by the sugar companies.[48] By dubious means, the executive of the MPCA declared the PPP candidates ineligible for office in the union and incumbent Richard Ishmael was re-elected President.[49] In 1959, in response to another PPP challenge, the MPCA Executive suspended the elections and declared Ishmael elected for a three-year term.[50] While uneasy about Ishmael's tactics, the colony's Trades Union Congress actively supported, and sympathized with, the MPCA's goal of preventing the PPP from obtaining a decisive influence in the sugar industry and labor movement.[51] As the PPP's star was rising, fear and concern about the growing strength of the Indian community in British Guiana's politics intensified ethnic and political mobilization among the other groups. In early 1959, the middle-class United Democratic Party (UDP) was merged with the PNC, creating a single party based upon Afro-Guianese communities. The largely black Trades Union Congress also began to support the PNC. The United Force was established as a party representing the Portuguese business community with token representation from conservative elements in other ethnic communities.[52] By late 1959, ethnic polarization in British Guiana was an undisputed fact of political life.

To shore up their difficult situation, the PNC and the Trades Union Congress approached labor and political groups in the United States for support. In April 1959, Forbes Burnham visited the United States where he continued his effort to discredit the PPP. He also approached New York Congressman Adam Clayton Powell about obtaining financial support that would help to strengthen his image and standing as a political leader among PNC constituents in Georgetown. Powell solicited an assessment of Burnham from the State Department and was told that Burnham compared unfavorably with the Jagans in acumen, discipline, and engagement in his political activities.[53] A delegation from the Trades Union Congress also visited the United States and apparently linked up with Burnham. With the active support of the American Federation of Labor-Congress of Industrial Organizations (AFL-CIO), the delegation met with officials of the State Department to discuss the situation in British Guiana. During the course of this meeting, the TUC delegation endorsed American aid for British Guiana even if such aid strengthened Jagan's image and standing. The TUC delegation also made it evident that the organization had a distinct preference for the PNC.[54]

Cheddi Jagan, accompanied by Frank Essex, the colony's financial secretary, also visited the United States in August 1959 to hold discussions with State Department and Development Loan Fund officials about American assistance for development projects in British Guiana. The visit followed upon talks in London about financing the proposed 1960-64 development plan for the colony. The British government authorized a plan of (G) $110 million over the period while Jagan had argued for planned expenditure of (G) $135 million. Of the proposed finances, Britain proposed to find (G) $60.4 million, with the remainder, (G) $49.6 million, being raised from domestic and other foreign sources. Jagan's visit to Washington resulted in meetings with officials of both the Department of State and the Development Loan Fund. At these meetings, Jagan made it evident that he was anxious to receive American financial assistance to improve the colony's infrastructure and its agricultural sector. In response to queries from American officials Jagan made it clear that he did not have high hopes for the success of the West Indian Federation and that his concern was to alleviate the problems confronting British Guiana. Jagan also solicited Department of Defense assistance in upgrading the airport in British Guiana that had remained under lease to the United States after 1945.[55] This latter request was symbolic of Jagan's moderation as it obviously implied that Jagan and the PPP were reconciled to the maintenance of American military rights in British Guiana. The presence of British officials at these discussions between Jagan and American officials implied that London was lending support to Jagan's quest for foreign assistance. Jagan's desire to accelerate the pace of economic growth in British Guiana to reduce the existing high levels of unemployment and underemployment had outpaced the capacity of the British government to finance these plans. Both Jagan and the British were hopeful that the Americans would fill the breech.

Upon his return to British Guiana, Jagan raised the issue of obtaining a loan from the Soviet Union to finance the ambitious development plans espoused by the PPP. After his discussions with the British government, and prior to his visit to the United States, Jagan had indicated that he was willing to explore the possibility of obtaining aid from Japan, India, and the Soviet Union in light of the inadequacy of British assistance. According to the American consul in British Guiana Jagan's announcement about possible Soviet aid was essentially a lever for forcing greater aid out of the West. In making this assessment, the Consul stated that "he (Jagan) has conditioned such a move on the unavailability of funds from the US and other Western countries, and upon the sanction of the Colonial Office. Such hedging establishes a large element of bluff.[56]

In addition, the chairman of the Booker Group supported Jagan's quest for foreign assistance and did not oppose Jagan's proposal about Soviet assistance.[57] The colony's financial secretary, Frank Essex, in discussion with the American consul said that provoking fears of a Communist menace would help to open American purse strings.[58] Jagan's proposal also seemed to enjoy considerable popular support.[59] Further evidence supporting the consul's view that Jagan was using Soviet assistance as a negotiating ploy came from Jagan himself. In a meeting with the American consul, Jagan was asked about the effect on investor confidence in British Guiana if Soviet assistance were to be given to the territory. In his response

> Jagan reiterated the assurances he had given the Canadian Trade Delegation last January, viz that the BG Government would scrupulously honor all commitments to private investors . . . . BG needs large scale government-to-government borrowings and if not forthcoming from the British and other Western countries, BG had the right to seek funds from the USSR so long as no strings were attached. After this fervently delivered statement Jagan stated that he had no plans at present for pursuing a Soviet loan; that private investors should have no fear about investing in BG; that the US should discount newspaper talk about "sinister Red designs on BG."[60]

In a subsequent meeting with the American consul general to Jamaica, Jagan indicated that he had not approached the Soviet Union for aid but felt that, given their aid to India and Egypt, it was an option that should not be dismissed. He further indicated that Britain was out to discredit him by withholding aid and that he was of the opinion that the British, not desirous of seeing American influence increase in British Guiana, were opposed to American assistance to the territory.[61] Jagan was clearly not above attempting to exploit the possible leverage that might exist in representing the United States as a potential savior from the British.

The American consul in Georgetown continued to reiterate the view that American assistance should be extended to British Guiana. He argued that the holding operation of the past five years would not be effective for the future and that Jagan's expectations of American assistance had been heightened by his visit to the United States.[62] By the end of 1959, American officials in Washington indicated that they were prepared to consider a well-developed loan of about (US) $5 million for British Guiana, while rejecting a (US) $34 million request as inadequately prepared.[63] This shift in the American position reflected a softening of the American hostility to assistance for British Guiana under the leadership of the PPP. It is not clear to what extent Jagan's moderation, the Soviet-assistance ploy, and British efforts to persuade the Americans to provide assistance helped to shift American policy. It seems that American policy by late 1959 was moving in a direction that foresaw the possibility of American assistance to the PPP government in British Guiana. It was also evident that Jagan had perceived the importance of moderating his ideological and political stance to obtain such American assistance. In effect, American assistance appeared to be a mechanism for opening a process of political accommodation between Jagan and the United States. Both parties had an interest in reaching an understanding. For Jagan also, it had become a critical index of his political legitimacy within British Guiana. In the case of the American government, its willingness to consider assistance to British Guiana was a useful inducement to influence the political climate in the colony.

The strategy of moderation by Jagan and the PPP won increasing accolades from British colonial officials. In late 1959, Governor Renison was transferred to Kenya being replaced by Sir Ralph Grey. As on previous occasions, the change of governors signaled a shift in policy by the Colonial Office. In early 1960, Jagan led a delegation to London to negotiate further constitutional devolution for the colony. After these discussions, it was announced that following new elections, elected officials would assume responsibility for internal affairs while foreign and defense policies would remain under the governor's authority. It was also agreed that after the introduction of the new constitution, scheduled for August 1961, independence for the colony "would be considered two years after the first general elections."[64] Implicit within this announcement was the promise that the winner of the general elections in 1961 would lead British Guiana to independence. The timing of Britain's withdrawal was also linked to the date set for the independence of the West Indian Federation. If the federation were to obtain an early date, so would British Guiana. A proposal from the opposition for the introduction of a system of proportional representation to replace the existing first-past-the-post electoral system was rejected by the British government. By early April 1960, the terms of independence for British Guiana had been set between the United Kingdom and nationalist leaders in the colony. The winner of the 1961 elections would assume control of an independent country by 1963, if not earlier. Further, it was clear that the British government was sufficiently impressed by Jagan's moderation, despite his continuous criticism of British aid to British Guiana, to accept the possibility of his leading the colony to independence.[65] The outcome of the negotiations for the colony's independence was a measure of the PPP's successful rehabilitation.

By early 1961, the Department of State was unwilling to challenge the British view and its policy reflected a willingness to work with Jagan. In June 1961, the World Bank approved a loan package for British Guiana for the promotion of small industries and for agricultural development.[66] Given the weighted voting system for loan approvals in operation at the World Bank, it was conceivable that the American government could have exercised enough leverage to block the loans if it so desired. In addition, the Kennedy administration in August 1961 indicated to the American embassy in Venezuela that it did not wish to deprive itself of the option of working with Jagan and was concerned about being accused of interfering with the election campaign underway in British Guiana.[67] The New York Times reported that there was concern about whether the PPP would opt for closer ties with Cuba under Castro and with the Soviet Union. Despite these fears among American policymakers, the paper reported that the Department of State believed that there was a possibility of working with Jagan.[68] The accuracy of the paper's depiction of American ambivalence about the PPP was confirmed in a telegram from Secretary of State Dean Rusk to the American embassy in Canada. Rusk sought the advice of the Canadian government about how to deal with the situation in British Guiana. According to Rusk:

> We seriously concerned at possible emergence in British Guiana of Communist or Castro-type regime. . . . FYI. HMG hold view Jagan is QTE salvageable UNQTE and best course for US is endeavor establish good relations with Jagan and seek win him over to West. Although we recognize Jagan is dominant political personality in British Guiana and that alternatives not attractive, we have considerable misgivings over following course advocated by HMG.[69]

The equation of the PPP and Jagan with Cuba under Fidel Castro reflected the traumatic effect of the Cuban Revolution upon American policymakers. The increasing radicalization of the Cuban Revolution and the Cuban decision to seek the political, economic, and military support of the Communist powers against American efforts to destroy the revolutionary government had fundamentally transformed American perceptions of the Caribbean.

From 1961 onward, Cuba under Castro's leadership effectively demonstrated that the Caribbean was no longer an exclusive American sphere of influence. It was a highly visible reminder of the inadequacies of American foreign policy in the Western Hemisphere. For American policymakers, the Cuban Revolution constituted an affront to American conceptions of the American experience. It was a triumph for anti-United States nationalism within Latin America. It also constituted additional evidence of the growing weight of the Soviet Union in international affairs with its ability to influence events in Asia, Africa, and the Western Hemisphere. Given this potent symbolic value, the Cuban Revolution traumatized American policymakers and led to an escalation of tensions that culminated in the missile crisis of 1962. It was in this context of highly charged debate about American policy in the Caribbean that the issue of independence for British Guiana began to assume a critical importance. Jagan's past, the ideological affinities of his wife and other leaders of the PPP, his unwillingness to embrace anti-Communist politics, the imperviousness of the majority of the Indian community in British Guiana to appeals to abandon the PPP, and the PPP's willingness to establish economic ties with the Communist world, all began to be assessed through lenses colored by the rabid anti-Castro hysteria that had been generated by the Cuban Revolution. The avenues of political debate in American politics were being closed under the impact of the Cuban Revolution, and the fear among American policymakers of another version of the "Who lost China?" debate. The budding accommodation between the United States and Jagan of the 1959-61 period was replaced by increasing American hostility to the PPP, and an American determination to prevent British Guiana from becoming independent under the PPP.

The shift in American policy from accommodation to opposition led to support for opposition groups in their efforts to oust the PPP through a campaign of violence, strikes, and other forms of confrontation. This campaign was conducted in parallel with an effort to persuade the British government to renege on its 1960 agreement with the nationalist leaders on the terms of independence for the colony. This was followed by a joint Anglo-American effort to oust the PPP and the creation of an anti-PPP coalition that assumed control over the transition to independence. In essence, the British government bowed to American pressures and allowed the latter to dictate the terms of British Guiana's independence. For the American government, setting the terms of British Guiana's independence was an effort to demonstrate its control over the Caribbean.

As the Kennedy administration agonized over the question of working with Jagan, it began to adopt a keen interest in the outcome of the August 1961 elections in British Guiana. It monitored the fortunes of the United Force (UF), the party founded by a wealthy entrepreneur of Portuguese extraction, Peter D'Aguiar, in 1960.[70] The formation of the United Force and the election campaign of 1961 provided further evidence of the racial polarization becoming pervasive in the colony's politics. The PPP had effectively become a party whose supporters were largely based in the rural Indian community of sugar workers, rice farmers, and small businessmen. The PNC drew its support from the urban centers and represented the working and the middle-class black community that dominated the civil service, the teaching profession, and the service industries. The UF represented middle-class and commercial groups dominated by Europeans, Christianized Indians, the Amerindian communities where the Roman Catholic and Anglican churches enjoyed long-established influence, and a sprinkling of supporters from other ethnic communities.

In preparation for the elections, the boundaries of the constituencies had been redrawn to the disadvantage of the PPP by a British official commission. The *New York Times* reported that Cheddi Jagan publicly criticized the boundaries but was unable to force any changes in them.[71] Despite this effort to strengthen the opposition's chances in the elections, the governor informed American officials in Washington that Jagan was perceived as more acceptable than Burnham. The latter was considered racist and untrustworthy.[72] The British were supportive of Jagan, but also sought to ensure that there would be a strong opposition that would keep the PPP in check. Nonetheless, after a bitter election campaign in which both the PNC and the UF sought to portray the PPP as communist, and in which race was the central mobilizing factor, the PPP won twenty seats to eleven for the PNC and four for the UF. Despite gaining only 42 percent of the vote, the PPP had won the elections while the bitterness engendered by the election campaign had created a vast gulf between Burnham and D'Aguiar. The PPP had helped to undermine the PNC by ordering its supporters to vote for the UF in constituencies where the PPP did not field a candidate.[73] Once again, the anti-Jagan forces found themselves unable to build a cohesive coalition against the PPP. The election campaign that all contenders knew would precede the British withdrawal had further intensified the ethnic polarization in the colony. Prior to the elections, the general secretary of the PNC, Sydney King, had raised the idea of exclusive zones in British Guiana for the various ethnic groups. He was promptly expelled from the party but his proposal was an explicit admission of the schisms within the society.[74] After the election, D'Aguiar raised the possibility of partitioning the country in conversation with the American consul in the colony.[75] The PPP's victory reflected solid support from the largely rural Indian population. The UF's attempt to field Indian candidates against the PPP in the rural constituencies was a major disaster for that party. It was again obvious that the opposition parties, even with electoral boundaries drawn in their favor, could not unseat the PPP under the existing electoral system.

Thus, while the 1961 election represented a personal and political vindication for Cheddi Jagan and the PPP, it had fostered the further polarization of the society and the heightening of racial tensions. It was a critical juncture in the evolution of the society. The central issue facing the PPP was maintaining the impetus necessary to achieve independence while presiding over a severely fractured population. At the best of times, it would have been an unenviable task fraught with many pitfalls. As the American and British governments moved to oust Jagan, the task became impossible.

Immediately after the PPP victory, the American and British governments held discussions in London about policy toward British Guiana. As a result of these discussions the United States opted to work in tandem with the British in trying to salvage Jagan. The State Department instructed the American consul in British Guiana that "Basic concept of new program is whole-hearted cross the board effort to cooperate with newly elected administration headed by Jagan and to foster effective association between British Guiana and the West."[76]

In advising the American consul that the new policy should be presented as an American response to the colony's move toward independence, and not the result of Anglo-American coordination, the State Department also indicated that Kennedy had agreed to meet with Jagan during the latter's proposed visit to the United States in October 1961. In addition to this meeting with Kennedy, the memorandum also indicated that the administration was prepared to provide support for the British Guiana development program:

> We have studied his economic development programme and have carefully reviewed comments he made here on subject. We glad work out with him modest U.S. program of assistance designed to help British Guyanese people toward their social and economic goals within framework of representative democracy and respect for human rights. For this purpose we are prepared to send special ICA representative from Washington to discuss with him specifically what might be done. . . . We would make every effort start promptly work on the ground.[77]

The reasons for this decision to work with Jagan were spelt out in a memorandum sent to the American embassy in Ottawa, Canada. The embassy was instructed to inform the Canadian government of the policy adopted by the Anglo-American Working Party and Canadian government assistance to British Guiana was solicited. According to the memorandum "Among factors contributing to decision were: (a) impracticality of any alternative cause of action; (b) dearth of effective political leadership apart from Jagan; and (c) recognition that coldness towards Jagan and withholding of aid could only accelerate his gravitation toward Soviet-Castro bloc."[78] The Kennedy administration had effectively committed itself to working with the PPP as British Guiana began to take the final steps toward independence. As an editorial in the *New York Times* put it: "If British Guiana is handled by the United States with some understanding, sophistication and sympathy there is every reason to hope it will become a desirable member of the inter-American system."[79] The key question was whether the Kennedy administration was endowed with the qualities listed by the editorial.

It was not only the Kennedy administration that shifted ground after the August election. Jagan himself issued explicit statements promising adherence to parliamentary democracy and expressing a desire to participate in the Alliance for Progress. He also reiterated the view that the PPP was not a Communist party. His efforts to reassure his critics and opponents extended even to the point of dropping Janet Jagan from the cabinet announced after the elections. Five members of the cabinet were Afro-Guianese and even the

British Guiana Trades Union Congress (BGTUC) came out with a statement indicating its willingness to work with the PPP government. Just before his departure for the United States, where he was scheduled to meet with President Kennedy, Jagan made it clear that he was prepared to establish a new relationship with the United States. On the issue of his socialist leanings, Jagan subsequently indicated that he did not perceive his ideological preferences as a constraint upon aid from the United States, since it was providing aid to Communist states, such as Yugoslavia and Poland.[80]

There was the expectation shared by the Kennedy administration and Jagan that the latter's visit to Washington would help to put relations on a new footing. Both sides hoped that the visit would result in their respective fears being assuaged. For the Americans, the Kennedy administration hoped that the meeting with Jagan would remove the fear of the PPP as a threat to American interests. For Jagan, it was the hope that Kennedy would extend development assistance to British Guiana. At the end of the visit, neither side was satisfied. During his stay in the United States, Jagan made it clear that after independence the country would seek membership in the Organization of American States, pursue a nonaligned foreign policy, and maintain a democratic system. He also professed his "socialist leanings" both in public forums and in his meeting with Kennedy and his advisors. His unwillingness to embrace an anti-Communist strategy was apparently unsettling to Kennedy and his advisors.[81] Despite a recommendation from the United States Agency for International Development (USAID) that the United States should offer aid to a maximum of $5 million and accept Jagan's view that he would seek development aid from other countries, including the Soviet Union Jagan left Washington without any firm commitment of development assistance.[82] While the unease of the Kennedy administration was serious enough to result in a decision to postpone the provision of development assistance to British Guiana, it was apparently not yet strong enough to result in a policy of not working with the PPP. The final report of Jagan's visit promised that an American mission would be sent to British Guiana to determine the areas where American assistance would best contribute to the colony's development. In a subsequent interview with Izvestia, Kennedy's comments on British Guiana and Jagan reflected a continuing measure of tolerance for Jagan. According to Kennedy:

> Mr. Jagan . . . who was recently elected Prime Minister in British Guiana, is a Marxist, but the United States doesn't object–because that choice was made by an honest election, which he won. If the people of any country choose to follow a Communist system in a free election, after a fair opportunity for a number of views to be presented, the United States would accept that.[83]

It was not a position that Kennedy maintained for very long.

In early 1962, the opposition parties in British Guiana, still embittered by the loss of the elections in August of the preceding year and fearful that the colony would proceed to independence under the PPP as the party of the Indo-Guianese community, decided on a test of strength. The PPP had introduced a budget, drafted by the Cambridge economist Nicholas Kaldor, calling for compulsory savings and higher taxes. In response the PNC, the TUC, and the UF called for a general strike to force revisions in the budget. The general strike was accompanied by a campaign of riots and arson in the capital city, Georgetown. British troops were introduced to quell the unrest. As a result of the violence, the PPP government was forced to withdraw the offending provisions.[84] The behavior of Governor Grey during the crisis seemed to reflect the first signs of British hesitation about Jagan's ability to lead the territory to independence. The governor, despite Jagan's recommendations to have the troops sent immediately to the capital from their base some twenty-seven miles away, did not request their dispatch until after the riots and arson had begun. He had also indirectly suggested that Jagan should resign.[85] According to the *New York Times*, he suggested that independence for the colony would be set back by the unrest.[86] The British government nonetheless confirmed that talks scheduled for May to discuss independence would be held as previously arranged.[87]

The apparent lack of confidence in Jagan displayed by the Governor may well have been due to the fact that the anti-PPP forces--the PNC, the TUC, and the UF--had demonstrated both their strength and willingness to collaborate in an effort to oust the PPP. The fear of independence under the PPP and the resulting polarization had been vividly demonstrated by the February disturbances. Once again, the political system of the colony was undergoing a process of realignment with the first evidence emerging of a viable anti-PPP alliance. It was certainly advisable for the British to hedge their bets.

The events of February 1962 also seem to have given the United States pause. On March 8, Kennedy circulated a memorandum to several members of the administration including the secretaries of State and Defense. In the memorandum, Kennedy stated:

> No final decision will be taken on our policy to British Guiana and the Jagan government until (a) the Secretary of State has a chance to discuss the matter with Lord Home in Geneva, and (b) Hugh Fraser completes his on-the- spot survey in British Guiana for the Colonial Office. The questions which we must answer before we reach our decision include the following: 1. Can Great Britain be persuaded to delay independence for a year? 2. If Great Britain refuses to delay the date of independence, would a new election before independence be possible? If so, would Jagan win or lose? If he lost, what are the alternatives? 3. What are the possibilities and limitations of United States action in the situation?[88]

The issues raised by Kennedy in the memorandum suggest that he was beginning to reconsider the policy of working with Jagan and the PPP. It also showed that he was seeking a meeting of minds with the British about changing that policy. But it seems that events in British Guiana were not the only motive for Kennedy's change of tack. The antipathy to Jagan ran very deeply among various members of Congress, the Central Intelligence Agency, and labor union officials in the United States. Even before Jagan's visit to the United States in October 1961, senators Thomas Dodd and Ernest Gruening had written Kennedy to express opposition to World Bank loans for British Guiana.[89] Congressman John H. Rousselot had cabled Kennedy in November 1961 to express his wish to "go on record as being unswervingly opposed to aid of any kind to Cheddi Jagan and his Marxist-Socialist-Communist government."[90] Representative Edna Kelly had also expressed opposition to aid for British Guiana.[91] Kelly and Dodd were democrats while Rousselot and Gruening were republicans, testifying to the bipartisan antipathy toward Jagan.[92] The extent of opposition to Jagan in the Congress was apparently enough to jeopardize aid to other countries.[93] Congressional opposition to aid for British Guiana extended even to teams sent by the Agency for International Development to determine whether American assistance should be offered to the colony. This opposition was mitigated when it was explained that the purpose of the teams was to facilitate the travel of operatives of the Central Intelligence Agency into British Guiana.[94] In May 1962, the *New York Times* reported that Burnham visited the United States for meetings at the United Nations in New York and with the State Department.[95] However, on the advice of the State Department, Arthur Schlesinger, Jr. sought to block a possible meeting with Kennedy. Apparently, there was concern that the AFL-CIO would be able to arrange such a meeting.[96] Nonetheless, Burnham was able to meet with Senator Dodd who reported their conversation to Kennedy. The conversation between Dodd and Burnham centered on the possibilities of provoking a split in the PPP and creating an anti-PPP coalition that could win new elections before independence. Dodd was told by the Kennedy administration that he would be kept "informed of the developments in British Guiana in view of his interest."[97] In September 1962, Dodd wrote to Dean Rusk complaining about the fact that the State Department was reluctant to support a housing project in British Guiana that would be financed by the United States and which would benefit Jagan's opponents. He also argued that public credit should be conferred upon Burnham for his role in obtaining American scholarships for students from British Guiana. Dodd was concerned to strengthen Burnham's standing in the colony's politics and volunteered to issue a statement affirming Burnham's role in the scholarship program.[98]

Serafino Romualdi, the director of the American Institute for Free Labor Development (AIFLD), shared Dodd's antipathy toward Jagan. His organization was funded by the American government through the Agency for International Development and provided training for pro-American trade union officials. From this position, Romualdi also sought to influence the development of an effective anti-Jagan alliance. In September 1962, Romualdi penned a report in which he indicated that "the trade union movement in British Guiana--supported by the ORIT-ICFTU, and most emphatically by their U.S. affiliates--rejects the theory that there is no alternative to the regime of Dr. Jagan."[99] By late 1962, it had become clear that the anti-Jagan forces in British Guiana had developed powerful allies in the United States who were pressing the Kennedy administration to switch its support to the opposition in British Guiana. As evidenced by the March memorandum, Kennedy himself had begun to rethink his policy of working with Jagan. Continuing pressure by influential American supporters of the anti-Jagan forces certainly seems to have contributed to the shift in policy toward the PPP.

At some point during 1962, the Kennedy administration decided to throw its weight behind the anti-Jagan forces in British Guiana and to force a delay in the colony's independence to allow for new elections. While Schlesinger claims that Rusk sent a letter to the British government early in 1962 reversing the policy of accommodation, evidence suggests that policy toward Jagan was still unresolved in June 1962.[100] Given Romualdi's and Dodd's interventions of September 1962, it would seem that either a decision had not been made before then, or that it was very tightly held to a trusted few.

In late September 1962, Kennedy met with Sir Alec Douglas Home in Washington to discuss Anglo-American cooperation against the Communist threat in the Caribbean. The British foreign secretary indicated that his country was unwilling to impose limitations on British trade with Cuba. However, paradoxically, he viewed Jagan's decision to increase economic and political ties with Cuba as a cause for concern to Britain. The *New York Times* reported that the two leaders agreed to Britain's assistance in mounting patrols in the Caribbean to ensure that Cuban agents and arms were not sent to British Guiana.[101] It may well have been this meeting where the two governments adopted a joint policy to force Jagan from office.[102]

This public shift in British policy toward cooperation with the Americans in containing the growth of Cuba-British Guiana relations followed a successful British effort to delay talks between the British government and the political leaders of the colony. Originally scheduled for May, the talks had been postponed until July and then rescheduled for late September. However, the talks did not open until late October, after the Kennedy-Home meeting of September. The *New York Times* reported that the official reason for the delays was the decision to await the submission of a report by the commission of inquiry into the disturbances of February 1962.[103] The commission was chaired by Sir Henry Wynn Parry of the United Kingdom. Its other members were Sir Edward Asafu-Adjaye of Ghana and G. D. Khosla of India. Its findings were released in early October. According to the *New York Times*, the report attributed the riots and disturbances of February 1962 to fear of the Communist tendencies of the PPP government. It minimized the significance of the racial tensions in the eruption of violence and rejected the notion that there had been a plot to overthrow the government.[104] In an earlier report on Jagan's testimony to the Parry Commission, the *New York Times* had carried the story that Jagan publicly acknowledged his admiration for Fidel Castro and Nikita Khrushchev. While he had admitted that he could be considered a Communist, he had qualified his statement by stipulating that he had no intention of introducing policies similar to those adopted by the Castro government.[105]

By the time of the opening of the talks on British Guiana's independence in London in late October 1962, the ideological and racial polarization of British Guiana was complete. Jagan's personal ideological preference and his willingness to establish relations with the Communist nations, had become the central issue in determining the colony's future. The Kennedy-Home meeting was a signal that the two governments had forged a common policy to remove the PPP and Jagan from power. There was little room to maneuver for Jagan whose increasing isolation did not appear to deter him from his efforts to develop relations with Eastern Europe. According to the *New York Times*, Jagan was seeking assistance for industrial development from Eastern European countries in late 1962.[106] It was in this context that the talks among the political leaders of British Guiana and the British government began. The PPP went into the talks seeking a timetable for the colony's independence. The opposition parties, the PNC and UF, reflecting their increasing cooperation, demanded new elections under a system of proportional representation prior to independence. Two weeks later the talks went into recess without any movement by any of the parties, and the British colonial secretary indicated that negotiations would continue under the chairmanship of Governor Sir Ralph Grey. The *New York Times* reported that he warned that deadlock among the parties would result in the British government imposing a solution.[107] The threat of British intervention only served to encourage the intransigence of the opposition since it seemed to imply British willingness to abandon Jagan and the PPP. Independence for the colony had clearly been relegated to a secondary status until the impasse among the three parties could be resolved.

The failure of the talks in October 1962 provided fresh momentum for the opposition to undermine Jagan. Jagan and Burnham began discussions to form a coalition government. Burnham refused to surrender the demand for an electoral system based upon proportional representation. Jagan's offer of new elections before independence with a legislature composed of two chambers, one elected on the existing first-past-the-post system and the other selected on the basis of proportional representation, was rejected.[108] Burnham's rejection of Jagan's offer may well have been influenced by a perception or knowledge of the thinking of the British and American governments. By early 1963, the failure of the talks in London and in the colony had heightened tensions. According to the *New York Times*, a struggle between pro-PPP and opposition-controlled unions for the right to represent workers at the government-owned

Rice Marketing Board in early April resulted in riots that targeted Indian-owned businesses and Indian vendors in the markets of the capital, Georgetown.[109] The anti-PPP sentiment was being transformed into intercommunal violence by the opposition. In late March, the PPP had introduced a Labour Relations Bill, patterned on the Wagner Act in the United States, to allow for balloting by workers to determine union representation.[110] After the riots of early April, the PPP made a serious effort to have the bill passed. While an obvious effort to settle recognition disputes, the bill also reflected the PPP's long-standing concern with acquiring control over the labor force in the sugar industry. There was no further interest in the effort to seize control of the MPCA from within, and the bill marked the return to the earlier strategy of trying to displace it with the PPP-backed Guyana Agricultural Workers Union (GAWU). If the MPCA were displaced by GAWU, the latter would also be able to assume a major role in the TUC, a major source of anti-Jagan sentiment.

The passage of the labor relations bill would have sounded the death knell for a major opposition force. The TUC's response provided further evidence of its strength and the sources of its support. It called a general strike throughout the colony. The strike-call was obeyed by the majority of the unions that they controlled, including the Civil Service Association to which most senior personnel in the government administration belonged. In the sugar industry, employers imposed a lockout that effectively prevented PPP supporters in the sugar industry from demonstrating that not all workers were willing to adhere to the call for a general strike.[111] Except for essential services, the colony had been effectively crippled. According to the *New York Times*, American and British trade unions helped to finance the general strike to the tune of $50,000 to $70,000 per week, over its eighty-day duration.[112] The AIFLD, at the instigation of Serafino Romualdi, also provided support in the form of organizers who helped to coordinate strike-related activities.[113] It appears that the intelligence services of both Britain and the United States were involved in the strike.[114] The general strike was accompanied by increasing intercommunal violence. The *New York Times* carried a story in early May about simultaneous police raids on the offices of the three major parties in the colony. In the offices of the ruling PPP, machetes, knives, and empty homemade bomb casings were confiscated. At the UF headquarters, no weapons were discovered, but at the offices of the PNC, arms and ammunition, explosives and detailed plans for a paramilitary organization were found.[115] The struggle between the PPP and its opponents had escalated to a dimension that revolved around more than bargaining rights for workers. As the conflict intensified, Jagan declared a state of emergency and the British government put troops on alert for dispatch to the colony. Jagan also offered his resignation on condition that new elections under the existing electoral system be held and independence be granted to the winner. He also turned to Cuba and the Soviet Union for supplies of fuel, flour, and other foodstuffs. In order to store the fuel supplied by the Cuban government, Jagan took over the storage facilities of the Shell Oil Company. This move was taken after the United States refused to allow the fuel to be stored at the colony's airport in the area leased to the United States in 1940.[116]

It is unclear whether the Cuban-Soviet assistance that arrived in mid-June was a major factor in British efforts to negotiate an end to the strike. A British trade union official, Robert Willis, was flown to the colony by British military aircraft to begin mediating the dispute. The anti-PPP labor unions apparently only accepted a negotiated solution when it became clear that foreign aid for the strike was in jeopardy. According to the *New York Times*, the Kennedy administration was concerned that the Cuban-Soviet assistance to Jagan was a harbinger of their greater involvement in the colony's affairs. These fears were communicated to the British and may have contributed to the strike's end.[117] The end of the strike was followed by Kennedy's decision to refuse aid to the PPP government in British Guiana. Kennedy's decision came in response to a letter that Jagan had sent him in April 1963 requesting a statement of whether the United States was willing to provide aid to British Guiana. Kennedy's decision was reportedly based on opposition to Jagan's willingness to seek ties with the Communist world, including Cuba, and the view that American aid would be futile unless the colony's racial and political conflicts were resolved.[118] The decision was communicated to Jagan after a meeting in London between President Kennedy and Prime Minister Macmillan. According to a report of the meeting published by the *New York Times*:

> Washington believes that Dr. Jagan is cast from the same mold as Premier Fidel Castro of Cuba, and that the Guyanese leftist's assumption of control would only heighten intolerably the American difficulties with Cuba. Dean Rusk, the Secretary of State, made these points clear to the British Government at Birch Grove and in London while President Kennedy was visiting 10 days ago. Prime Minister Macmillan assured President Kennedy at Birch Grove that independence was not contemplated now. One possible action that Mr. Rusk found acceptable was the introduction of proportional representation for voting in British Guiana. Such a system would reduce the strength of single parties and would allow many parties to share control of the Government. The hope is that it would bring a coalition of Dr. Jagan's opponents into office.[119]

The June 1963 meeting in London seems to have set the stage for the Anglo-American effort to oust Jagan to assume new momentum. The anti-PPP forces had failed to force Jagan's resignation during the general strike and it was clear that a new tack would have to be tried. Immediately after the end of the strike British Colonial Secretary Duncan Sandys visited British Guiana and with his encouragement, talks began between Jagan and Burnham to form a coalition government. The *New York Times* reported that upon his return to Britain, Sandys declared that he had given the parties in British Guiana until October to reach an agreement. Failing such agreement, the British government would impose a solution.[120] By late September the talks between the PPP and the PNC had failed to provide an agreement. As in earlier meetings, the PNC's demand for an electoral system based on proportional representation and the PPP's refusal to accept that demand was the source of the impasse.[121] Early in the talks, the PNC had also sought an equal number of cabinet positions in any coalition government. It was obvious that the PNC's intransigence was being fed by a perception that the PPP was vulnerable. The *New York Times* reported the subsequent call by the Republican leadership in the American Congress for Kennedy to pressure the British into withholding independence from British Guiana. This was undoubtedly further ammunition for the anti-Jagan forces since the American government seemed intent on preventing Jagan from leading the country into independence.[122] The failure of the talks between the PPP and the PNC meant that talks would have to resume in London under the auspices of the colonial secretary. These talks were scheduled for late October. On their way to London, during a stopover in New York, Burnham and D'Aguiar both expressed the view that the talks would only result in a solution imposed by Duncan Sandys.[123] It was evident that the two leaders were not prepared to shift ground.

As the opposition leaders forecasted, the talks among the Guyanese delegations did not resolve their differences. The *New York Times* reported that they had agreed to sign a joint letter to Sandys requesting him to devise a solution to the impasse as they did not wish to delay independence for the colony.[124] Sandys's solution was a new constitution with an electoral system based upon proportional representation; elections under the new constitution; and plans for independence to be delayed until after the new elections. The solution reflected the triumph of the anti-PPP forces. Jagan accused Britain of subservience to the United States and declared the PPP free to reject the Sandys solution.[125]

Jagan immediately began a campaign of opposition to the policies of the British government. He wrote to British Prime Minister Alec Douglas Home, rejecting the Sandys decision and requested the intervention of the UN Secretary General, U Thant.[126] In January 1964, Jagan protested the decision to replace Governor Sir Ralph Grey with the South African Sir Richard Luyt. The PPP later boycotted the swearing-in ceremony for the new governor.[127] Gene Meakins, an American adviser to the TUC, was expelled from the colony.[128] The PPP also sought the support of the Labour party in Britain to prevent the introduction of proportional representation in the colony. This effort was abandoned in late April by the British Labour party.[129] In early May the PPP shifted tack. A strike was called in the sugar industry and intercommunal violence resumed. By late May, a state of emergency was declared and more British troops had to be flown into the territory in an effort to maintain control. In mid-June, Governor Luyt assumed emergency powers and detained several members of Parliament belonging to the PPP. These detentions removed the PPP majority in the legislature. Without a functioning legislature, the governor was the sole authority in the colony.[130]

An effort by Prime Minister Eric Williams of Trinidad and Tobago to mediate the conflict failed. Williams blamed the intransigence of both the PPP and its opponents. He later proposed a seven-point plan for UN intervention and for the UN to assume responsibility for administering the colony. The British government rejected the plan as it had previously responded to UN efforts to involve itself in the colony's affairs.[131] Evidently, the political system in British Guiana was so polarized that there was little, if any, capacity for compromise. British policy seemed to be intent on maintaining the polarization until the elections were held.

The victory of the Labour party in the British general elections of mid-October brought no respite for Jagan and the PPP. Jagan went to London immediately after the elections in an effort to persuade the new government to review British policy to British Guiana.[132] Despite his importuning, the Labour government announced that the elections set for December in the colony would go ahead as scheduled.[133] The *New York Times* reported that Dean Rusk, the American secretary of state, had reiterated his country's views to his British counterpart, Patrick Gordon-Walker. As a result, the Wilson government was bowing to American pressures to continue policy in British Guiana initiated by its predecessor.[134] The ensuing election confirmed the ethnic polarization in the colony. The PPP obtained 45.8 percent of the vote, the PNC got 40.5 percent and the United Force 12.4 percent. The votes mirrored the ethnic composition of the electorate. The combined percentages of the anti-PPP parties allowed them to establish a coalition government dominated by the PNC. Finally, an effective anti-PPP coalition had assumed power in the colony. Even after their victory, the anti-PPP groups continued to receive funding from American intelligence sources with the approval of the British government.[135] It had taken eleven years to oust the PPP from its preeminent position in British Guiana's political life. It had required the collaboration of the British, the Americans, and the anti-PPP forces to achieve this objective. The British collaboration with the United States represented the recognition that its colonies were passing into the American sphere of influence in the Caribbean. For the Americans, the campaign against the PPP reflected policy driven by a fear of ideological pluralism in the Caribbean and the traumatic effect of the Cuban Revolution upon American policymakers. The anti-PPP forces had recognized the shift in influence over British Guiana's future as Britain withdrew from the Caribbean. They exploited the growing influence of the Americans and the American fear of the PPP to full advantage. By 1962, this strategy represented their only hope of emerging as an alternative to the PPP.

For the PPP and for the other Caribbean territories, events in British Guiana had revealed the level of American antipathy to anti-Western ideologies or groups. It was a further indication of American intolerance of forces that did not accept American-defined limits upon foreign and domestic policies in its sphere of influence. It was a signal failure of the PPP to recognize the volatility of American policy in dealing with non-Western nationalism and the innate conservatism of the Kennedy administration. Even nonalignment in foreign policy by a state within the Western hemisphere was considered anathema to American policymakers. The PPP had also not understood that after Suez and the resignation of Eden, British policymakers were very cognizant of the need to court American goodwill. Given the importance of the Caribbean to American policymakers, especially in the wake of the Cuban Revolution and the missile crisis, it was inevitable that the British would seek to accommodate American policy. In the final analysis, it revealed that the transfer of power in the Caribbean was a dual process--West Indian independence from Britain also marked passage into the American sphere of influence. It was an inevitable sequel to the Bases-for-Destroyers Deal of 1940 that had symbolized the continued British retrenchment from the Caribbean and its replacement by American dominance.

NOTES

1. See Thomas Spinner, *A Political and Social History of Guyana* (Boulder, Colo.: Westview Press, 1984), 55-56. Spinner's monograph is a useful treatise on the recent history of Guyana (British Guiana) and was used extensively in the preparation of this chapter.

2. 741D.00/1-1254. Dispatch, Maddox to DOS, January 12, 1954. R.G. 59, State Decimal File, Box 3543.

3. Spinner, *Guyana*, 56-59

4. 741D.00/2-455. Dispatch, Maddox to DOS, February 4, 1955. R.G. 59, State Decimal File, Box 3205; and, Spinner, *Guyana*, 61-64

5. 841D. 062/2-1155. Dispatch, Steins to DOS, February 11, 1955. R.G. 59, State Decimal File, Box 4451.

6. 841B. 062/8-2654. Dispatch, Hamlin to DOS, August 26, 1954. R.G. 59, State Decimal File, Box 4812.

7. 741D. 00/6-1455. Dispatch, Maddox to DOS, June 14, 1955. R.G. 59, State Decimal File, Box 3205.

8. 741D. 00/9-2355. Dispatch, Cope to DOS, September 23, 1955. R.G. 59, State Decimal File, Box 3205.

9. 741D. 11/7-2655. Dispatch, Maddox to DOS, July 26, 1955. R.G. 59, State Decimal File, Box 3205.

10. 741D. 11/10-2755. Dispatch, Cope to DOS, October 27, 1955. R.G. 59, State Decimal File, Box 3205.

11. 741D. 00/12-755. Dispatch, Jenkins to DOS, December 7, 1955. R.G. 59, State Decimal File, Box 4451.

12. 741D. 00/3-656. Dispatch, Jenkins to DOS, March 6, 1956, and 741D. 11/3-656, Cope to DOS, March 6, 1956. R.G. 59, State Decimal File, Box 3205.

13. 741D. 00/5-1656. Dispatch, Jenkins to DOS, May 16, 1956. R.G. 59, State Decimal File, Box 3205; and Spinner, *Guyana*, 61.

14. 741D. 00/10-2256. Dispatch, Cope to DOS, October 22, 1956. R.G. 59, State Decimal File, Box 3205.

15. Ibid.

16. 741D. 00/5-456. Dispatch, Jenkins to DOS, May 4, 1956. R.G. 59, State Decimal File, Box 3205.

17. 741D. 00/12-2856. Dispatch, Cope to DOS, December 28, 1956. R.G. 59, State Decimal File, Box 3205.

18. Ibid.

19. 741D. 00/5-157. Dispatch, Cope to DOS, May 1, 1957, and 741D. 00/5-857. Dispatch, Cope to DOS, May 8, 1957. R.G. 59, State Decimal File, Box 3205.

20. Spinner, *Guyana*, 72; and Roy A. Glasgow, *Guyana: Race and Politics among East Indians and Africans* (The Hague: Martinus Nijhoff, 1970), 110.

21. 741D. 00/6-656. Dispatch, Jenkins to DOS, June 6, 1956. R.G. 59, State Decimal File, Box 3205.

22. Spinner, *Guyana*, 71

23. 741D. 00/6-2857. Dispatch, Cope to DOS, June 26, 1957. R.G. 59, State Decimal File, Box 3205.

24. Ibid.

25. 741D. 00/7-2657. Memorandum of Conversation, Participants: Sir Patrick Renison, D. A. Humphrey, Douglas Williams, C. Burke Elbrick, Marselis C. Parsons, Coulter D. Hyler, and Frank D. Taylor; July 26, 1957. R.G. 59, State Decimal File, Box 3205.

26. Spinner, *Guyana*, 72-73

27. 741D. 00/2057. Dispatch, Cope to DOS, August 20, 1957. R.G. 59, State Decimal File, Box 3205.

28. 741D. 00/8-1657. Dispatch, Cope to DOS, August 16, 1957. R.G. 59, State Decimal File, Box 3205.

29. 741D. 00/8-1657. Telegram, Herter to American Consulate, Georgetown, August 16, 1957. R.G. 59, State Decimal File, Box 3205.

30. 841D. 00/10-2857. Dispatch, Cope to DOS, October 28, 1957. R.G. 59, State Decimal File, Box 4451.

31. 741D. 00/8-2057. Dispatch, Cope to DOS, August 20, 1957. R.G. 59, State Decimal File, Box 3205.

32. 741D. 00/12-1057. Memorandum, Dale to Jones, December 10, 1957. R.G. 59, State Decimal File, Box 3205.

33. Ibid.

34. 741D. 00/7-958. Dispatch, Cope to DOS, July 9, 1958. R.G. 59, State Decimal File, Box 3205.

35. 841D. 061/5-1558. Dispatch, Cope to DOS, May 15, 1958. R.G. 59, State Decimal File, Box 4451.

36. 841D. 00/2-1458. Dispatch, Cope to DOS, February 14, 1958. R.G. 59, State Decimal File, Box 4451.

37. 741D. 00/6-2458. Dispatch, Cope to DOS, June 24, 1958. R.G. 59, State Decimal File, Box 3205.

38. 841D. 061/7-1458. Dispatch, cope to DOS, July 14, 1958; and, 841D. 10/8-158. Dispatch, Cope to DOS, August 1, 1958. R.G. 59, State Decimal File, box 4451.

39. Ibid.

40. 741F. 00/6-2058. Memorandum of Conversation, Participants: Dale, Burn, Wilson, and Douglas Williams, June 20, 1958. R.G. 59, State Decimal File, Box 3206.

41. 841D. 10/7-1758. Telegram, Dulles to American Embassy, London, July 22, 1958. R.G. 59, State Decimal File, Box 4451.

42. 841D. 00TA/10-3158. Memorandum, Dale to Jandrey, October 31, 1958. R.G. 59, State Decimal File, Box 4451.

43. 741D. 03/11-1258. Dispatch, Woods to DOS, November 12, 1958. R.G. 59, State Decimal File, Box 3205.

44. 741D. 03/6-458. Dispatch, Orebaugh to DOS, June 4, 1958. R.G. 59, State Decimal File, Box 3205.

45. 841D. 00TA/2-2459. Dispatch, Woods to DOS, February 24, 1959. R.G. 59, State Decimal File, Box 4451.

46. By mid-1958, Jagan apparently was describing himself as a Democratic Socialist and was looking to the Communist party of India as a model. See 741D. 03/7-258. Dispatch, Cope to DOS, July 2, 1958. R.G. 59, State Decimal File, Box 3205.

47. 741D. 00/5-1559. Dispatch, Woods to DOS, May 15, 1959. R.G. 59, State Decimal File, Box 3205.

48. 741D. 00/1-358. Dispatch, Cope to DOS, January 3, 1958. R.G. 59, State Decimal File, Box 3205.

49. 741D. 00/1-2958. Dispatch, Dye to DOS, January 29, 1958. R.G. 59, State Decimal File, Box 3205.

50. 841D. 00/3-1959. Dispatch, Woods to DOS, March 13, 1959. R.G. 59, State Decimal File, Box 4451.

51. 741D. 00/1-2058. Dispatch, cope to DOS, January 20, 1958; and, 741D. 00/1-2958. Dispatch, Dye to DOS, January 29, 1958. R.G. 59, State Decimal File, Box 3205.

52. For discussion of some of the shifts in British Guiana's ethnic politics, see Spinner, *Guyana*, 74-81.

53. 741D. 00/4-2459. Memorandum of Conversation, Participants: Adam Clayton Powell, Florence Kenlin, William Dale, and North Burn, April 24, 1959. R.G. 59, State Decimal File, Box 3205.

54. 841D. 062/4-1459. Memorandum of Conversation, Participants: Rupert Tello, Wendell Bobb, Harry Pollitt, Douglas Williams, Harold Edwards, Don Goot, Irving Cheslaw, Warrick Elrod, and North Burn, April 14, 1959. R.G. 59, State Decimal File, Box 4451.

55. 741D. 5-MSP/8-1759. Memorandum of Conversation, Participants: Cheddi Jagan, Frank Essex, Michael Woods, Mr. Perry, Mr. Menapace, Mr. Hutchinson, Mr. Sergeant, August 17, 1959. R.G. 59, State Decimal File, Box 3205(?).

56. 841D. 10/8-2659. Dispatch, Woods to DOS, August 26, 1959. R.G. 59, State Decimal File, Box 4451.

57. Ibid.

58. Ibid.

59. 841D. 00-TA/9-1859. Dispatch, Woods to DOS, September 18, 1959. R.G. 59, State Decimal File, Box 4451.

60. 841D. 10/9-959. Dispatch, Woods to DOS, September 9, 1959. R.G. 59, State Decimal File, Box 4451.

61. 841D. 00/11-2759, Dispatch, McGregor to DOS, November 27, 1959. R.G. 59, State Decimal File, Box 4451(?).

62. 841D. 00-TA/9-1859. Dispatch, Woods to DOS, September 18, 1959. R.G. 59, State Decimal File, Box 4451.

63. 841D. 10/12-1559. Telegram, Henderson to American Consulate, Georgetown, December 15, 1959. R.G. 59, State Decimal File, Box 4451.

64. "Guiana's Charter Effective in '61," *New York Times*, April 1, 1960.

65. Governor Sir Ralph Grey expressed this view to American policymakers in Washington in early 1961. See Memorandum for the record, "Visit to Washington of Sir Ralph Grey, Governor of British Guiana", April 28, 1961. Schlesinger White House File, Box WH-3A, JFKL.

66. "Loan to British Guiana," *New York Times*, June 15, 1961.

67. Telegram, Rusk to American Embassy, Caracas, August 19, 1961. Papers of President Kennedy NSF, Countries, Box No. 14A, JFKL.

68. "U.S. Is Watching Guiana Election," *New York Times*, August 18, 1961.

69. Telegram, Rusk to American Embassy, Ottawa, August 12, 1961. Papers of President Kennedy, NSF, Countries, Box No. 14A, JFKL.

70. Telegram, Ball to American Consulate, Georgetown, August 7, 1961. Papers of President Kennedy, NSF, Countries, Box No. 14A, JFKL.

71. "Jagan Plans Protest," *New York Times*, January 9, 1961.

72. See "Visit to Washington of Sir Ralph Gray, Governor of British Guiana."

73. Telegram, Melby to Secretary of State, August 25, 1961. Papers of President Kennedy, NSF, Countries, Box No. 14A, JFKL.

74. Spinner, *Guyana*, 79.

75. Telegram, Melby to Secretary of State, August 25, 1961. Papers of President Kennedy, NSF, Countries, Box No. 14A, JFKL.

76. Telegram, Bowles to American Consul, Georgetown, September 25, 1961. Papers of President Kennedy, NSF, Countries, Box No. 14A, JFKL.

77. Ibid.

78. Telegram, Bowles to American Embassy, Ottawa, September 29, 1961. Papers of President Kennedy, NSF, Countries, Box No. 14A, JFKL.

79. Editorial, *New York Times*, August 23, 1961.

80. Telegram, Christensen to Secretary of State, October 13, 1961. Papers of President Kennedy, NSF, Countries, Box No. 14A, JFKL.

81. Spinner, *Guyana*, 83-85 and Arthur Schlesinger, Jr., *A Thousand Days* (Cambridge: Houghton Mifflin, 1965), 773-79.

82. USAID Position Paper, Premier Cheddi Jagan's visit to Washington, October 23-25, 1961: "Economic Assistance to British Guiana," October 17, 1961. Papers of President Kennedy, NSF, Countries, Box No. 14A, JFKL.

83. "Transcript of Interview Granted by Kennedy to Soviet Government News Agency," *New York Times*, 29 November, 1961.

84. Spinner, *Guyana*, 94-98.

85. Ibid., 97.

86. "Guianans Bitter in the Wake of Riot," *New York Times*, February 25, 1965.

87. "Jagan Aide Holds Troops Came Late," *New York Times*, February 23, 1965. However, the talks were later suspended until October 1962.

88. National Security Action Memorandum no. 135, John F. Kennedy to the Secretary of State, March 8, 1962. *Declassified Documents Reference Service*, 9, no. 2. 1983(WH 001370).

89. Letter, Thomas Dodd and Ernest Gruening to John F. Kennedy, September 6, 1961. Papers of President Kennedy, WH Central Files, Box 43, JFKL.

90. Cable, John H. Rousselot to John F. Kennedy, November 6, 1961. Papers of President Kennedy, WH Central Files, Box 43.

91. Letter, Lawrence F. O'Brien to Edna F. Kelly, November 7, 1961. Papers of President Kennedy, WH Central Files, box 43.

92. Senator Thomas Dodd's capacity to influence Kennedy's foreign policy seems to be worthy of an intensive study. Dodd's rabid anticommunism, his use of his seniority within the Democratic party to pursue his own initiatives, and his willingness to embrace nationalists who displayed anti-Communist credentials were also evident in his attempts to influence the Kennedy administration's policy toward the Belgian Congo. His influence on the Kennedy administration's policy is treated in Richard D. Mahoney *JFK: Ordeal in Africa* (New York: Oxford University Press, 1983), 110 and 146.

93. Spinner, *Guyana*, p. 85

94. Interview of Fowler Hamilton by Edwin R. Bayel, August 18, 1964. Oral History Project, JFKL.

95. "Guiana Leader off for U.S." *New York Times*, April 30, 1962.

96. Memorandum, Schlesinger to O'Donnell, (n.d.). Schlesinger WH Files, Box 3A. JFKL. Schlesinger, in his published memoirs of his service in the Kennedy administration, expressed the view that Burnham impressed American officials during his visit as a viable alternative to Jagan. See, Schlesinger, *A Thousand Days*, 778-79.

97. Memorandum for the Files, Ralph A. Dungan, May 22, 1962. Schlesinger WH Files, Box 3A, JFKL.

98. Letter, Dodd to Rusk, September 17, 1962. Papers of President Kennedy, WH Central Files, Box 236, JFKL.

99. Report, "More About Cheddi Jagan," Serafino Romualdi, September 17, 1962. Schlesinger WH Files, Writings Box W-3, JFKL.

100. Spinner, *Guyana*, 85. Spinner accepts Schlesinger's description of the step taken by Rusk. However, in May 1962, the *New York Times* carried a report of a U.S. economic mission visiting British Guiana and quoted an unidentified American official saying: "If Dr. Jagan had given clear evidence of a moderate approach it would not have been necessary to send a mission before he got any money." "U.S. Gets Mixed Advice on Aid to British Guiana," *New York Times*, 20 May 1962. Schlesinger subsequently wrote Kennedy in June advising him that George Ball had expressed reservations about State Department proposals for policy toward British Guiana, and that the department had provisionally withdrawn its memorandum to the president. This would suggest that U.S. policy to the colony was still not completely resolved in late June 1962. See, Memorandum, Schlesinger to Kennedy, June 21, 1962. Schlesinger WH Files, Box WH-3A, JFKL.

101. "President Meets with Lord Home on Curbing Cuba," *New York Times*, October 1, 1962.

102. Until further declassification reveals both the process and content of Anglo-American discussions on British Guiana, the exact timing of this decision remains unclear. However, there seems to have been some private understanding on British Guiana between Lord Home and the American government. McGeorge Bundy, the national security adviser, referred to that understanding in a memorandum to President Lyndon Johnson. See Memorandum for the President, March 2, 1964. Memos of the Special Assistant for National Security Affairs: McGeorge Bundy to President Johnson, 1963-66. Microfilm, reel 1, University Press of America, Frederick, Maryland.

103. "Guiana Chief angry over delay in talks," New York Times, July 4, 1962.

104. "Guiana Riot Inquiry blames Fear of a Red Trend in Regime," *New York Times*, October 4, 1962.

105. "Jagan Agrees He Fits Description of a Red," *New York Times*, June 23, 1962.

106. "Jagan Clarifies Reports of Deal With Soviet Bloc," *New York Times*, October 29, 1962.

107. "Parley on Guiana Ends in Deadlock," *New York Times*, November 7, 1962.

108. Spinner, *Guyana*, 100.

109. "Guiana Factions Renew Violence," *New York Times*, April 4, 1963.

110. Cheddi Jagan, "Letter to the Editor," *New York Times*, June 28, 1963.

111. Spinner, *Guyana*, 101.

112. "Guiana Labor Uneasy," *New York Times*, July 7, 1963. In 1967, it was reported that strikes in British Guiana in 1962 and 1963 were financed by the CIA using the American affiliate of the Public Service International that had its headquarters in London. See "C.I.A. Men Aided Strikes in Guiana against Dr. Jagan," *New York Times*, February 22, 1967.

113. Letter, Romualdi to Ralph A. Dungan, July 19, 1963. Papers of President Kennedy, WH Central Files, Box 43, JFKL. In this letter to Dungan who was a special

assistant to the president, Romualdi revealed that after his visit to British Guiana in April 1962, AIFLD decided to extend support to the anti-Jagan BGTUC.

114. In October 1964, Labor Foreign Secretary Patrick Gordon Walker visited the United States. He was expected by his American hosts to authorize the continuation of Anglo-American cooperation to oust Jagan. See Briefing Book, Visit of Foreign Secretary Gordon Walker, October 26-27, 1964. *Declassified Documents Quarterly Catalogue* 5, no.4, (1979), State Department 451B. In 1965, an even more pointed reference to the collaboration was revealed in a memorandum to Rusk, explaining the purpose of the British ambassador's meeting with the secretary of state: "Sir Patrick is expected to advise you officially that the British government agrees to authorize continued covert assistance to the anti-Jagan parties in British Guiana. . . . He may also express the hope that the cooperation now existing between our intelligence services will be continued." Memorandum, Davis to the Secretary, July 9, 1965. *Declassified Documents Quarterly Catalogue* 3, no.2, (1977), State Department 116B.

115. "Guiana Police Seize Arms and Arrest 3," *New York Times*, May 5, 1963.

116. "7 Shell Oil Tanks Seized by Guiana," *New York Times*, June 23, 1963.

117. "Guiana's Labor Uneasy," *New York Times*, July 7, 1963.

118. "Kennedy Refuses Aid to Guiana; Ties to Reds Termed Reason," *New York Times*, July 9, 1963.

119. "U.S. Said to Press for Jagan's Ouster," *New York Times*, July 10, 1963.

120. "Britain Delays Action on Racial Strife in Guiana," *New York Times*, July 17, 1963; and, "British Give Guiana Deadline for Peace," *New York Times*, July 18, 1963.

121. "Talks Fail To Bring Guiana Party Peace," *New York Times*, September 20, 1963.

122. "Republicans in Washington Fight Guiana Independence," *New York Times*, September 27, 1963.

123. "2 Rivals of Jagan Call Peace Remote," *New York Times*, October 19, 1963.

124. "Guiana Requests Imposed Charter," *New York Times*, October 26, 1963.

125. "Britain Demands Proportional Election in Guiana," *New York Times*, November 1, 1963.

126. "Jagan Denounces Britain's Plan on Independence," *New York Times*, November 12, 1963.

127. "Guiana Governor Sworn: Jagan Boycotts Ceremony," *New York Times*, March 8, 1964.

128. "Unionist Appeals Ouster," *New York Times*, January 4, 1964.

129. "Labor Party Drops Pro-Jagan Motion," *New York Times*, April 28, 1964.

130. "British Assume Full Guiana Rule," *New York Times*, June, 14 1964.

131. "U.N. Intervention in Guiana Sought," *New York Times*, July 16, 1964.

132. "Jagan Says Britons Seek to Defeat Him," *New York Times*, October 23, 1964.

133. "British Guiana's Dec. 7 Poll Is Set, London Tells Jagan," *New York Times*, October 30, 1964.

134. "Jagan Rebuffed on Independence," *New York Times*, October 31, 1964. On November 1, the *New York Times* carried a denial of U.S. pressure on Britain: "United

States sources indicated today that the decision of Britain's Labor Party Government to go ahead with a legislative election in British Guiana Dec. 7 had been reached without pressure from Washington and with American agreement.

They added that the decision should be regarded not as a concession to United States views but as a continuation of standing British policy as developed under the Conservative Government. The outcome of the elections will influence the British in deciding whether to grant early independence to their self-governing colony, it was said." See "U.S. Denies Pressing London over Guiana," *New York Times*, November 1, 1964.

135. Memorandum, Davis to Secretary, July 9, 1965. *Declassified Documents Quarterly Catalogue* 3, no. 2 (1977), State Department 116B.

7

Conclusion

The evolution of American policy toward the West Indies over the period 1940-64 is a case study of American responses to the growth of non-European nationalism and the decolonization of European imperial systems. It is also an evaluation of the importance of anticolonial sentiment as a factor influencing American foreign policy toward Europe and the rest of the world. From the 1930s to the end of World War II, American anticolonialism was largely directed against mercantilist policies used by the major powers to close imperial markets to foreign competition. These mercantilist policies had been implemented as a response to the collapse of the international trade and payments order during the 1920s. American criticism of colonialism reflected economic imperatives as the country struggled with the consequences of the depression of the late 1920s and 1930s. By 1942, American anticolonial rhetoric began to be influenced by the increasing demands of non-European nationalists for an end to European imperial systems. The spurt of American enthusiasm for, and endorsement of, non-European nationalism was influenced by the revelation of the bankruptcy of colonial rule in Asia as Japanese armies swept through the area. This enthusiasm represented both a response to popular sentiment and an attempt by the Roosevelt administration to neutralize Japan's championship of an Asia for Asians policy.

A significant component of American popular support for non-European nationalism came from the black American community that likened the situation of the subjects of European colonial rule to their own experience within the American political system. American anticolonial rhetoric during 1942 reflected an appeal to diverse domestic and foreign constituencies to build support for the American war effort. Its endorsement of non-European nationalism during 1942 and its efforts to broaden the application of the Atlantic Charter to the European colonies put America on a path to confrontation with its European allies. However, as the domestic climate cooled after 1942, and with the Allies gaining the upper hand in the war from

1943 on, American enthusiasm for non-European nationalism began to wane. By the end of the war and after Roosevelt's death, American policy began to reflect an increasing preoccupation with underwriting the anti-Communist coalition of European states.

This shift in focus of American policy resulted in a reassessment of American support for non-European nationalism after 1945. This reassessment of anti-colonialism as a factor in American foreign policy resulted in its refinement into an instrument of its anti-Communist strategy. As a consequence of this shift, American support for non-European nationalism became conditional upon such nationalism serving the American global strategy of containment of the communist states and their allies. The anti-Communist credentials of nationalist movements became a litmus-test for American support. Even then, American policy increasingly reflected support for the reassertion and maintenance of European colonial rule between 1945 and 1952.

European economic recovery required the mobilization of non-European resources to support postwar reconstruction. The continuation of mercantilist trade regimes within European empires after 1945, with tacit American support after 1947, was also necessary for European recovery. The visible weakness of Europe, including Britain, and the fear that such weakness would undermine the anti-Communist coalition of European states were critical to the American willingness to support the reassertion of European imperial authority. Buffeted by the costs of two major wars in less than a generation, the European colonial powers were in desperate need of both their empires and American assistance to bolster their recovery.

After 1945, the United States sought to utilize support for both non-European nationalism and European empire as instruments of its anti-Communist strategy. While support for non-European nationalism could be invoked to discredit the Soviet Union and burnish the American self-portrayal as an exemplar of anticolonialism, reality required a much more pragmatic stance in support of the European colonial powers.

It was this paradox that informed American responses to the decolonization process. The tensions generated by this gap between the rhetoric and actual policy emerged in the late 1940s as the United States confronted the dilemmas of Indonesian and Indochinese nationalists challenging their Dutch and French imperial masters. At various stages in the struggle between the Dutch and the Indonesian nationalists, the United States supported one side or the other, finally coming out in support of the nationalists. However, in the case of Indochina, American support was directed toward supporting French efforts to isolate and destroy the Vietnamese nationalist movement. While supporting one set of non-European nationalists against its ally, Holland, the United States refused to do the same for the Vietnamese against the French. This paradox in American policy manifested itself repeatedly as the decolonization process moved from Asia to North Africa, sub-Saharan Africa, and the Caribbean.

An examination of American policy toward the West Indies over the period 1940-64 demonstrates the parallels between the American responses to West Indian nationalism and its attitude to the decolonization process elsewhere. Beginning in 1940, American policymakers began to interact with the emergent nationalist movement of these colonies. Their sensitivity to the existing state of crisis in the West Indies was heightened by the fact that there had also been unrest in its own Caribbean colonies, Puerto Rico and the U.S. Virgin Islands, during the 1930s. In Puerto Rico, nationalist agitation had accompanied the unrest, and there was a growing demand for political reform that continued during the war.

Events in Asia also contributed to this heightened American sensitivity to the demands of non-European nationalists. Japan's military campaign in early 1942 rapidly transformed the map of Asia as the European and American colonies fell to Japanese forces. These Japanese military victories coincided with increasing unrest among black American communities in the United States. White American leaders championed anticolonialism in 1942 as a means of attracting support from black American constituencies for both the war effort and their own partisan purposes. These efforts to win support from the black American constituencies were in response to the latter's mobilization to demand equality within American society as the price of their participation in the war against the Axis powers. In 1942, unrest in the West Indian colonies resulting from the deteriorating economic situation, the use of American troops to quell that unrest, and fears of the impact of these events on black American opinion impelled the Roosevelt administration to pressure Britain into implementing far-reaching reforms in the West Indies. These reforms were major concessions to nationalist demands in the region. American enthusiasm for anticolonialism during 1942 was a response to the worsening security situation in the Caribbean and pressures from domestic constituencies to champion anticolonialism. It also reflected a fear that there would be a repeat of the events in Asia where Japan's military successes had revealed the bankruptcy of the colonial order.

Thus American policy in 1942 represented the first sign that anticolonialism was being transformed from an instrument of foreign economic policy into a device for winning support from domestic constituencies, and a tactic of security enhancement. It was a point of transition for American support for non-European nationalism. Security considerations were becoming paramount in American approaches to European colonialism. As Robert Dallek has shown, American policy toward Burma in 1942, where Roosevelt displayed little sympathy for nationalist aspirations, was diametrically opposed to policy toward India.[1] The support for Indian nationalists by the Roosevelt administration obviously reflected the greater importance India played in American strategy in Asia. Security concerns and support for non-European nationalism had become intertwined in the minds of American policymakers.[2] This linkage between American security concerns and policy towards non-European nationalism continued into the postwar period. American policy had shifted from an early endorsement of anticolonialism toward support for the European colonial powers.

Its participation in the Caribbean Commission and the decline of Taussig's influence within the ranks of the Truman administration were obvious indicators of the shift in American policy toward the West Indies. The restoration of a mercantilist trade regime in the West Indies after 1947, and West Indian discomfort with the strictures of this regime did not seem to elicit any American effort to pursue an aggressive trade policy in the region. As in other parts of the world, American policy was influenced by the priority given to British economic recovery. The reduction of the American military presence in these colonies was one indicator of the low sense of threat to the United States in the Western Hemisphere. In effect, without the conditions that had precipitated the American entry into and efforts to influence events in the West Indies, American policy displayed little enthusiasm for nationalist sentiment in the region and elsewhere. Other than in Indonesia, the Truman administration made little effort to champion the cause of non-European nationalism. The security of America's allies in Europe was of preeminent concern and there was no desire to jeopardize their status and influence in the non-European world.

The electoral victory of a radical nationalist movement in British Guiana in 1953 forced the conservative, newly installed Eisenhower administration to confront the growing militancy of non-European nationalism. While prepared to urge European powers to seek an accommodation with the burgeoning nationalist challenge within their empires, the Eisenhower administration was not above providing American support for attempts to suppress nationalist movements considered radical. The American support for Britain's military intervention in British Guiana in 1953 provided evidence of this policy in the first year of the administration. Similarly, in 1960, American policy in the Congo was directed at the suppression of the Lumumbist faction of the nationalist movement. This hostility to radical nationalism was accompanied by a deference to British policy in the Caribbean that seemed to contradict the public expressions of support for the right to self-determination for colonial subjects. Even in the case of an enthusiastically pro-American nationalist movement in British Honduras, the State Department was reluctant to support the nationalist challenge to colonial rule. It explicitly preferred to give priority to comity in Anglo-American relations on wider issues rather than strain the relationship by supporting nationalist demands for accelerating the pace of decolonization. This position was adopted well after the Suez crisis that has been perceived as a major turning point in American support for non-European nationalism.[3]

Finally, as the British began to withdraw from the West Indies, American policy reflected slight sensitivity to nationalist sentiment in these colonies. It took the prolonged and heated campaign by West Indian nationalist leaders to force the American government to concede that the Bases-for-Destroyers Agreement should be voided and replaced by a treaty negotiated among the West Indian, British and American governments. This lack of sensitivity to West Indian nationalism was accompanied by a determined effort to impose limits upon the ideological and political orientations of the nationalist movements in the West Indies. The attempt to unseat Eric Williams, though abortive, nevertheless reflected American intolerance of nationalist challenges to its rights in the West Indies. The identification of C. L. R. James, the West Indian nationalist of Trotskyite persuasion, as a threat to the West provided further evidence of American unwillingness to accept radical nationalists. Prior to the American covert intervention in British Guiana from 1962 onward, American efforts to intervene in Trinidad's politics represented the most serious attempt to impose its views upon West Indian nationalists. It was a signal of the American intention to incorporate the West Indies into its historic sphere of influence in the Caribbean.

American policy towards British Guiana over the period 1957-64 reflected the paradoxes of American policy toward the decolonization process in the Caribbean and wider international system. From 1953-57, American policy had actively supported British efforts to reverse the process of constitutional devolution as a means of undermining the People's Progressive Party. American concerns about the ideological orientation of the PPP and its militant anticolonialism served as a catalyst for renewed activism in the British West Indies. Again, as in the period 1940-42, security considerations were defining the American response to non-European nationalism. The PPP's return to office in 1957 revealed the failure of British and American policy. While it had suffered a serious split, the PPP retained its credibility and appeal within British Guiana. Confronted by the PPP's legitimacy, the moderation of its ideological and political stance, and British willingness to work with the Party, American policy shifted toward accommodation with the PPP. As on other occasions, American policy followed British shifts and demonstrated American deference to its European partners. There seemed to be little capacity for American policymakers to pursue an independent policy toward decolonization.

The Kennedy administration initially opted to continue the search for accommodation with the PPP. However, under the impact of the radicalization of the Cuban Revolution, the desperate strength of the anti-PPP forces in British Guiana, and pressure from domestic supporters of the anti-PPP forces, the Kennedy administration shifted tack. Fearing that an independent Guyana under the PPP would represent another Cuba in the American sphere of influence, American policymakers began a campaign to force Jagan from office with the active support of the British government and the opposition parties in the colony. In spite of the PPP's assurances that it would maintain an electoral democracy, provide guarantees to foreign investors, and pursue a nonaligned foreign policy, American policymakers lacked the sophistication necessary to deal with the PPP as a government. In the final analysis, American policy toward British Guiana from 1962 onward was driven by fear of the domestic repercussions of maintaining the policy of accommodation set in 1961. The conception of British Guiana as another Cuba had little to do with the policies of the PPP, and more to do with the hysteria unleashed in the United States by the radicalization of the Cuban Revolution. The greater the Cuban success in defying American attempts to overthrow the Castro government, the more desperate was the American effort to reassert its hegemony in the Caribbean. The PPP government fell victim to an American policy it did not understand and against which it had little defense.

In looking over the entire 1940-64 period, it is interesting to perceive the shift that had taken place among the various actors. During 1940-42, American policy had concentrated upon structural transformation of the West Indian economy, and the introduction of a new political dispensation in the colonies. By 1964, American policy stressed the necessity for ideological conformity in the region and fealty to the West in its conflict with the Communist states. Britain had been transformed from an imperial power, confident of its durability, to a declining power, dependent upon its relationship with the United States to maintain a semblance of its status as a major power. Its retreat from the Caribbean, begun at the end of the nineteenth century, continued unabated. For the West Indian territories, the problem of economic diversification had yet to be resolved. Agricultural exports, including sugar, remained dependent upon access to a protected market in Britain. Jamaica, British Guiana, Barbados, and Trinidad had managed to create fairly viable economies and were actively pursuing strategies of industrialization. For the majority of the other territories, continued dependence on Britain was the order of the day. And finally, independence marked the passage of these territories from British colonialism to American hegemony.

These changes in the Anglo-American-West Indian relationship mirrored the processes of change in the wider international system. Nationalism and decolonization had helped to force the realignment of power in the international system. The Western European powers were weakened by the collapse of their empires while American influence had reached unprecedented proportions. However, rather than validate American anticolonialism, the decolonization process in the Caribbean and the wider world revealed the fundamental ambiguity of American claims to be a champion of self-determination.

NOTES

1. Robert Dallek, *Franklin D. Roosevelt and American Foreign Policy, 1932-1945* (New York: Oxford University Press, 1979), 327-28.

2. See Gary R. Hess, *America Encounters India, 1941-47* (Baltimore: Johns Hopkins Press, 1971), 74. Hess argues that the Roosevelt administration viewed "willingness to support the Allied cause and to accept postponement of freedom . . . . (as) a test of colonial people's worthiness" to win American support for their right to independence.

3. Seyom Brown, *The Faces of Power* (New York: Columbia University Press, 1968), 104-8.

Bibliography

PRIMARY SOURCES

Franklin D. Roosevelt Library: Papers of C. W. Taussig
Eisenhower Library: Papers of Dwight D. Eisenhower as President
John F. Kennedy Library: Papers of Arthur Schlesinger, Jr., White House Files
National Archives: Department of State, Record Group 59, Decimal File, and Intelligence Reports.
Public Records Office: Foreign Office Files, FO/371.
Published Collections:
Foreign Relations of the United States 1945, Department of State.
Declassified Documents Reference Service, University Press of America.
Declassified Documents Quarterly Catalogue, University Press of America.

SECONDARY SOURCES

Books

Ambrose, Stephen E. *Eisenhower: The President*. London: George Allen and Unwin, 1984.

Anderson, T. H. *The United States, Great Britain and the Cold War, 1944-1947*. Columbia: University of Missouri Press, 1981.

Andic, F. M. and T. G. Matthews. (eds.) *The Caribbean in Transition*. Rio Piedras,P.R.: Institute of Caribbean Studies, 1965.

Ayearst, Morley. *The British West Indies: The Search for Self-Government*. New York: New York University Press, 1960.

Baldwin, David. *Economic Development and American Foreign Policy, 1943-1962*. Chicago: University of Chicago Press, 1966.

Barker, Elizabeth. *The British between the Superpowers, 1945-1950.* London: Macmillan, 1983.

Barnhart, Michael A. *Japan Prepares for Total War: The Search for Economic Security, 1919-1941.* Ithaca: Cornell University Press, 1987.

Baylis, J. *Anglo-American Defence Relations, 1939-1980.* London: Macmillan, 1981.

Bell, Wendell. (ed.) *The Democratic Revolution in the West Indies.* Cambridge: Schenkman Publishing Company, 1967.

Berman, William C. *The Politics of Civil Rights in the Truman Administration.* Columbus: Ohio State University Press, 1970.

Best, Lloyd, and Kari Levitt. *Externally-Propelled Growth in the Caribbean: Selected Essays.* Montreal: McGill University, 1967.

Blanshard, Paul. *Democracy and Empire in the Caribbean.* New York: Macmillan, 1947

Boahen, A. Adu. *African Perspectives on Colonialism.* Baltimore: The Johns Hopkins University Press, 1987.

Blum, Robert M. *Drawing the Line: The Origin of the American Containment Policy in East Asia.* New York: W. W. Norton, 1982.

Brown, Seyom. *The Faces of Power: Constancy and Change in United States Foreign Policy from Truman to Johnson.* New York: Columbia University Press, 1968.

Bryce-Laporte, Roy S., and Delores M. Mortimer. *Caribbean Immigration to the United States.* Washington D.C.: Smithsonian Institution, 1983.

Bunche, Ralph J. *The Political Status of the Negro in the Age of FDR.* Chicago: University of Chicago Press, 1973.

Burk, Robert F. *The Eisenhower Administration and Black Civil Rights.* Knoxville: University of Tennessee Press, 1984.

Campbell, Charles S. *Anglo-American Understanding, 1898-1903.* Baltimore: The Johns Hopkins Press, 1957.

Cayton, Horace R., and St. Clair Drake. *Black Metropolis.* London: Jonathan Cape, 1946.

Clark, Sir R. *Anglo-American Collaboration in War and Peace, 1942-1949.* Oxford: Clarendon Press, 1982.

Collier, John. *America's Colonial Record.* London: Fabian Publications Ltd., 1947.

Conn, Stetson, and Byron Fairchild. *United States Army in World War II: The Western Hemisphere.* Washington, D.C.: Department of the Army, 1960.

Corkran, Herbert, Jr. *Patterns of International Co-operation in the Caribbean, 1942-1969.* Dallas: Southern Methodist University Press, 1970.

Crassweller, Robert D. *The Caribbean Community: Changing Societies and U.S. Policy.* New York: Praeger Publishers, 1972.

Cruse, Harold. *The Crisis of the Negro Intellectual.* New York: William Morrow, 1967.

Dallek, Robert. *Franklin D. Roosevelt and American Foreign Policy, 1932-1945.* New York: Oxford University Press, 1979.

Davie, Maurice R. *Negroes in American Society.* New York: McGraw-Hill, 1949.

de Kadt, E. *Patterns of Foreign Influence in the Caribbean.* London: Oxford University Press, 1972

Demas, William. *The Economics of Development in Small Countries with Special Reference to the Caribbean.* Montreal: McGill University Press, 1965.

Dickson, David. *United States Foreign Policy Towards Sub-Saharan Africa.* Lanham: University Press of America, 1985.

Dilks, D. (ed.) *Retreat from Power: Studies in Britain's Foreign Policy of the 20th Century.* London: Macmillan, 1981.

Divine, Robert A. *Eisenhower and the Cold War.* New York: Oxford University Press, 1981.

Dobson, Alan P. *U.S. Wartime Aid to Britain, 1940-46.* New York: St. Martin's Press, 1986.

Draper, Theodore. *American Communism and Soviet Russia.* New York: Viking Press, 1960.

Dulles, Foster R. *The Imperial Years.* New York: Thomas Cromwell, 1956.

Eckes, Alfred E., Jr. *The United States and the Global Struggle for Minerals.* Austin: University of Texas Press, 1979.

Feinberg, Richard E. *The Intemperate Zone: The Third World Challenge to United States Foreign Policy.* New York: W.W. Norton, 1983.

Ferrell, Robert H. (ed.) *The Eisenhower Diaries.* New York: W.W. Norton, 1981.

Fox, Annette Baker. *Freedom and Welfare in the Caribbean: A Colonial Dilemma.* New York: Harcourt Brace, 1949.

Frazier, Franklin E., and Eric Williams. *The Economic Future of the Caribbean.* Washington, D.C.: Howard University Press, 1944.

Freeland, Richard M. *The Truman Doctrine and the Origins of McCarthyism: Foreign Policy, Domestic Policy, and Internal Security, 1946-1948.* New York: Alfred A. Knopf, 1971.

Fried, Richard M. *Nightmare in Red: The McCarthy Era in Perspective.* New York: Oxford University Press, 1990

Gaddis, John Lewis. *The United States and the Origins of the Cold War, 1941-1947.* New York: Columbia University Press, 1972.

------. *Strategies of Containment.* New York: Oxford University Press, 1982.

Gallagher, John. *The Decline, Revival and Fall of the British Empire.* Cambridge: Cambridge University Press, 1982.

Gardner, Lloyd. *Economic Aspects of New Deal Diplomacy.* Madison: University of Wisconsin Press, 1964.

Gardner, Richard N. *Sterling-Dollar Diplomacy*, 2nd ed. London: McGraw-Hill, 1969. 2nd edition.

Geiss, Immanuel. *The Pan-African Movement*. London: Methuen University Paperback, 1974.

Girvan, Norman. *Foreign Capital and Economic Underdevelopment in Jamaica*. Jamaica: University of the West Indies, 1971.

Goldsworthy, David. *Colonial Issues in British Politics, 1945-1961: From "Colonial Development" to "Wind of Change."* Oxford: Clarendon Press, 1971.

Graham, Ronald. *The Aluminium Industry and the Third World*. London: Zed, 1982.

Green, David. *The Containment of Latin America*. New York: Quadrangle Books, 1971.

Greenstein, Fred I. *The Hidden Hand Presidency: Eisenhower as Leader*. New York: Basic Books, 1982.

Gupta, Partha Sarathi *Imperialism and the British Labour Movement, 1914-1964*. London: Macmillan, 1975.

Hargreaves, J. D. *Decolonization in Africa*. London: Longman, 1988.

Hathaway, Robert M. *Ambiguous Partnership: Britain and America, 1944-1947*. New York: Columbia University Press, 1981.

Henry, Frances. (ed.) *Ethnicity in the Americas*. The Hague: Monton Publishers, 1976.

Hinden, Rita. *Empire and After: A Study of British Imperial Attitudes*. London: Essential Books Ltd., 1949.

Hoopes, Townsend. *The Devil and John Foster Dulles*. Boston: Little, Brown, 1973.

Hopkins, A. G. *An Economic History of West Africa*. London: Longman, 1973.

Horne, Gerald. *Black and Red: W.E.B. Dubois and the Afro-American Response to the Cold War, 1944-1963*. Albany: State University of New York Press, 1986.

Horowitz, David. *The Free World Colossus*. New York: Hill and Wang, 1965.

Hudson, G. F., R. Lowenthal, and R. MacFarquhar. *The Sino-Soviet Dispute*. New York: Frederick A. Praeger, 1961.

Huggins, H.D. *Aluminium in Changing Communities*. Jamaica: University of the West Indies, 1965.

James, C. L. R. *The Case for West Indian Self-Government*. London: L. & V. Woolf, 1933.

Jefferson, Owen. *The Post-War Economic Development of Jamaica*. Jamaica: Institute of Social and Economic Research, 1972.

Kaufman, Burton I. *Trade and Aid: Eisenhower's Foreign Policy, 1953-1961*. Baltimore: Johns Hopkins University Press, 1982.

Kneer, Warren G. *Great Britiain and the Caribbean, 1901-1913: A Study in Anglo-American Relations*. East Lansing: Michigan State University Press, 1975.

Knowles, Yereth K. *Beyond the Caribbean States: A History of Regional Co-operation in the Commonwealth Caribbean*. Puerto Rico: Caribbean Institute and Study Center for Latin America, 1972.

Kolko, Gabriel. *The Politics of War: The World and United States Foreign Policy, 1943-1945*. New York: Random House, 1968.

Kolko, Gabriel, and Joyce Kolko. *The Limits of Power: The World and United States Foreign Policy 1945-1954*. New York: Harper and Row, 1972.

Lafeber, Walter *America, Russia and the Cold War, 1945-1975*, 3rd. ed. New York: John Wiley and Sons, 1976.

LaGuerre, John Gaffar. *The Social and Political Thought of the Colonial Intelligentsia*. Jamaica: Institute of Social and Economic Research, 1982.

Langley, J. Ayodele. *Pan-Africanism and Nationalism in West Africa, 1900-1945*. London: Oxford Press, 1973.

Langley, Lester D. *The United States and the Caribbean, 1900-1970*. Athens: University of Georgia Press, 1982.

Larson, Deborah Welch. *Origins of Containment: A Psychological Explanation*. Princeton: Princeton University Press, 1985.

Lee, J. M. *Colonial Development and Good Government*. Oxford: Clarendon Press, 1967.

Leutze, James R. *Bargaining for Supremacy: Anglo-American Naval Collaboration, 1937-1941*. Chapel Hill: University of North Carolina Press, 1977.

Lewis, Gordon K. *The Growth of the Modern West Indies*. London: MacGibbon and Kee, 1968.

Louis, William Roger. *Imperialism at Bay, 1941-1945*. Oxford: Clarendon Press, 1977.

Louis, William Roger and Prosser Gifford. (eds.) *The Transfer of Power in Africa: Decolonization, 1940-1960*. New Haven: Yale University Press, 1982.

------. *The British Empire in the Middle East, 1945-1951*. New York: Oxford University press, 1984.

------. and Headley Bull. (eds.) *The Special Relationship: Anglo-American Relations since 1945*. New York: Oxford University Press, 1986.

Lowenthal, David. *The West Indies Federation*. New York: Columbia University Press, 1961.

Mahoney, Richard D. *JFK: Ordeal in Africa*. New York: Oxford University Press, 1983.

Marshall, D. Bruce. *The French Colonial Myth and Constitution-Making in the Fourth Republic*. New Haven: Yale University Press, 1973.

McCoy, Donald, and Richard Ruetten. *Quest and Response: Minority Rights and the Truman Administration*. Lawrence: University of Kansas Press, 1973.

McMahon, Robert J. *Colonialism and Cold War: The United States and the Struggle for Indonesian Independence, 1945-1949*. Ithaca: Cornell University Press, 1981.

Meyer, F. V. *Britain's Colonies in World Trade*. London: Oxford University Press, 1948.

------. *Britain, the Sterling Area, and Europe*. Cambridge: Bowes & Bowes, 1952.

Milward, Alan S. *The Reconstruction of Western Europe, 1945-51*. Berkeley: University of California Press, 1984.

Mintz, Sidney W., and Sally Price. *Caribbean Contours*. Baltimore: Johns Hopkins University Press, 1985.

Mordecai, John. *The West Indies: The Federal Negotiations*. London: Allen & Unwin, 1968.

Morgan, D.J. *The Official History of Colonial Development*. vols. 1-5. London: Macmillan, 1980.

Morgan, Kenneth O. *Labour in Power, 1945-51*. New York: Oxford University Press, 1984.

Munro, Dana G. *Intervention and Dollar Diplomacy in the Caribbean, 1900-1921*. Princeton: Princeton University Press, 1964.

Munroe, Trevor. *The Politics Of Constitutional Decolonization: Jamaica, 1944-62*. Jamaica: University of the West Indies, 1984.

Nagai, Yonosuke, and Akira Iriye. *The Origins of the Cold War in Asia*. Tokyo: University of Tokyo Press, 1977.

Naison, Mark. *Communists in Harlem During the Depression*. Chicago: University of Illinois Press, 1983.

Nelson, Anna Kasten (ed.) *The State Department Policy Planning Papers, 1947-1949*. New York: Garland Publishing, 1983.

Nicholas, H. G. (ed.) *Washington Despatches, 1941-1945: Weekly Political Reports from the British Embassy*. Chicago: University of Chicago Press, 1981.

Noer, Thomas J. *Cold War and Black Liberation: The United States and White Rule in Africa, 1948-1968*. Columbia: University of Missouri Press, 1985.

Owen, Roger, and Bob Sutcliffe (eds.) *Studies in the Theory of Imperialism*. London: Longman, 1972.

Packenham, Robert A. *Liberal America and the Third World*. Princeton: Princeton University Press, 1973.

Palme Dutt, R. *The Crisis of Britain and the Empire*. London: Lawrence & Wishart, 1953.

Palmer, Ransford W. *Caribbean Dependence on the United States Economy*. New York: Praeger Publishers, 1979.

Pastor, Robert A. *Congress and the Politics of U.S. Foreign Economic Policy, 1929-1976*. Berkeley: University of California Press, 1980.

Paterson, Thomas G. *On Every Front: The Making of the Cold War*. New York: W. W. Norton, 1979.

------. (ed.) *Kennedy's Quest for Victory*. New York: Oxford University Press, 1989.

Pelling, Henry. *The Labour Governments, 1945-1951*. New York: St. Martin's Press, 1984.

Perkins, Whitney T. *Constraint of Empire: United States and Caribbean Interventions*. Westport: Greenwood Press, 1981.

Pollard, Robert A. *Economic Security and the Origins of the Cold War, 1945-1950*. New York: Columbia University Press, 1985.

Proudfoot, Mary. *Britain and the United States in the Caribbean*. London: Faber & Faber, 1954.

Poole, Bernard L. *The Caribbean Commission: Background of Co-operation in the West Indies*. Columbia: University of South Carolina Press, 1951.

Post, Ken. *Strike the Iron*. vols. 1- 2. Atlantic Highlands, N.J.: Humanities Press, 1981.

Reynolds, David. *The Creation of the Anglo-American Alliance, 1937-1941*. Chapel Hill: University of North Carolina Press, 1982.

Roosevelt, Theodore. *Colonial Policies of the United States*. New York: Doubleday, Doran & Company, 1937.

Rose, Lisle A. *Dubious Victory*. Kent, Ohio: Kent State University Press, 1973.

------. *Roots of Tragedy: The United States and the Struggle for Asia, 1945-1953*. Westport, Conn: Greenwood Press, 1976.

Rosen, S. McKee. *The Combined Boards of the Second World War*. New York: Columbia University Press, 1951.

Rothwell, Victor. *Britain and the Cold War, 1941-47*. London: Jonathan Cape, 1982.

Rubin, Barry. *Secrets of State*. New York: Oxford University Press, 1987.

Ryan, Selwyn D. *Race and Nationalism in Trinidad and Tobago*. Toronto: University of Toronto Press, 1972.

Sbrega, John J. *Anglo-American Relations and Colonialism in East Asia*. New York: Garland Publishing, 1983.

Simey, T. S. *Welfare and Planning in the West Indies*. Oxford: Clarendon Press, 1946.

Smith, M. G. *The Plural Society in the British West Indies*. Berkeley: University of California Press, 1974.

Smith, Tony *The French Stake in Algeria*. Ithaca: Cornell University Press, 1978.

------. *The Pattern of Imperialism*. Cambridge: Cambridge University Press, 1981.

Spinner, Thomas J., Jr. *A Political and Social History of Guyana, 1945-1983.* Boulder, Colo.: Westview Press, 1984.

Strausz-Hupe, Robert, and Harry W. Hazard (eds.) *The Idea of Colonialism.* London: Atlantic Books, 1958.

Stueck, William Whitney, Jr., *The Road to Confrontation: American Policy toward China and Korea, 1947-1950.* Chapel Hill: University of North Carolina Press, 1981.

Sutton, Paul K. *Forged from the Love of Liberty.* Trinidad: Longman Caribbean, 1981.

Szulc, Tad. *The United States and the Caribbean* Englewood Cliffs, N.J.: Prentice-Hall, 1971.

Thorne, Christopher. *Allies of A Kind: The United States, Great Britain and the War against Japan, 1941-1945.* London: Hamilton, 1978.

Tugwell, Rexford G. *The Democratic Roosevelt.* New York: Doubleday, 1957.

van Alstyne, R. W. *The Rising American Empire.* Oxford: Basil Blackwell, 1960.

von Albertini, Rudolf. *European Colonial Rule, 1880-1940.* Oxford: Clio Press, 1982.

Wall, Irwin M. *L'influence americaine sur la politique française 1945-1954.* Paris: Balland, 1989.

Wallace, Elizabeth. *The British Caribbean.* Toronto: University of Toronto Press, 1977.

Watt, Cameron D. *Succeeding John Bull.* Cambridge: Cambridge University Press, 1984.

Weston, R. F. *Racism in United States Imperialism.* Columbia: University of South Carolina Press, 1972.

Wilgus, Alva C. (ed.) *The Caribbean: Contemporary International Relations.* Gainesville: University of Florida Press, 1957.

------. *The Caribbean: Peoples, Problems and Prospects.* Gainesville: University of Florida Press, 1962.

------. *The Caribbean: Its Hemispheric Role.* Gainesville: University of Florida Press, 1967.

Whitaker, Arthur P. *The Western Hemisphere Idea.* New York: Cornell University Press, 1954.

Yergin, Daniel *Shattered Peace: The Origins of the Cold War and the National Security State.* Boston: Houghton Miffin Company, 1977.

Zagoria, Donald *The Sino-Soviet Conflict, 1956-1961.* Princeton: Princeton University Press, 1962.

Articles

Abbott, George C. "A Re-examination of the 1929 Colonial Development Act." *Economic History Review* 24, no. 1 (1971), 68-81.

Abrams, Richard M. "United States Intervention Abroad." *American Historical Review* 79, no. 1 (1974), 72-102.

Adamthwaite, Anthony "Britain and the World, 1945-49: The View from the Foreign Office." *International Affairs* 61, no. 2 (1985), 223-36.

Ajayi, J .F .A. and R. A. Austen. "Hopkins on Economic Imperialism in West Africa." *Economic History Review* 25, no. 2 (1972), 303-12.

Allen, William R. "The International Trade Philosophy of Cordell Hull, 1907-1933." *American Economic Review* 43, no. 1 (1953), 101-16.

Anderson, Stuart. "Racial Anglo-Saxonism and the American Response to the Boer War." *Diplomatic History* 2, no. 3 (1978), 219-36.

Anstey, Caroline. "The Projection of British Socialism: Foreign Office Publicity and American Opinion, 1945-1950." *Journal of Contemporary History* 19 (1984), 417-51.

Archibald, C. "The Failure of the West Indies Federation." *World Today* 18, no.6 (1962), 233-42.

Barrow, Christine. "Ownership and Control of Resources in Barbados: 1834 to the present." *Social and Economic Studies* 32, no. 3 (1983), 83-120.

Basdeo, Sahadeo. "Colonial Policy and Labour Organization in the British Caribbean 1937-1939: An Issue in Political Sovereignty." *Boletin de Estudios Latinoamericanos y del Caribe* 31 (1981), 119-29.

------. "The Role of the British Labour Movement in the Development of Labour Organization in Trinidad 1929-1938." *Social and Economic Studies* 31, no. 1 (1982), 40-73.

------. "Walter Citrine and the British Caribbean Workers Movement during the Moyne Commission Hearing, 1938-9." *Journal of Caribbean History* 18, no. 2, (1983), 43-59.

Baylis, John. "Defence Policy Analysis and the Study of Changes in Post-War British Defence Policy." *International Relations* 4, no. 4, (1973), 383-99.

Beck, Kent M. "Necessary Lies, Hidden Truths: Cuba in the 1960 campaign." *Diplomatic History* 8, no. 1 (1984), 37-61.

Bell, P. W. "Colonialism as a Problem in American Foreign Policy." *World Politics* 5, no. 1 (1952), 86-109.

Bell, Wendell. "Equality and Social Justice: Foundations of Nationalism in the Caribbean." *Caribbean Studies* 20, no. 2 (1980), 3-36.

Ben-Zvi, Abraham. "In Pursuit of National Security: A Juxtaposition of American Images and Policies." *Journal of Strategic Studies* 4, no. 4 (1981), 386-414.

Berle, A. A. "The Cuban Crisis: Failure of American Foreign Policy." *Foreign Affairs* 39, no. 1 (1960), 40-55.

Bhana, Surendra. "Puerto Rico and the Truman Administration, 1945-47: Self-Government `Little by Little.'" *Prologue* 5, no. 3 (1973), 155-66.

Bolland, O. Nigel. "Systems of Domination after Slavery: The Control of Land and Labor in the British West Indies after 1838." *Comparative Studies in Society and History* 23, no. 4 (1981), 591-619.

Bowen, Gordon L. "U.S. Policy toward Guatemala 1954 to 1963." *Armed Forces and Society* 10, no. 2 (1984), 165-91.

Bowen, N., and E. J. Hughes. "Guatemala, 1954: Intervention and Jurisdiction." *International Relations* 4, no. 1 (1972), 78-93.

Boyce, R.W.D. "America, Europe, and the Triumph of Imperial Protectionism in Britain, 1929-30." *Millennium* 3, no. 1 (1974), 53-70.

Buchan, Alastair. "American perceptions of the post-war world." *British Journal of International Studies* 3, no. 3 (1977), 331-39.

Buckley, Roger. "Joining the Club: The Japanese Question and Anglo-American Peace Diplomacy, 1950-1951." *Modern Asian Studies* 19, no. 2 (1985), 299-319.

Child, John. "From `Color' to `Rainbow': U.S. Strategic Planning for Latin America, 1919-1945." *Journal of International Studies* 21, no. 2 (1979), 233-59.

Clarke, Colin G. "The Quest for Independence in the Caribbean." *Journal of Latin American Studies* 9, no. 2 (1977); 337-45.

------. "Colonialism and its Social and Cultural Consequences in the Caribbean." *Journal of Latin American Studies* 15, no. 2 (1983), 491-503.

Clymer, Kenton J. "The Education of William Phillips: Self-Determination and American Policy Towards India, 1942-45." *Diplomatic History*, 8, no. 1 (1984), 13-36.

Colbert, Evelyn. "The Road Not Taken: Decolonization and Independence in Indonesia and Indochina." *Foreign Affairs* 51, no. 3 (1973), 608-28.

Collart, Yves. "Limites à la Décolonization." *Relations Internationales*, no. 18 (1979), 115-30.

Conniff, Michael L. "Black Labor on a White Canal: West Indians in Panama, 1940-1980." *Latin American Institute Research Paper Series*, no. 11 (1983), University of New Mexico.

Croft, Stuart. "British Policy towards Western Europe, 1947-9: The Best of Possible Worlds." *International Affairs* 64, no. 4 (1988), 617-29.

Cromwell, William C. "The Marshall Plan, Britain and the Cold War." *Review of International Studies* 8, no. 4 (1982), 233-49.

Dalfiume, Richard. "The Forgotten Years of the Negro Revolution." *Journal of American History* 55, no. 1 (1968), 90-106.

Darwin, John. "British Decolonization since 1945: A Pattern or a Puzzle." *Journal of Imperial and Commonwealth History* 12, no. 2 (1984) 187-209.

Davis, George. "Laos: Roots of American Involvement." *Millennium* 11, no. 2 (1973), 27-43.

De Galindez, Jesus. "Government and Politics in Puerto Rico: New Formula for Self-Government." *International Affairs* 30, no. 3 (1954), 331-41.

Divine, Robert A. "The Cold War and the Election of 1948." *Journal of American History* 59, no. 1 (1972), 90-110.

Dobson, Alan P. "The Kennedy Administration and Economic Warfare Against Communism." *International Affairs* 64, no. 4 (1988), 599-616.

Doenecke, Justus D. "Non-Interventionism on the Left: The Keep America out of the War Congress, 1938-1941." *Journal of Contemporary History* 12, no. 2 (1977), 221-36.

Dulles, Foster Rhea, and Gerald E. Ridinger. "The Anti-Colonial Policies of Franklin D. Roosevelt." *Political Science Quarterly* 70, no. 1 (1955) 1-18.

Dulles, John Foster. "Policy for Security and Peace." *Foreign Affairs* 32, no. 3 (1954), 353-64.

------. "Challenge and Response in United States Foreign Policy." *Foreign Affairs* 36, no. 1 (1957), 25-43.

Ekoko, A. Edho. "The British Attitude Towards Germany's Colonial Irredentism in Africa in the Inter-War Years." *Journal of Contemporary History* 14, no. 2 (1979), 287-307.

Emerson, Rupert. "Reflections on the Indonesian Case." *World Politics* 1, no. 1 (1948), 59-81.

------. "The United Nations and Colonialism." *International Relations* 3, no. 10 (1970), 766-81.

Emerson, Rupert, and Martin Kilson. "The American Dilemma in a Changing World: The Rise of Africa and the Negro American." *Daedalus* 94 no. 4 (1965), 1055-84.

Falk, Richard. "The Failure of American Foreign Policy to Adjust to the End of the Postwar World." *Current Research on Peace and Violence* 6, nos. 2-3 (1983), 77-113.

Farrell, Terrence. "Arthur Lewis and the Case for Caribbean Industrialization." *Social and Economic Studies* 29, no. 4 (1980), 52-75.

Field, James A., Jr. "American Imperialism: The `Worst' Chapter in Almost Any Book." *American Historical Review*, 83, no. 3 (1978), 664-83.

Fielder, Peter C. "The Pattern of Super-Power Crises." *International Relations* 3, no. 7 (1969), 498-510.

Frieden, Jeff "Sectoral Conflict and Foreign Economic Policy, 1914-40." *International Organization* 42, no. 1 (1988), 59-90.

Frieden, Jeffrey A. "The Economics of Intervention: American Overseas Investments and Relations with Underdeveloped Areas, 1890-1950." *Comparative Studies in Society and History* 31, no. 1 (1989), 55-80.

Gaddis, John Lewis. "Was the Truman Doctrine a Real Turning Point?" *Foreign Affairs* 52, no. 2 (1974), 386-402.

------. "Containment: A Reassessment." *Foreign Affairs* 55, no. 4 (1977), 873-87.

------. "Containment: Its Past and Future." *International Security* 5, no. 4 (1981), 74-102.

------. "The Rise, Fall and Future of Detente." *Foreign Affairs* 62, no. 2 (1983).

Garson, Robert A. "American Foreign Policy and the Limits of Power: Eastern Europe, 1946-1950." *Journal of Contemporary History* 21, no. 3 (1986), 347-66.

George, Alexander L. "American Policy-Making and the North Korean Aggression." *World Politics* 7, no. 2 (1955).

Griffith, Robert. "The Political Context of McCarthyism." *The Review of Politics* 33, no. 1 (1971), 24-35.

Gilchrist, Henry. "The United Nations: Colonial Questions at the San Francisco Conference." *American Political Science Review* 39, no. 5 (1945), 982-92.

Gonzalez, Edward. "Castro's Revolution, Cuban Communist Appeals and the Soviet Response." *World Politics* 21, no. 1 (1968), 39-68.

Graebner, Norman. "Whither Containment?" *International Journal* 24, no. 2 (1969), 246-63.

Green, William A. "The Creolization of Caribbean History." *Journal of Imperial and Commonwealth History* 14, no. 3 (1986), 149-69.

Haines, Gerald K. "Under the Eagle's Wing: The Franklin Roosevelt Administration Forges an American Hemisphere." *Diplomatic History* 1, no. 4 (1977), 373-88.

------. "American Myopia and the Japanese Monroe Doctrine, 1931-1941." *Prologue* 13, no. 2 (1981), 101-14.

Harbutt, Fraser. "Churchill, Hopkins, and the `other' Americans: An Alternative Perspective on Anglo-American Relations, 1941-1945." *International History Review* 8, no. 2 (1986), 236-62.

Henry, Keith S. "The Black Political Tradition in New York: A Conjunction of Political Cultures." *Journal of Black Studies* 7, no. 4 (1977), 455-84.

Herring, George C., Jr. "The United States and British Bankruptcy, 1944-1945: Responsibilities Deferred." *Political Science Quarterly* 86, no. 2 (1971), 260-80.

------. "The Truman Administration and the Restoration of French Sovereignty in Indo-China." *Diplomatic History* 1, no. 2 (1977), 97-117.

Hess, Gary. "United States Policy and the Origins of the French-Viet Minh War, 1945-46." *Peace and Change* 3, nos.2-3 (1975), 21-33.

------. "The First American Commitment in Indo-China: The Acceptance of the `Bao Dai' Solution", 1950." *Diplomatic History* 2, no. 4 (1978), 331-50.

Hinds, Allister E. "Sterling and Imperial Policy, 1945-51" *Journal of Imperial and Commonwealth History* 15, no. 2 (1987), 148-69.

Hoffman, Stanley. "Old Wine, Old Bottles: American Foreign Policy and the Politics of Nostalgia." *Millennium* 9, no. 2 (1980), 91-107.

Hogan, Michael. "Revival and Reform: America's Twentieth-Century Search for a New Economic Order Abroad." *Diplomatic History* 8, no. 4 (1984), 287-310.

Holland, R. F. "The Imperial Factor In British Strategies from Attlee to Macmillan, 1945-63." *Journal of Imperial and Commonwealth History* 12, no. 2 (1984), 187-208.

Holsti, Ole R., and James N. Rosenau. "Vietnam, Consensus, and the Belief Systems of American Leaders." *World Politics* 32, no. 1 (1979), 1-56.

------. "U.S. Leadership in a Shrinking World: The Breakdown of Consensuses and the Emergence of Conflicting Belief Systems." *World Politics* 35, no. 3 (1983), 368-92.

Hosoya, Chihiro. "Japan, China, The United States and the United Kingdom, 1951-52: Che Case of the `Yoshida Letter.'" *International Affairs* 60, no. 2 (1984), 247-59.

Immerman, Richard H. "Guatemala as Cold War History." *Political Science Quarterly* 95, no. 4 (1980-81), 629-53.

Johnson, Caswell. "The Emergence of Political Unionism in Economies of British Colonial Origin: The Cases of Jamaica and Trinidad." *American Journal of Economics and Sociology* 39, nos. 2 & 3 (1980), 151-64 and 237-48.

Johnson, Howard. "The United States and the Establishment of the Anglo-American Caribbean Commission." *Journal of Caribbean History* 19, no. 1 (1984), 9-46.

------. " The Anglo-American Caribbean Commission and the Extension of American Influence in the British Caribbean, 1942-1945." *Journal of Commonwealth and Comparative Politics* 22, no. 2 (1984), 180-203.

Kaufman, Burton I. "The United States Response to the Soviet Economic Offensive of the 1950s." *Diplomatic History* 2, no. 2 (1978), 153-66.

Keal, Paul. "Contemporary Understanding about Spheres of Influence." *Review of International Studies* 9, no. 2 (1983), 155-72.

Kennedy, Paul M. "Strategy versus Finance in Twentieth-Century Great Britain." *International History Review* 11, no. 1 (1981), 44-61.

Kepley, David R. "The Senate and the Great debate of 1951." *Prologue* 14, no. 4 (1982), 213-26.

Kimball, Warren F. " `Beggar My Neighbor': America and the British Interim Finance Crisis, 1940-1941." *Journal of Economic History* 29, no. 4 (1969), 758-72.

------. "Lend-Lease and the Open Door: The Temptation of British Opulence, 1937-1942." *Political Science Quarterly* 86, no. 2 (1971), 232-59.

Kindleberger, Charles P. "The Marshall Plan and the Cold War." *International Journal* 23, no. 3 (1968), 369-82.

Knight, Wayne. "Labourite Britain: America's Sure Friend." *Diplomatic History* 7, no. 4 (1983).

Krakau, Knud. "American Foreign Relations: A National Style." *Diplomatic History* 8, no. 3 (1984), 253-72.

LaFeber, Walter. "Roosevelt, Churchill, and Indochina:1942-45." *American Historical Review* 80, no. 5 (1975), 1277-95.

------. "The `Lion in the Path': The U.S. Emergence as a World Power." *Political Science Quarterly* 101, no. 5 (1986), 705-18.

LaGuerre, J. Gafar. "The Moyne Commission and the Jamaican Left." *Social and Economic Studies* 31, no. 3 (1982).

Lake, David A. "The State and American Trade Strategy in the Pre-Hegemonic Era." *International Organization* 42, no. 1 (1988), 33-58.

Lattimore, Owen. "The Fight for Democracy in Asia." *Foreign Affairs* 20, no. 4 (1942), 694-704.

Laurence, K. O. "Colonialism in Trinidad and Tobago." *Caribbean Quarterly* 9, no. 3 (1963), 44-56.

Lee, C. H. "The Effects of the Depression on Primary Producing Countries." *Journal of Contemporary History* 4, no. 4 (1969), 187-200.

Lees, Lorraine M. "The American Decision to Assist Tito,1948-1949." *Diplomatic History* 2, no. 4 (1978), 407-22.

Louis, William Roger. "American anti-colonialism and the Dissolution of the British Empire." *International Affairs* 61, no. 3 (1985), 395-420.

Lowenthal, Mark M. "Roosevelt and the Coming of the War: The Search for United States Policy, 1937-42." *Journal of Contemporary History* 16, no. 3 (1981), 413-40.

Macmillan, Mona. "The Making of Warning from the West Indies." *Journal of Commonwealth and Comparative Politics* 18, no. 2 (1980).

Maddock, R. T. "The Politics of Trade--The American Experience since 1945." *International Relations* 6, no. 1 (1978), 272-301.

Mark, Eduard. "The Question of Containment: A Reply to John Lewis Gaddis." *Foreign Affairs* 56, no. 2 (1978), 430-41.

Marvel, W. Macy. "Drift and Intrigue: United States Relations with the Viet-Minh, 1945." *Millennium* 4, no. 1 (1975), 10-27.

Mayers, David. "Eisenhower's Containment Policy and the Major Communist Powers, 1953-1956." *International History Review* 5, no. 1 (1983), 59-83.

McLellan, David S. "Who Fathered Containment? A Discussion." *International Studies Quarterly* 17, no. 2 (1973), 205-26.

McMahon, Robert J. "Eisenhower and Third World Nationalism: A Critique of the Revisionists." *Political Science Quarterly* 101, no. 3 (1986), 453-73.

Meredith, David. "The British Government and Colonial Economic Policy, 1919-1939." *Economic History Review* 28, no. 3 (1975), 484-99.

Metz, Steven. "American Attitudes Toward Decolonization in Africa." *Political Science Quarterly* 99, no. 3 (1984), 515-34.

Morley, Morris H. "Reinterpreting the State-Class Relationship: American Corporations and U.S. Policy towards Cuba, 1959-1960." *Comparative Politics* 16, no. 1 (1983), 67-83.

Munroe, Trevor. "The Marxist Left in Jamaica 1940-1950." Working Paper no. 15 (1978), University of the West Indies.

Myers, Frank. "Conscription and the Politics of Military Strategy in the Attlee Government." *Journal of Strategic Studies* 7, no. 1 (1984), 55-73.

Nachmani, Amikam. " `It's a Matter of Getting the Mixture Right': Britain's Post-War Relations with America in the Middle East." *Journal of Contemporary History* 18, no. 1 (1983), 117-40.

Nettleford, Rex. "Manley and The Politics of Jamaica." *Social and Economic Studies* 20, no. 3 (1971 supplement), 1-78.

Newman, Robert P. "The Self-Inflicted Wound: The China White Paper of 1949." *Prologue* 14, no. 3 (1982), 141-56.

Newton, C. C. S. "The Sterling Crisis of 1947 and the British Response to the Marshall Plan." *Economic History Review*. 37, no. 3 (1984), 391-408.

Ovendale, Ritchie. "Britain, The United States, and the Cold War in South-East Asia, 1949-1950." *International Affairs* 58, no. 3 (1982), 447-64.

Palmer, Annette. "Black American Soldiers in Trinidad, 1942-44: Wartime Politics in a Colonial Society." *Journal of Imperial and Commonwealth History* 14, no. 3 (1986), 203-18.

Pastor, Robert A. "Explaining U.S. Policy toward the Caribbean Basin: Fixed and Emerging Images." *World Politics* 38, no. 3 (1986), 483-515.

Pazos, Javier. "Cuba--Was a Deal Possible in '59?" *The New Republic* 148, no. 1 (1963), 10-1.

Peffer, Nathaniel. "Southeastern Asia in Escrow." *Foreign Affairs* 20, no. 3 (1942), 503-16.

Pelz, Stephen. "John F. Kennedy's Vietnam War Decisions." *Journal of Strategic Studies* 4, no. 4 (1981), 356-85.

Plank, J. "The Caribbean: Intervention, When and How?" *Foreign Affairs* 44, no. 1 (1965).

Pomerance, M. "The United States and Self-determination: Perspectives on the Wilsonian Conception." *American Journal of International Law* 70, no. 1 (1976), 1-27.

Powers, R. J. "Containment: From Greece to Vietnam--and Back?" *Western Political Quarterly* 22, no. 4 (1969), 846-61.

------. "Who Fathered Containment?" *International Studies Quarterly* 15, no. 4 (1971), 526-43.

Pritchard, R. John. "The Far East as an Influence on the Chamberlain Government's Pre-War European Policies." *Millennium* 2, no. 3 (1973-74), 7-23.

Rahman, Habibur. "British Post-Second World War Military Planning for the Middle East." *Journal of Strategic Studies* 5, no. 4 (1982), 511-30.

Reynolds, David. "A `Special Relationship'?: America, Britain and the International Order since 1945." *International Affairs* 62, no. 1 (1985-86), 1-20.

Rollins, Judith. "Part of a Whole: The Interdependence of the Civil Rights Movement and Other Social Movements." *Phylon* 47, no. 1 (1986), 61-70.

Roskin, Michael. "From Pearl Harbor to Vietnam: Shifting Generational Paradigms and Foreign Policy." *Political Science Quarterly* 89, no. 3 (1974), 563-88.

Ross, Douglas A. "Middle Powers as Extra-Regional Balancer Powers: Canada, India, and Indochina, 1945-1962." *Pacific Affairs* 55, no. 2 (1982), 185-209.

Rotter, Andrew J. "The Triangular Route to Vietnam: The United States, Great Britain, and Southeast Asia, 1945-1950." *International History Review* 6, no. 3 (1984), 404-22.

Rubin, Barry. "Anglo-American Relations in Saudi Arabia, 1941-45." *Journal of Contemporary History* 14, no. 2 (1979), 253-69.

Saunders, Richard M. "Military Force in the Foreign Policy of the Eisenhower Presidency." *Political Science Quarterly* 100, no. 1 (1985), 97-116.

Sbrega, John J. "The Anticolonial Policies of Franklin D. Roosevelt: A Reappraisal." *Political Science Quarterly* 101, no. 1 (1986), 65-84.

Schaller, Michael. "Securing the Great Crescent: Occupied Japan and the Origins of Containment in Southeast Asia." *Journal of American History* 69, no. 2 (1982), 392-414.

Schonberger, Howard. "Peacemaking in Asia: The United States, Great Britain, and the Japanese Decision to Recognize Nationalist China, 1951-52." *Diplomatic History* 10, no. 1 (1986), 59-74.

Sella, Amnon. "Khalkin-Gol: The Forgotten War." *Journal of Contemporary History* 18, no. 4 (1983), 651-87.

Sitkoff, Harvard. "Racial Militancy and Interracial Violence in the Second World War." *Journal of American History* 58, no. 3 (1971), 661-81.

Steele, Richard W. "The Pulse of the People: Franklin D. Roosevelt and the Gauging of American Public Opinion." *Journal of Contemporary History* 9, no. 4 (1974), 195-216.

Tarling, Nicholas. "The United Kingdom and the Origins of the Colombo Plan." *Journal of Commonwealth and Comparative Politics* 24, no. 1 (1986), 3-34.

Tillapaugh, J. "Closed Hemisphere and Open World? The Dispute over Regional Security at the U.N. Conference, 1945." *Diplomatic History* 2, no. 1 (1978), 25-42.

Tomlinson, B. R. "Indo-British Relations in the Post-Colonial Era: The Sterling Balances Negotiations, 1947-49." *Journal of Imperial and Commonwealth History* 13, no. 3 (1985), 142-162.

Tonnesson, Stein. "The Longest War: Indochina, 1945-75." *Journal of Peace Research* 22, no. 1 (1985), 9-29.

Twitchett, Kenneth J. "The American National Interest and the Anti-Colonial Crusade." *International Relations* 3, no. 4 (1967), 273-95.

------. "The United States and Le Tiers Monde." *International Relations* 3, no. 5 (1968), 328-54.

Wells, Samuel F., Jr. "Sounding the Tocsin: NSC 68 and the Soviet Threat." *International Security* 4, no. 2 (1979), 116-58.

Williams, J. E. "The Colombo Conference and Communist Insurgency in South and South East Asia." *International Relations* 4, no. 1 (1972), 94-107.

------. "The Joint Declaration on the colonies: An Issue in Anglo-American relations, 1942-1944." *British Journal of International Studies* 2, no. 3 (1976), 267-92.

Windass, G. S. "The Cuban Crisis and World Order." *International Relations* 3, no. 1 (1966), 1-15.

------. "Indonesia and the U.N.: Legalism, Politics, and Law." *International Relations* 3, no. 8 (1969), 578-98.

X. "The Sources of Soviet Conduct." *Foreign Affairs* 25, no. 4 (1947), 566-82.

Yasahura, Yoko. "Japan, Communist China, and Export Controls in Asia, 1948-52." *Diplomatic History* 10, no. 1 (1986), 75-89.

Young, Lowell T. "Franklin D. Roosevelt and America's Islets: Acquisition of Territory in the Caribbean and in the Pacific" *The Historian* 35, no. 2 (1972-73), 205-20.

Unpublished Works

Baptiste, Fitz A. "*The European Possessions in the Caribbean during World War II: Discussions of Conflict and Cooperation.*" Ph.D. diss., University of the West Indies (1981).

Burn, North. "*United States Base Rights in the British West Indies, 1940-1962.*" Ph.D. diss., Tufts University (1964).

Cravens, Raymond L. "*The Constitutional and Political Status of the Non-Contiguous Areas of the United States.*" Ph.D. diss., University of Kentucky-Lexington (1958).

Lewis, Patrick. "*A Historical Analysis of the Development of the Union-Party System in the Commonwealth Caribbean, 1935-68.*" Ph.D. diss., University of Cincinnati (1974).

Palmer, Annette. "*The United States and the Commonwealth Caribbean, 1940-45.*" Ph.D. diss., Fordham University (1979).

St. Hill, C.A.P. "*The Chaguaramas Question.*" M.Sc. thesis, University of the West Indies, Jamaica (1967).

Newspapers

New York Times (USA)
Daily Gleaner (Jamaica)
Daily Chronicle (British Guiana)
Advocate (Barbados)
Guardian (Trinidad)

Index

About the Author

CARY FRASER is a Visiting Fellow at the Princeton Center for International Studies and has written articles on American policy toward decolonization.

QM LIBRARY
(MILE END)

Lightning Source UK Ltd.
Milton Keynes UK
08 September 2010

159584UK00005B/95/P

F2131 FRA

QM Library

23 1349799 0

WITHDRAWN
FROM STOCK
QMUL LIBRARY

AMBIVALENT ANTI-COLONIALISM

Recent Titles in
Contributions in Latin American Studies

Modernization and Stagnation: Latin American Agriculture into the 1990s
Michael J. Twomey and Ann Helwege, editors

State Formation in Central America: The Struggle for Autonomy, Development, and Democracy
Howard H. Lentner

Cuba and the Future
Donald E. Schulz, editor